LIVE AS A MAN.
DIE AS A MAN.
BECOME A MAN.

WAY OF THE MODERN DAY SAMURAI

A true story about living according to the Samurai Code of Honor in the modern world by Enson Inoue.

ISBN: 1495961605
ISBN 13: 9781495961601

Dedicated to my Mother, Father, Brother Egan, and to my Yamatodamashii Ichizoku for whom I would die today if I had the chance.

"A Samurai that goes into battle with the will to die,
Will surely live.
While the Samurai who goes into battle to survive
Will surely die.
Where the body may die,
The spirit will rise."

Acknowledgements

I would like to thank my Mother and Father for raising me and for the sacrifices they made to give me all a child could ask for. They taught me values and beliefs that are so embedded in my soul that I would willingly die for them.

Thank you Egan, my brother, for being the role model I needed in my younger days and being the reason why I don't smoke cigarettes or drink alcohol to this day.

I am grateful for having the best friend in the world, Darren Suzuki. He has been with me through thick and thin and I wouldn't be here today if he wasn't by my side.

I would like to thank Tommy Hackett, Lanning Lee, Burton Richardson, Brandon Bosworth, Chris Rudd and my mother Evangeline Inoue for their contributions to the book.

Thank you also to Hody Jae Huh, Yamatodamashii Ichizoku's official photographer, for the photos throughout the years and Susumu Nagao for his awesome fight pictures.

Much aloha to my sister Alice Leary Inoue for her guidance, support, and wisdom. She helped me step-by-step to make this book a reality...

I'd like to thank my Tarling, SJ McCann for putting all the finishing touches together. Without her help this book would still be stuck in my computer.

...and to my beloved boy, Shooto who left me for Doggy Heaven 4 years ago. He was an American Red-nosed Pitbull pup from Egan's dogs and was born in Hawaii. At three months old, I brought him over to Japan and he was with me 90% of the time for 14 years. He was a companion, brother and best friend all in one and I miss him dearly. Rest in peace and be nice to the other doggies in Doggy Heaven.

Last but not at all least, I would like to give a shout out to my Yamatodamashii Ichizoku that spreads out all over the world.

TABLE OF CONTENTS

FOREWORD

This book has been in the making for 5 years and I am very happy to be able to present you with Volume One of my life story. Aside from my desire to put out a good product, there have been numerous events that have delayed the progress. The most impactful event that delayed the progress of this book happened on March 11, 2011. A 9.0 magnitude earthquake hit Japan, triggering a Tsunami that demolished the east coast of northern Japan, the country I fell in love with and have called home for 24 years.

Surges that reached heights of over 100 feet swept over the coast of Japan killing over 15,000 people and leaving over 200,000 homeless. Then, as if that wasn't enough there was a meltdown of three nuclear reactors resulting in 100,000 more losing their homes. I've been on over 30 missions and counting to bring much needed supplies and aid to these unfortunate people of North Japan.

I currently have a business called Destiny Forever LLC where I hand make bracelets with gem stones that help supplement my trips up North, and a portion of sales from this book will also help fund my missions to bring aid to these people.

Another event that delayed the progress was my "Walk Across Japan", which required me to put everything on hold as I walked 1360 miles from Hokkaido to Kyushu. It took me 67 days, which raised over $12,000 for the people of North Japan.

Although I am raising funds to help the people of Japan, this book was not written for financial purposes. The purpose of this book was to put on paper my philosophy of life that has evolved and still continues to develop through the trials and tribulations from my experiences in life. As a MMA fighter I have touched many in various walks of life and although my fighting career has come to an end, I am still blessed with the ability to continue inspiring people outside of the ring.

I decided to write this book to explain my "way of life", hoping it can inspire more to live the life that I will live until the day I die, "The Yamatodamashii Way" or "The Way of the Samurai". It's about living a life of compassion and honor, encompassing integrity and loyalty, which is the basis for all things that are important in one's life. I believe that living the way of *Yamatodamashii* is the ultimate way to live. I may never attain it, but plan to strive to get as close as I can until the day I die.

Yamatodamashii is a way of life!!!

A Special Message From Fighter to Fighter

"I don't really look up to a whole lot of fighters, but Enson had a big impact on me. A lot of guys fight just to win, fight and not get hurt. But those guys, they would rather die than give up.

Igor Vovchanchyn was a killer back when Enson fought him. He was in his prime, murdering people... and Enson stood his ground and didn't give up. I was amazed by his perseverance; how he kept going like he didn't have a care in the world. He was just out there, fighting -- the way I think MMA should be. We're different from boxing. He has a true warrior spirit and not every fighter has that. Even some champions don't have a true warrior spirit, but Enson does.

Some people only want to fight people they know they can beat. It's not a challenge if you know you can beat them. Some fighters know they're getting beat and they just turtle up or they just tap out right away. And honestly, I don't look up to guys like that. Why should I?

It's not about a record. Just because some fighter is undefeated, doesn't mean he has the best fighting spirit. Maybe he's a good athlete. Maybe he's got a game plan for everybody. That doesn't mean he has samurai spirit – that's what I call it.

A lot of warriors came out of Enson's day. He was one of the founders of the sport, fighting over in Japan when it was the biggest show on the planet. This was before the UFC rose. I don't know if a lot of new fans understand that back then, PRIDE, in Japan -- that was the show. That was the "Mecca." They had the toughest fighters on the planet, and Enson was one of them. There were a couple of other killers out there, but only a few I look up to."

– Quinton Ramone "Rampage" Jackson

INTRODUCTION

My reputation today is of a modern day samurai. It was emphasized most in my "Kill or Be Killed" fight style, but what many fail to realize is that my beliefs and strengths started at a very precious young age. I would like to share with all of you many of the experiences in my life that have molded me into the man I am today. These experiences have fostered the beliefs I am willing to die for at any moment.

Pain is Temporary and Pride is Forever.
My Dear friend Danny... Please forgive me.

There are some things in your life that you forget in a year, many more in 5 years. Then there are a select few that leave deep footprints in your heart, which you remember for the rest of your life as though it only happened yesterday. These that leave footprints in your heart can never be forgotten. They sit in the shadows of your mind, very rarely becoming visible, but when they do, they are as vivid and clear as the day they happened. Some of these select few are just memories that linger in your memory banks and some are like a *diamond in the rough* that are etched so deep in your heart that it plays a big part in the person that you are today. I'd like to share with you one that happened about 38 years ago when I was just an innocent elementary school boy...

When I was 9, I was attending Manoa Elementary School, where 80% of the kids were Japanese-American. Located in Manoa Valley, it was a peaceful school where violence and crime was very rare. Both of my parents were schoolteachers and they got home at 5 or 6pm. Therefore, when the school dismissal bell rang at 2:15pm, I had a lot of free time to kill. Some days I would go to the stream and fish or hang out in the park for hours with my best friend Darren and my cousin Gary. There were also times that I would just go home and play with my dogs Tora and Bucky, or shoot hoops in my driveway. On some of those days, about 2-3 times a week for about a month to be exact, a 14 year old boy named Danny, would meet me at the park to kick his soccer ball around or to just hang out. I really enjoyed his company.

Then one day, one just like any other day, Danny and I were kicking his soccer ball around in Manoa Park when out in the distance I noticed five or six Hawaiian boys about the same age as Danny heading towards us. As they got closer I could hear them calling him "Haole Boy" and other derogatory names like "fag," "homo," "wimp," and more of the same. I realized that these boys were kids from Danny's school, Stevenson Intermediate School, which was a school comprised of a mixture of the meek timid kids from Manoa Elementary with the bigger, scary Hawaiian kids from Papakolea and Pauoa.

It was where all the kids from Manoa Valley would be transferred to, after completing elementary school. Most of the Japanese -American kids, who were physically smaller, dreaded the day they would be transferred to Stevenson.

As those Hawaiian boys got closer, I could see fear building up in Danny, making me scared and petrified, wishing it was all a dream. Before I knew it, the boys began beating up Danny, not saying a word to me or acknowledging my presence. I froze. I was too scared to help Danny and too scared to even utter the word, "stop." I just watched and prayed that it would end soon or that this was all just a dream.

After what seemed like an eternity, Danny was curled up on the ground, beaten and at their mercy. Then, as if beating Danny wasn't enough, one of the boys picked up a piece of dog shit and put it on Danny's head and eventually tried to make him eat it. Danny was crying, they were laughing, and I was terrified. When they had their fill of humiliating Danny, they walked off, laughing and punching each other in play, disappearing in the distance just as suddenly as they appeared.

So many thoughts rushed through my head; so many emotions churned like a typhoon in my soul. Why didn't I help Danny? Why couldn't I stand up for my friend? I quickly walked up to Danny, leaned over to him and asked him if he was okay. Danny then started getting up without looking at me, brushed off the grass on his clothes and just walked away without saying a word. I felt so lost and alone, like I betrayed Danny. As I slowly walked home, my heart ached. I wanted to rewind the hands of time. I wished I had one more chance to do something, anything to help Danny.

I had been afraid to get involved. Fearing that I would be beaten up too, possibly getting hurt enough to be hospitalized with a broken bone or some sort of fracture. What I didn't realize at the time was that the scar this incident left, etched in my heart was by far incomparable to any broken bone I may have suffered. What I came to understand is that, any physical injury I may have been afflicted with if I stood up for Danny, would be so small and minute compared to the scar in my heart I still have today from not standing up for a dear friend. Any injury I would have sustained would have healed and been long forgotten within a few months, but the emotional damage I received from not standing up for Danny to this day still hurts in my heart as if it were yesterday. Unbelievably, 38 years, nearly four decades later, my heart hurts so much as I recall that horrible day. It feels like someone is squeezing my heart in a vice. Was Danny angry at me? Was he too embarrassed to face me again? Still today, I wonder how Danny is and where he is. Does he even remember me? Does that humiliation still linger in his heart? Is he even alive? Will I ever see him again? I also wonder if he even remembers this day like I do, or is it just a faded memory of his childhood. These are questions that were left unanswered, for that was the last time I ever saw Danny again.

For me, this incident made a big impact in my life, playing a major part of what kind of man I am today. Never, ever again will I betray a friend like I did, on that day in the park. I would rather die than put myself through the pain and the guilt of sacrificing someone important in my life for my safety. The pain of a broken arm or a fractured leg is nothing compared to the pain of scarring my pride and endangering my honor as a man.

I have people that are close to my heart called my *Family*. In Japanese *Family* is translated as *Ichizoku*. There are numerous people that without a split second of hesitation, I could die for. For these people, my *Yamatodamashii Ichizoku*, I would be honored to die for and vice versa, I know they would for me. Dying is easier than living life with no honor. Physical pain is no comparison to the pain in your heart one will feel by hurting your pride. Enduring any pain, setback, or even death to keep your all-important pride intact is so very important. Without pride there is no honor. Without honor you are not a man. If I cannot be a man of honor I would rather die. A man without honor is better off dead.

"I'd rather die tomorrow for something, than live forever for nothing."

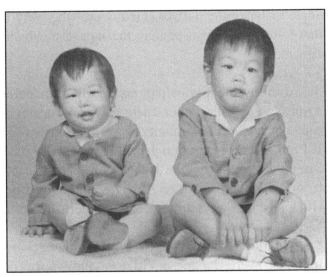

Me (left) and Egan, 1969.

Chapter 1
THE BEGINNING

Although I am fourth generation Japanese-American, my blood is pure Japanese. However, because I was born in Hawaii, making my nationality American I spoke no Japanese. During World War II, colonies of Japanese emigrated away from Japan to try to create better lives for their families. The biggest migration would be to three places: Brazil, California, and Hawaii.

My great-grandparents originating from Kyushu and Hiroshima, migrated to Hawaii, where they were forced to live within a totally different language and culture. However, they were determined to continue the purity of the Japanese bloodline through discouraging mixed race marriages. They were very proud of their Japanese heritage so they held on tight to the Japanese customs and beliefs, unusually more than the

Japanese people in Japan themselves. That is probably why I am some-times told that I am more Japanese than the Japanese, which to me is a great compliment.

In my family, from my great-grandparents, to my grandparents, all the way down to my mother and father, there were no interracial marriag-es. The Japanese-American community was a tight group so my blood, even though I am fourth generation Japanese-American, is 100% pure Japanese. I am no different from the Japanese in Japan except that I hold a passport from the United States of America and, having been born in Hawaii, my language and ways are more like Americans.

The Japanese language was also lost through the generations. My great-grandparents, were Japanese citizens and spoke no English. Because of this, my brother Egan and I needed our grandparents to translate in order to communicate with them. My grandparents needed to speak Japanese to communicate with their parents and needed to speak English to survive in Hawaii so they spoke both broken Japanese and broken English. They had just enough Japanese to communicate with their parents and just enough English to survive and get around in Hawaii.

Because my grandparents spoke English, although broken, my mother and father didn't need to learn the Japanese language. My parents were fluent in English with a few Japanese words here and there. The fourth generation, Egan and I, spoke absolutely no Japanese. Our primary lan-guage was English.

My family was very sports orientated and also very much involved in the martial arts. My grandfather was a 4th degree black belt in Karate and my mother was a brown belt; even Egan was on his way to getting his black belt. Therefore, it was assumed that I too would follow likewise so I was enrolled in a Karate class. I felt ready and eager to begin Karate.

So here, at the young age of five, the baby of the family, I set foot in a local Karate dojo with my first martial arts teacher, Darryl Lee. The

2

first two classes weren't too bad. I learned katas, the basic stance, basic punches and blocks. I was actually beginning to enjoy Karate, though the hardest part was memorizing the katas. Then, on the third day it all went downhill. The class was moving through the same routine. But this time, after we were told to get into our basic stance, Sensei Lee began walking around the dojo checking everyone's stance. He was giving everyone's stance a swift firm check with a sweeping kick to one of our legs. I was confident and proud to be in my Karate stance. When my turn came around, as much as I felt sure my stance was okay, I was getting more and more butterflies the closer Sensei Lee got to me.

When my turn came, I braced myself for his kick and to my surprise I was swept flat on my ass. My stance must have sucked because with one swift sweep Sensei Lee kicked my legs out from under me. I didn't know what to feel. I felt lost like an alien who was beamed down to earth and as helpless as a newborn deer taking his first steps. Then suddenly tears began streaming down my cheeks and like something took control of me I got up and ran out of class, out of the Dojo, down the stairs and to the nearest pay phone. My first instinct was to get home back to the sanctuary of my home and my parents where I felt safe.

However, I was faced with two major setbacks: I didn't have loose change to make the call and I couldn't reach the phone. My desire to get home was so strong I pushed my shame aside and walked over to a construction worker who was doing construction on the main road and said, "Excuse me sir, can I have 15 cents to make a call?" The surprised construction worker looked at me and without a moment's hesitation he reached into his pocket and pulled out a quarter. As he was trying to hand it to me instead of reaching out my hand I said, "988-4811." The construction worker glanced over at the phone and realized that I couldn't reach the coin slot or the dial. He smiled, took the phone off the hook, handed it to me, inserted the quarter and dialed, 9-8-8-4-8-1-1. When my mother answered the phone my emotions took control of me and I screamed, bawling, "Pick me up!!! I hate Karate!!!"

I never returned to that Karate class and I don't remember getting any pressure from my mother or father to go back or getting a talk from them to be a man. As far as I was concerned, I was done with the martial arts.

The culture we were brought up in was typically American, but in our household we held on strong to some Japanese traditions and beliefs. For example we didn't wear any outdoor footwear indoors, neither did we clip our fingernails at night and we didn't put our feet anywhere the head would go. It was a unique mixture of the traditional American "Ladies First" way and the quiet but effective humble Japanese style, never boasting about what you can do but instead letting actions speak for themselves. This style of the Japanese I really respect.

I grew up in a nice and peaceful community called Manoa Valley in Honolulu, where the majority of the residents are Japanese-American. However after graduating from Manoa Elementary School, everyone who didn't transfer to a private school transferred to the rougher Stevenson Intermediate School. All the Japanese-Americans dreaded going to Stevenson because it combined four other districts, which included some rowdy Hawaiians and Samoans. The Japanese were always targeted because we were so much smaller and weaker.

As an elementary school kid, I was a rascal and sometimes it got me into trouble. I especially remember one of these times when I was forced to do something I never expected to do. I was in the 5th grade and sometimes after school, instead of walking home my father would pick us up at the gym. On this particular day, my cousin Gary and I were running around and playing in the gym. I can't remember exactly what we did but somehow we pissed off one of the biggest 6th graders in the school, Glen Cambra. He was trying to catch us but because he was so big he couldn't move fast enough. I was taunting him, knowing my father would soon be coming to pick me up so I just had to stay out of reach until then.

Finally, when my father arrived, Gary and I ran behind my father, feeling safe and protected. I continued making faces at Glen to further taunt him, when suddenly my father stepped aside and said, "What? They making trouble? Go get them." I couldn't believe my ears. I felt like a poodle barking at a Pitbull knowing he has a chain around his neck only to realize that the chain wasn't connected to anything. I looked at Glen and he looked at us with a grin like he was about to devour two chunks of steak. Gary and I had no choice. We couldn't run with my father watching so taking on the big man was the only way. I decided to take the initiative and went in for the attack. I ran up to Glen and gave him a big front thrust kick square into his belly. To my surprise he didn't budge. Instead, I bounced off him and fell to the ground. As I got up, Glen began preparing to close in on me, when suddenly Gary went rushing towards Glen and began to wrestle with him. I soon joined in until we took control of him. Glen lost his fire to fight and said, "Your Father is waiting. You guys better go." so without anyone getting hurt the fight was over.

On the way home my father told us that if we make trouble, we will need to fight our own battles. At this young age of 11, I was taught a big lesson. I was taught that I must take responsibility for my actions and fight my own battles.

From the numerous stories I had heard about Stevenson, my first day at this new school had me scared and uneasy. At the first lunch break, I noticed that all the groups were segregated. The Vietnamese hung out in one corner, the geeks in another, the scary Hawaiians and Samoans in the far corner, and the Japanese in another corner. We all dreaded the Hawaiians because they were big, scary-looking, very noisy and disorderly. They would intimidate us with the older ones picking out certain guys and taking their lunch money. There were times my friends and I gave them our lunch money because we were afraid of getting beaten up.

One day my father found out that I was giving away my lunch money. Instead of calling the principal, he called me in for a talk. When I walked in the room he got straight to the point: "Hey, I hear that some of the Hawaiian boys at school have been taking your lunch money."

My heart practically stopped and I froze, not saying anything. He continued: "What's the matter with you? You can't stand up for yourself? Well, the next time you decide to give up your lunch money because you're scared of the Hawaiians, you can fight with me when you come home!" Now my father was like God to me, so the last person I would ever want to fight was my Dad! I would rather fight five Hawaiians all at once instead of fight my father.

The following week, sooner than I expected, the time came. I saw the Hawaiians coming my way and my heart began to pound. Just as they were approaching me, the school bell rang, signifying the end of the day. Everyday, we all sprinted for the bus to get a seat and my muscles twitched, wanting to get up and run for the bus. If I ran, I would avoid this confrontation, but I knew it was inevitable. I felt that the sooner it happened, the better. So instead of running, I just sat where I was. Sure enough, the leader of the gang, Billy, walked straight up to me and said, "Hey Japanese boy, I like some money so I can buy juice!"

My heart began to pound ten times faster. I thought to myself, "Oh, shit! Here goes!" I took a deep breath, looked up at Billy, and in a soft voice said, "No." Billy was much bigger than me and was considered crazy. I was scared, but the words of my father were stuck in my head. He stopped in his tracks — as if he'd seen a ghost — then blurted out, "What?! What the fuck did you just say?!" Without hesitation I repeated in a louder voice, "No." He took a step back, took off his shirt and said, "You stupid Jap, now I'm going to fuck you up!" Don't ask me why, but back then when guys got into fights they always took off their shirt. He didn't attack but instead he began jumping around with his shirt off, screaming obscenities at me and telling me that I was going to die today. Then a Hawaiian girl came and screamed at me, "You stupid Japanese boy, just give him your money or he going put you in the hospital!"

Just as we were starting to fight, a bunch of campus walkers came up and broke us apart. I wasn't struggling much, but it seemed that Billy's fury escalated just as he was grabbed. That confused me: He had enough time to "fuck me up" before the campus walkers came but didn't. I was terrified but definitely didn't show it. I stood facing him without taking my eyes off of him, even for a second. They pulled Billy into a room. I left to catch my bus home.

The news of this incident seemed to have spread around campus, and I got a new type of respect from all the other students, except from Billy and his gang- Billy, Puna, and Avis. Billy's boys, would stare me down, give me the middle finger, and shout obscenities at me every chance they had. However, the funny thing is that it was all verbal abuse and they never laid a hand on me. Also, I no longer had to run to the bus stop to guarantee myself a seat on the school bus. My seat was always saved so I was able to stroll down to the bus stop, taking my time, while the others ran ahead. The newfound fear and respect felt good but interestingly, I wasn't ready for it.

Because I was so young, I didn't really understand what it meant and didn't know how to handle it properly.. It felt good to be spoken to by kids with fear in their voices. Going on day-by-day knowing everyone feared me felt so good and unfortunately, I took advantage of the fear in a very bad way.

Instead of stopping the hijacking and bullying, I turned around and began hijacking all the other guys in the Japanese community, taking over right where the Hawaiian bullies left off. I was blinded by the instant surge of power and lost control of it. Consequently, I began hijacking and bullying others, forgetting what it felt like being on the other end.

There was an instance where I would collect from a fellow student, Clinton Choy, $20 dollars a week for protection from me. I would also make him carry my books to class even though his next class wasn't the same as mine.

I turned into something I hated. I learned that standing up for myself not only made me feel better about who I was but it changed what people thought of me. The power felt good and I craved more of it. Unknowingly, I was thrown on to the wrong path. It was the path of a person who did whatever he wanted, enjoying himself at the expense of others.

However, the positive thing that was embedded in my soul was the courage to stand up for myself in the midst of fear. Still today, whether it's a 300 pound muscle man, ten gangsters, or a prominent Yakuza figure, I will stand up for myself until the end, even if it would mean dying. If I didn't do anything wrong and it was to protect my honor or my family, I would die today if I had to, without a split second of hesitation.

Ironically, I ran into Billy about seven years ago at a McDonald's. I recognized him, and I'm sure he recognized me, too. Surprisingly, he was a lot smaller than me now. He glanced over at me for a moment, looked away, and never looked back my way. As I recalled the past, I chuckled to myself and decided to let him be. After all, he played a big part in helping me to become the man I've become today! Maybe I should have thanked him.

"Live as a Man. Die as a Man. Become a Man."

When I first saw this saying it was in the office of Mr. Fujita, a Yakuza I knew well and I thought nothing of it. The only thing I observed was that the order of the sentences was wrong. Dying was the last thing you do so I questioned why it was in the middle?

I asked Mr. Fujita and he explained that all the trials and tribulations one encounters in life are little tests to prepare you for the ultimate test of death! The strength in your heart and the undying fire in your spirit, a split second before your death, will determine if you passed the ultimate test of dying. If you die as a coward, you will have failed the final test and therefore, did not become a man. On the other hand, if you died with fire in your heart which entailed fighting and being strong until the very end, then you will have passed the final horrific test of death and have become a man.

However, living life like a man is something I try to do every day for it grooms you for the ultimate moment of facing death. I'm still in the process of building the strength in my heart to be able to die as a Man and there are episodes in my life that assure me that I'm on the right path.

Chapter 2

GUIDED TO THE RIGHT ROAD... A GOOD CHANGE

At Stevenson Intermediate School, I was forced to change. My change at Stevenson was for the good but at the time, I wasn't able to recognize what the right course was and how to stay on it since I was still young. I went from a quiet boy who was being hijacked, to an assertive boy who stood up for himself, to an overly proud boy, who began himself, hijacking and bullying other fellow students.

I spent two years in Stevenson Intermediate and was preparing for my 3rd and final year before moving on to Roosevelt High School. I was to rule Stevenson in my final year, even more dominantly, for I would now be the in highest grade level of the school. It would be like my last hurrah before moving to Roosevelt where I would become part of the youngest grade level of the school. A part of me dreaded the move to Roosevelt but another part of me felt anxious and eager inside because I believed that there was an opportunity to conquer and bully fellow students on a bigger scale, meaning more power.

However, my parents had different plans. They had enrolled me in a small private school called University Laboratory School (UHS). It was a school of mixed races with very small classes with a total enrollment of approximately 500 students. I was excited over this change but also a bit lost and insecure to have been taken from my newly conquered turf at Stevenson to a school totally unfamiliar to me.

I remember my first day at UHS: new grounds, new faces, and a bit of insecurity being so unfamiliar to the new surroundings. It was a small school, very quiet and very homely. My new classmates were nice and the campus was very clean.

And then, just when I was just getting comfortable at my new stomping grounds, I came across something startling. As I was changing classes and walking past the cafeteria, on my first day of school, I noticed huge Samoan and Hawaiian students sitting on the benches outside of the class. One of them stood out and his name was Saleva'a. He was about 300 lbs.! I had never been up close to these large-sized guys before. They were scary looking and three times bigger than Billy from Stevenson. When I walked by, I felt no intimidation. They just kept to their business, almost as if they didn't see me. There were no stares or threats., Something was different. I was confused.

As time passed, I found out that these huge guys I always saw hanging out at the cafeteria were football and basketball players for the school, not thugs like I encountered at Stevenson. It was interesting that I felt no desire to conquer or control my surrounding peers and I didn't know whether it was because of the positive vibe I got off these guys or the size of them. We became friends and little did I know, I was being steered back on to the right path.

Although I was back on the right track, I still felt the battle within me trying to keep the Stevenson Enson under control.

An incident occurred on my first week back that reminded me I still was the warrior who stood up for myself, no matter what. It was a very rainy day and the roads in the school were flooding. It was a challenge to stay dry moving from class to class. At lunch break, with my two (to be) good friends, Ray and Kenny, I headed to the cafeteria huddled together under one umbrella trying to stay dry. There was a huge puddle near the cafeteria close to a speed bump where muddy rainwater was accumulated. Just as we were passing the puddle, two older basketball players, Randy and Darin, came running towards us drenched from the rain, yelling and running. They ran right through the puddle and kicked the muddy water up, getting all three of us all wet. I stopped looked down at my soaked clothes and said to Ray and Kenny, "That's fucked up! We can't let them get away with this! Let's go fuck them up!" It surprised me that these guys deliberately chose to fulfill their need to have fun and attention, oblivious to how they would affect those around them.

I could see in Ray and Kenny's eyes that they wanted nothing to do with what I was feeling. I tried to convince them, telling them that there were three of us and just two of them so we could take them on. They declined. This upset me even more. I knew in my heart that something had to be done about this wrong that was done to us. I just couldn't let it go so I took off alone and headed towards the direction these basketball players went with the intent to put these pranksters in their place. When I finally got to where they were, I realized that my 5'8" 175 pound frame was no match to these two upper classmen, with one of them a towering 6'1". The only problem was that my blood was boiling too much to even care, so I approached them and angrily yelled, "What?! You guys think that was funny?! You fucking punks?!"

They seemed startled to see me standing in front of them alone calling them out. Then the bigger guy Darin looked at me and said, "What, Japanese boy! You want trouble?" Just then I realized that things were going to get ugly and I could feel myself switching to "I don't give a fuck, let's go crazy" mode. I was a bit disappointed to have trouble at my new school so soon but I was angry and so I didn't care. I was wondering how my first "two- on-one" would go and got ready for war.

People heard the commotion and a big crowd began to gather. I didn't care. All I saw were the two basketball players and everything else was a blur. Then just as things were about to begin I heard a voice from the crowd, "Eh! Beat it! Leave the Japanese boy alone!" I turned and was surprised to see the big 300 lb. football player, Saleva'a, pushing his way through the crowd walking towards us. When he got close he turned to the two basketball players and told them to leave. Then he turned to me and said, "Eh, Japanese boy. If they bother you again let me know," and he walked off. I didn't know what to say and I was really grateful for what he did. The fire in my heart was still there and now burned with the strength of appreciation! This I found wasn't necessarily always a good thing. When mixed with the strong loyalty I had for my friends, it oftentimes got me in tight spots. Although my move to a private school lessened the trouble I was getting into and presumably, being guided onto a better path, I still found myself on the wrong road at times. The fire inside of me made street fights a regular thing and I jumped at any chance to back up friends against rival gangs.

Then there was a humbling incident that took place that gave me a wake-up call making me realize that I wasn't as tough as I thought I was.

It happened one day while I was warming up for a game. A friend pulled up in his car and informed me that the gang he belonged to was challenged to fight another gang from the countryside. Not hesitating or giving a second thought to leaving the game and excited to back him up against this rival gang, I yelled to my teammate, Ryan Kato, to grab my bat and join me. We jumped over the outfield fence and into my friend's car and we were off on our way.

When we got to the meeting place, I felt safe to see that we had about 20-30 guys gathered. The rival gang hadn't arrived yet, so we talked, laughed and clowned around as we waited for their arrival. We waited for only about 10 minutes when four cars pulled up across the street from where we were. When they got out it seemed like they had about the same amount of guys as we had.

"This is going to be crazy", I thought. I was imagining how many guys I was going to drop as I stood in the front of our group holding my baseball bat in my hand. The two guys that had the dispute met in the middle, as the rest of us waited for one of his guys to jump in. We weren't going to intervene as long as it was a fair one-on-one fight. They began arguing and emotions were escalating. The other guy began walking backwards towards the car he arrived in. He then bent over, picked something up and as he came walking from around the car, he began raising his right hand in which he held a gun. He raised it in the air so everyone could see it and then pointed it at my friend, whom he was arguing with.

It really scared me because my friend wasn't backing off. He raised his arms in the air and shouted, "Shoot me! Go right ahead and shoot me!" The good thing was that, as my friend was saying this he was backing away and the tension in the gunman seemed to simmer down. When my friend backed off far away enough where the gunman felt safe, he took the focus of the gun off my friend and began pointing it in our direction. "Holy shit!!!" I thought, "He's going to shoot us!" He ran the gun along the line of us standing across the street slowly as if to be picking out whom he was going to shoot.

As the gun passed by me, I waited for him to shoot but he didn't. He continued down the line until he got a bit past the middle of us. When he was almost to the end of the line, one of the guys freaked out and began to run. We were already on edge and he sparked panic and everyone began to scatter. It was unexpected and I also began to run. I remember running and imagining the bullet hitting me from behind, wondering how it was going to feel.

I dove behind a parked car as I noticed some of our guys running past me in panic, some scaling fences, trying to distance themselves from the gunman. I was ashamed of running but relieved no one got shot. After a few minutes things quieted down. I peered from behind the car towards the gunman and I noticed they were all getting into their cars to leave.

I felt ashamed and wondered if what I did was the act of cowardice. Everyone on our side ran. Would it have been honorable to be the only one to remain standing? I was uneasy as all kinds of thoughts ran through my head. It was all over and we returned to our baseball game and I knew for sure that I needed a lot of work building my spirit before I could consider myself real man.

I graduated from UHS in 1985 and enrolled at the University of Hawaii. While in high school I was a four-letter varsity athlete in baseball, basketball, volleyball, and track. On the side, I was also playing racquetball very seriously at the local sports club. Out of all the sports I played, baseball and racquetball were my passion. I remember having dreams as a youngster of becoming a professional baseball player so immediately after enrolling at the University, I walked down to the athletic department to find out when the tryouts for the baseball team would be.

From childhood times I always had dreams of being a professional baseball player. Picture taken in 1982.

14

Although I made the Star Bulletin State All-Star Team, I wasn't scouted so I had to go to tryouts as a walk-on. In high school the positions I played were pitcher and center field. However, because the level for college ball was so much higher, I could only tryout for right field. Tryouts went well, but unfortunately, I was cut on the final cuts. For the final cut the coaches didn't even tell us in person. Instead, the names of those selected would be posted on a bulletin board and only the names on the list would be allowed to show up for practice. The nervousness I felt as I was scanning the names, as well as the heartbreak I felt when I did not see my name listed, crushed me. Despite the disappointment, I contemplated trying out again the following year. As time went by and my participation in racquetball increased, I decided to hang up my glove for baseball and pursue racquetball instead. Egan was already one of the top-10 racquetball players in the world so I made plans to follow in his footsteps.

Chapter 3

New Venture – Racquetball

I still remember my racquetball days and how it began. I was 16 years old with a passion and love for the ocean. There wasn't a single day that passed that I wasn't in the ocean, surfing or diving. Some days I would even wake up at 5 a.m., drive down to the surf spot and sit on the rocks waiting for sunrise. I wanted to surf so bad I couldn't even wait for the sun to rise. There were even days when I would paddle out in the dark, shivering from the cold while waiting for the sun to rise. Even when the sun was setting, I would be out there until the last second of sunlight, paddling back to shore in the dark. It was the sensation of riding a wave, which was an indescribable feeling of just me and my board, riding Nature's swells from the depths, far from land.

Surfing at Diamond Head, Hawaii circa 1983.

The desire to ride the swells was so strong that I would venture out alone if none of my friends could go. With my other love, diving, I would go alone even though that was one of the biggest "no-no's" of water sports. I would tell my parents I was going diving with someone although I was going alone.

One of my favorite pastimes – night diving, 1987.

Many nights when everyone was out on the town I was underwater in another world. When my head was above the surface I could hear the cars honking, people laughing, or the wind blowing. But the moment, I submerged below the surface, I could not hear a thing except my own breathing. There was peace and calm as if I were in another world. I was so content with my surfing and diving that I didn't need anything else.

When my parents invited Egan and I one day to join them at a sports club, the Oahu Athletic Club, I was reluctant to go. It was an adult fitness club where my parents would go to play racquetball and on Sundays the members were allowed to bring their children to enjoy the club's facilities. I remember the first time I went with them was on the day the surf was flat and I had no plans for the afternoon. It was a beautiful club with cool air conditioning, a nice aroma and soft carpet.

My first impression of racquetball, before actually playing, was that is was a simple and easy game to play, until we started playing. Egan and I were running all over the court chasing the ball that took weird and unpredictable bounces changed its courses and going in totally different directions. Even though the racquets had a huge face, I was actually missing the whole ball. Egan and I were huffing and puffing as my mother ran me all over the court easily beating me without a challenge. All I could think about was how much better surfing or diving was and I really didn't care if I ever did this racquetball shit again. Damn, I thought, even a day of flat surf was better than this. I had a horrible time and I vowed never to come back again. Egan was different. He couldn't stand that he couldn't beat Mom and a fire was lit.

My parents invited us every Sunday to join them and, although Egan would go, I was always busy surfing, diving, or just sitting around the house. Then, months later, Egan entered his first racquetball tournament and I went to cheer him on. To my surprise he wasn't running like a chicken without a head as I recalled on our first day. He anticipated where the ball would bounce and he didn't whiff any balls. Wow, I knew now that even Egan would beat me and this racquetball thing was not for me.

As the months went by, Egan continued to consistently practice every day and eventually began winning tournaments until he was in the top division. He also brought home trophies and medals which made me decide to give it another try.

Chapter 4
EGAN MY ROLE MODEL

With Egan's help in training and as a role model, I also began to win tournaments and that's when a new passion was born. However, I never could discipline myself like Egan. The hours he spent in the court, the early morning training and the hours of cross training he would do were incredible and it paid off. He also never smoked, drank or went out partying. Instead he was at the racquetball courts. I admired Egan so I also never smoked or drank but just couldn't find it in me to be so disciplined in the training. It paid off for Egan because in only a couple years he was already the Hawaii State Champ and had racquet, clothing and even shoe sponsors. He then began entering some of the professional tour events and fared well enough to begin to follow the Pro Tour full time.

I was getting better and even won some Hawaii state titles but not nearly as dominant as Egan was. Egan shared with me some racquets, shoes and because we wore the same size clothing, he was able provide clothing for me too. I even began following the Pro Tour trying to follow in my older brothers footsteps. My parents were paying my airline tickets and I was jumping in Egan's hotel room, which his sponsors provided for him. Egan eventually became World Champion and even at one time was ranked the #1 racquetball player in the world. I, on the other hand, was struggling and wasn't playing as nearly the level Egan was. My highest world rank was #28, which was not so good in the racquetball world.

Because racquetball was such a fast sport, television wasn't interested in it and the sport began hurting. Egan was the hardest hitter on the pro tour and had been clocked hitting the ball at 191 mph. Even the average player hit the ball about at 140 mph, which was too fast for the television cameras to catch. The number of Pro events was dwindling and I just couldn't seem to break into the top 24. Breaking into the top 24 was essential because only the top 24 players would receive a spot in the main draw, while all the other touring pros and the local players would have to play off for 8 spots. I would have to sometimes play three matches the day before the main draw just to qualify. Then the qualifiers would be thrown into the main draw getting matched up with one of the top 16. I wasn't consistently qualifying so my rank never got higher than #28.

Chapter 5

Houston Texas' National Amateur Racquetball Championships – Riot

Every year Egan and I entered one of the biggest amateur racquetball tournaments in the United States, the U.S. Nationals. It was the qualifying tournament that decided the team who would represent the United States in the World Games. Egan had just won his way into the best eight and I was in the middle of a match in the round of 16's against James Lorello. The match was close, with me taking the first set and James winning the second set, putting us in a tiebreaker. During the tiebreaker, James' supporters started to heckle me and started to get louder and louder. They were cheering whenever I made a mistake and made comments like "lucky" and "dog-shit" whenever I made a good shot. Egan was up there in the gallery amongst all those assholes, standing right next to them. I was down in the court trying my best to ignore them because I knew that one of their objectives was to upset me and take me out of my game. Then at 8-8 in the tiebreaker to 11, I appealed a shot James hit and one of the hecklers yelled, "What a crock of shit! It was a perfect shot!" That's when I think Egan had enough of these guys shit because I saw him have a word with this asshole. He got pushed; then all hell broke loose.

It was a 20 feet high to climb to get to the gallery where Egan was, too high to climb. I knew Egan was alone so I had to get up there. However, before I began to make my way to the gallery, I looked at James and thought of attacking him first but decided it would waste precious time and I had to reach Egan as soon as possible. I dropped my racquet and went up the stairs on a full sprint up to the gallery to join Egan. When I finally got up to the gallery, there was such a huge mob of people that I couldn't get through to Egan so I climbed up to the top of the bleachers and scoped out where Egan was. I noticed one guy who was the main aggressor so I hurried out to the edge of the top bleacher, zeroed in on him, and like a superhero, jumped smack dab right on top of my target. I landed with my arms wrapped around his face so I squeezed his face and began pulling him away from Egan.

There was so much ruckus, so many people but I was just focused on this one guy. Then suddenly, I felt some huge arms wrap around me and then I was literally lifted off my feet. I was struggling, kicking, and punching but I never got free. I knew that whoever was holding me was definitely a tough dude and was taking some licks. They finally dragged me out of the gallery and I had three guys pinning me down on the ground. I was determined to get out but I couldn't move. As things began to calm down I noticed the guy who carried me out of the arena was an ex NFL football player, about 6 feet 4 inches tall, and huge! They separated us from James' supporters and brought us to a back room. I remember saying, "I'm going to kill you!" to Egan's attacker and the big ex NFL football player kindly told me, "Be careful. Don't say that. You could get in big trouble just for saying something like that." I took his advice and shut up, waiting for a chance to break away and get back James' group. Then the Commissioner, Jim Hiser walked into the room and wanted to know our side of the story so he could try to come to a solution to the problem. We were then escorted back to our hotel room and were told to wait for a call from the commissioner of racquetball.

An hour later the commissioner called and said that he wanted James and I to finish the match in a back court, that he would referee with no spectators, just me and James. Egan then called his manager, Dr. Lorenze and told him the situation. Dr. Lorenze told Egan, fuck the commission and go back home to Hawaii on the next flight out... and we did just that. Egan was the defending World Champion and the favorite to win the Nationals so with him leaving was a big blow to the commission and the racquetball community. However to my surprise, although we left on our own, in the next *National Racquetball* magazine, the gutless commission claimed that they sent us home. It is sad to have such spineless people in this world.

Chapter 6

FIRST BIG MOVE AWAY
FROM HOME

By 1987, I was determined to make more sacrifices to improve my game. I decided to move away from Hawaii to the U.S. mainland so I could be closer to the pro tour and stop being a burden to my parents. I chose Texas because of its central location allowing me to be close to any pro tournaments in the mainland U.S. Texas had many top pro players with many small satellite tournaments that I could play in to get more court time that would help improve my game. I also had met a Club Pro by the name of Gene White who gave me an open invitation to come stay with him in Dallas.

I had it all planned out without anyone's knowledge. After my first year at the University of Hawaii, I decided not to register for the following year and planned my move to Texas. I quietly sold all my belongings to save up money for the move. I also worked part time at Hawaiian Island Creations, a surf shop and delivered newspapers in the morning to increase my savings.

In the summer of that year, Egan and I participated in a big amateur tournament in Houston. After the tournament was over, I remember being silent until the last moment when Egan and I were leaving the hotel and was about to jump into a taxi heading to the airport to catch our plane,, I looked over to Egan and said, "I'm going to stay. I'm going to catch a bus to Dallas and look up Gene. Tell Mom that I stayed." Without hesitation, Egan said okay, jumped into the taxi and was gone.

Watching the taxi pull farther and farther away, I began to realize that I was now on my own. No Egan to take care of me, or watch over me. I felt lost and alone. Then I wondered if I had made a wrong move. I began to walk to the Greyhound bus station lugging all of my luggage with me. I bought my bus ticket to Dallas, found a window seat and as I observed all the foreign landscape of Texas, I couldn't help but wonder if I had made the wrong decision.

The bus arrived at the Dallas Greyhound Bus Station. I got off and walked to the taxi stand. All I had was the business card of the sports club where Gene worked at, so I jumped into a taxi and showed him the card. Then, I realized that I had not contacted Gene but I was confident he would be at work.

The taxi pulled up in front of a beautiful sports club and I got out and walked over to the front desk lugging my luggage and asked for Gene. The girl at the front promptly answered, "Gene? Oh it's his day off to-day." Oh shit!, I thought, what was I going to do. I asked her to call him but there was no answer. He wasn't home. Now the feeling of being lost and alone was at its peak and I literally felt like crying. I wanted to go home and I wished I could rewind the hands of time so I could jump in the taxi with Egan.

I didn't know what to do so I just sat in front of the front desk pondering what I should do when I heard a familiar voice say, "Howdy Enson, what are you doing here?" I looked up and it was Gene. I was a lucky man. He had come to practice racquetball on his day off and although he didn't expect me, he welcomed me into his home. I stayed with Gene for a couple of weeks until I found a job and eventually my own apartment.

Following in my brother's footsteps on the racquetball court.

I found an apartment at a complex near the Dallas Fort Worth Airport called Oaks at Centerport, which ironically had a racquetball court. I pulled in side cash teaching private lessons and was doing okay until I made the big mistake of buying a car. I found it parked in a parking lot with a "For Sale" sign on it. It was priced at $500, which was almost all I had. I really needed a car so I made the purchase only to have it break down a week later. I was out of money and now I didn't have a car.

I went job searching and got lucky. I was hired at a sports club called Racquetball Resorts, where I taught racquetball and restrung and re-gripped racquets. The pay was good and the best part about it was that I was allowed to take off work and participate in the pro events – it was the perfect set up. The only problem was that I had to wait a month before the first paycheck and I was out of cash. I refused to ask my parents for money so I was down to eating one baloney sandwich a day. It was such a struggle. I tried many different eating techniques. One technique was to eat a bite every 4 hours and make it last the whole day. That technique made me feel hungry all day so I tried sucking it up until the night and ate the whole sandwich before bed. I also thought of tiring myself out by doing laps in the pool but that only made me hungrier. I eventually ended up losing about 15 pounds but was alive and kicking when my first paycheck came in.

The paychecks were steady and a good flow of income was coming in from the lessons, re-gripping and re-stringing. Everything was going smooth with a nice apartment to stay in that was only 10 minutes away from Racquetball Resorts. I found it exciting to shop for household goods and filling up my apartment. However, I also realized how much my mother did for me. The laundry, cleaning, groceries, cooking, etc. was really a chore to do. Sometimes I would come home from training too tired to cook dinner and finally eating something unhealthy or a TV dinner..

I eventually got two roommates, Guy Humphrey from Kansas City and Carl Otsuka from Hawaii. Guy was a racquetball buddy and we trained together and traveled to tournaments. Carl was a high school classmate who wanted to try his hand at living away from home.

Living in Texas, chasing my racquetball dreams.

A year passed and everything was going well until one day I was informed by the manager that there was going to be an ownership change and he wasn't sure how it was going to affect me. A week later I was called in by the new management and told that I wasn't going to be able to travel to all the pro events and if I did I would have to take a pay cut for the days I was away. This defeated the whole purpose of my move so after deep thought I decided to move back to Hawaii.

The move was sad. I had to sell everything I had and say goodbye to all my new friends in Texas. The members at the club didn't want me to leave so they started a petition to keep me but I had my mind made up that I was leaving. I thanked them and knew I would miss them but was also looking forward to moving back home. The racquet stringer I bought to string racquets was too big to bring back to Hawaii so I put it up for sale. One of the fellow pro racquetball players, Dave Watson, originally from Oklahoma, wanted to purchase it. However, to my disappointment, Dave didn't have the cash so I told him he can transfer the money to me later and that was the last I heard of him. He must have decided that he didn't want to pay and just stopped answering my calls. Dave, if you're out there, do the right thing, pay up!

It was nice to be home but traveling from Hawaii to tournaments was too costly and so I began to consider the worth of this pursuit. Also, I wasn't excelling like Egan and I wasn't getting sponsorship from any big company. I remember the last tournament of the last season on the pro tour which was a national tournament, the biggest of the year and worth double the points to your ranking. I had qualified and was matched up to the #12 ranked player in the world, Dan Obremski. Dan was a good-looking GQ-type and was in top shape but I knew I had the tools to upset him, which would allow me to break into the top 24 and guarantee me a spot in the main draw, without having to qualify. I was pumped because this was my chance. I had to win 3 out of 5 games to 11 and I was on fire beating Dan the first 2 games. I lost the 3rd but found myself up 10-8 serving for the match in the 4th game. One more point and I would have won, which meant I finally would break into the top 24. I served, and we had a great rally until he misplaced a shot which gave me a perfect set up in mid court. This was a shot that pro players would bury 100 times out of a 100. My heart began to race knowing the game was over and I was going to be finally ranked in the top 24. It felt like slow motion as the ball dropped right in front of me in the perfect spot to hit a winner and end the game. I raised my racquet up over my head preparing for the shot, shuffled my feet so my body was in the perfect spot to take my shot, stepped into the ball, took a full, smooth stroke and like a gunshot ringing through the air my racquet met the ball. The ball went whistling towards the front wall only to skip on the floor before hitting the front wall. My heart dropped. How could this have happened? I hit the shot into the ground losing me the rally and eventually the match. I missed the perfect shot, lost the match, and never broke into the top 24.

The following year the pro tour cut the amount of tournaments in half and I had a big decision to make on whether to continue playing racquetball or to go back to school. I gave it a shot for a full two years and my parents were spending a lot of money flying me to tournaments without me showing good results. I had to be real here and decided to go back to school and say goodbye to the racquetball pro tour. I was broken. That one shot ended my racquetball career and till this day I can still see that perfect shot so vividly as if it were right in front of me, waiting for me to hit a winner to win the most important match in my racquetball career. I was haunted by that missed shot for almost a decade until God showed me why I missed that shot and why it was one of the best things that ever happened in my life.

Chapter 7

ROAD TO JIU-JITSU...
MY NEXT LOVE

I enrolled back at the University of Hawaii and felt I was ready to get back into the studying. However, I felt like there was something missing. After racquetball I had a lot of pent-up energy and I felt that martial arts would be a great way to vent it. Although my negative experience with Karate put a bad taste in my mouth for martial arts, I still felt the need to train. Being a smaller Japanese in Hawaii you had to fight for survival and street brawls were a common thing so I always wanted to be prepared. After Karate I tried many different martial arts. There was Hapkido/Tae Kwon Do, awesome aggressive arts but I'm as flexible as a 2 X 4 so my progress in Tae Kwon Do was limited and my stiffness limited me to being able to execute 90% of the techniques.

I trained a variety of martial arts and I narrowed it down to the two I felt would cover me the best on the streets: Muay Thai was for when one didn't have direct contact with one's aggressor and Wing Chun for when one makes contact with him. I liked Wing Chun, especially the sticky hands technique, even though I was never really that good. I also did Muay Thai and I especially liked the solid basics of Muay Thai. It had me kicking my banana tree in my yard, which made my mother think I was losing my mind. Although I really took an interest in Wing Chun and Muay Thai, still something was missing. I didn't feel complete and again resumed searching.

When I enrolled at the University of Hawaii, I noticed that they offered a variety of non-credit martial arts courses. Scanning down the list of non-credit courses, Aikido caught my eye. I remember seeing an old Aikido master defend himself from 12 attackers and I wanted to see what that was about so I signed up for Aikido class.

It was slow and hard to execute. The idea was to harmonize with your opponent's energy. The problem was that every opponent exerted a different energy and every fight required one to feel the opponent's energy, harmonize with it before flowing with it and eventually redirect it.

Even if you fought the same opponent numerous times, he still would be exerting a different level of energy on every encounter. So I confronted my teacher and asked him how would I be able to use this on the street with this theory and he answered, "It will take many years to be able to execute Aikido, sometimes 50-60 years." What? I was still immature and young and I felt like I needed something NOW! 50-60 years from now, I would hopefully not be getting into street fights so that wouldn't do me any good. I felt that I needed something that I could use tomorrow. Then I began to wonder if there was such an art. I completed the three-month course and stopped going to class for want of something more practical.

I felt there were still holes in my armor. I didn't know what they were and I was uneasy. Then one day, while I was walking to class at the University of Hawaii, there was a skinny Brazilian guy, Romolo, passing out flyers for this grappling art from Brazil called Gracie Jiu-Jitsu. I had to hurry to class so I set up a meeting with Romolo the next day. We met in the cafeteria and Romolo showed me the Gracie Jiu-Jitsu in Action video. I watched the video and was impressed at what I saw. The Gracie Jiu-Jitsu practitioners were destroying everyone from Karate, wrestling, to street fighting with ease.

What really left an impression on me was the last fight on the video where Rickson Gracie fought a street brawler named Zulu. At the time in Hawaii it was believed that the bigger guy was usually stronger and Zulu out-weighed Rickson by over 80 pounds. As I watched the video, I was impressed with the defense Rickson had from the bottom. Then, to my amazement, the smaller Rickson Gracie slipped to Zulus back, wrapped his arms around his neck and choked Zulu out into submission.

I was sold! That little Brazilian guy just choked out a huge black street fighter and in my heart I knew I had to learn Gracie Jiu-Jitsu. Romolo told me that it was one of the non-credit courses at the university so the following day I went straight down and signed up. I was excited! This was it!!! Combining the kicks and elbow strikes of Muay Thai, the close fighting in Wing Chun and the ground fighting of Jiu-Jitsu would be ideal. I would become the complete fighter with the ability to defend myself on the streets on any aspect of hand-to-hand combat. I couldn't wait to begin.

On my first day of Jiu-Jitsu class, Relson Gracie stood at the front of the class speaking to us in his broken English just like the movies. He made us do some stretching exercises and then told us to partner up. "Yeah!" I thought that we were now going to learn how to fight!!! I expected to get down and dirty like the video I saw and was surprised when I saw a girl partner up with a guy. We then did some weird exercises like,when someone grabs you here, you grab his wrist and then step here, do this and subdue him. To be honest I was disappointed. I wanted to learn what I saw on the video, 80 kg Rickson Gracie submitting the 120 kg huge barbarian, Zulu. Move after move and nothing changed. A full 90 minutes of self-defense techniques that I didn't feel were realistic in a real street fight. I knew that it was only the first class but I was impatient.

After class, I waited for most of the students to leave and then approached Relson. He was chatting with Romolo and a small black belt student named Romero who only weighed about 70 kilos. Relson extended his hand in a friendly manner and said in his broken English, "Thank you for coming my friend."

I shook his hand but then said, "I want to spar. I want to see how good your Gracie Jiu-Jitsu is." He looked surprised at first but suddenly turned to the little Brazilian guy Romero and signaled him to spar with me. Of course this was still a friendly confrontation so no strikes were going to be thrown and we were just going to wrestle. Not only was Romero small, he was skinny with little or no muscle. I looked over at this little Brazilian guy walking towards me and thought, "I don't care how good his technique is, my power will control and dominate, no matter what." It was beyond my comprehension that a small guy like Romero would be able to do anything to me.

So we took to the mat and before I could get ready he shot in and took me to the ground. I wasn't worried and so I just turned around and began to stand up. Romero was so small that I felt no resistance but as I got up he jumped on my back. I tried to get him off but he was stuck to me like a turtle's shell. Before I could realize I was in trouble, I felt his arm wrap around my neck like a vice. The squeeze came so fast I couldn't breathe nor scream and I knew I was helpless so I tapped. I don't think it went past a minute so I asked him to give me another chance.

Again he took me down and again I turned my back and again I was forced to tap out from another rear naked choke. I was frustrated! He got lucky again??? What's going on??? I turned to Romero and signaled I wanted another try and he casually said okay. It was like a walk in the park for him and I felt like a child being subdued by an adult even though I was the much bigger guy. Finally when I was easily subdued for the third time, my frustration turned to a mixture of disbelief and amazement. I wasn't angry – I was in awe.

I then turned to Relson and begged him, "Teach me this please! I need to learn this!" He laughed as he said, "In time my friend, in time." I was sold! From that day on I was obsessed with Gracie Jiu-Jitsu (GJJ) and couldn't get enough.

As the days passed and I trained GJJ every day, I couldn't believe that such an amazing art was still undiscovered. I attended classes on every weekday at the UH studio and in the evenings on Tuesday and Thursdays in the garage at his house. In addition, I gathered the top belts together and we trained together on our own on Saturdays. I couldn't get enough!

I even helped promote GJJ by setting up booths on campus so students could see this amazing art. I also set up seminars at schools, dormitories and at events in Hawaii. I became Relson's spokesman at all the seminars since Relson's English was hard to understand.

Whenever my mother didn't know where I was she would just call Relson's house and find me. I lived, breathed, and ate GJJ.

Chapter 8
Street Fight In Seattle

Three months after my first GJJ class, there was a street fight I got into that proved the effectiveness of GJJ. This incident happened when Egan and I went down to downtown Seattle to play in a professional racquetball tournament. Up until the trip to Seattle, I had been training Gracie Jiu-Jitsu for only three months, but it wasn't a normal person's three months because I trained every day of the week and twice a day on Tuesdays and Thursdays.

After the racquetball tournament was over, Egan and I stayed an extra three days to check out the town with Guy Humphrey, who lived with me in Texas where we created a bond and is like a brother to me.. . Guy was a very good racquetball player and although he was only about 140 pounds he hit the ball a ton. He also had the pride of a lion and didn't take shit from anybody, which sometimes got him into trouble.

Guy Humphreys and I hanging out in Texas.

One night, in our hotel room I began to show them some Gracie Jiu-Jitsu moves. Both Egan and Guy knew nothing about Jiu-Jitsu, so I was a bit cocky when I was twisting them up and telling them that if you know Gracie Jiu-Jitsu, size didn't matter. From mount to arm bar to guillotine to slipper choke, I was having my way with them. Then when all the horseplay was done we all decided to jump in Guy's rent-a-car and go out looking for some chicks.

We were driving around downtown Seattle when a carload of girls pulled up on our left as we were stopped in a three-lane street. We asked them where they were going. They said they were going to a club and if we wanted to go we should follow them. However, when the light turned green they hung a left and, although we were in the middle lane, Guy hung a left turn too. Then we heard a screech of skidding tires and "bang", another car crashed right into the side of us.

As we got out of the car to check the damage, we were met by an en-raged muscular black guy. He was huge, pissed off, and coming towards us. You could see his trap muscles bulging through his t-shirt and his eyes were round and beady like he was high on drugs. He got out of his car, noticed that Guy was the driver and walked straight up to him and got right into Guy's face. This guy was about 240 pounds and he was screaming at 140 pound Guy, "What is the matter with you?! You fuckin' idiot!!! I'm going to kill you now!"

We had checked the traffic signs and sure enough from the left lane you could turn left or go straight and from the middle lane, which was the lane we were in, you could only go straight. Thus, we were 100% wrong and that explained why this black guy was so infuriated. He looked as if he were about to strangle Guy so I felt I had to do something.

Now I was in the middle of a rock and a hard place. After bragging about how good Gracie Jiu-Jitsu was and if I didn't help I would really look like someone who talks the talk but doesn't walk the walk. Egan was about 50 meters away on a pay phone calling the police when I walked over to the black guy and said, "Hey, why don't you calm down and wait for the police to arrive." Then all of his anger shifted over to me, and he began screaming, "Calm down?! Calm down?! Who the fuck are you? Now I'm going to kill you, motherfucker!"

"Oh shit!" I thought. What have I done? Now this guy built like a bear wants to kill me!!! He then began to poke his fingers in my chest as he continued screaming obscenities to me, getting closer and closer to my face. I backed off and said in a bit nicer tone, "Hey, we don't want any trouble. Let's wait for the cops to come." It seemed like he didn't hear me because he walked up to me again and continued screaming in my face. I could feel the spit hitting my face as he was screaming so I stepped back once more. Now that was twice I have stepped back and it seemed like he was getting angrier and more aggressive every time I took a step back. Therefore, I told myself that if he steps up to me a third time I'm going to need to take an offensive stance. Then, as much as I prayed he didn't come forward again, he did. This is it I thought. So when he came into reach, I just reacted, grabbed his head, put him in a headlock, and flipped him to the ground. I don't remember how but I ended up in the mount and instinctively hit him with a flurry of three or four punches.

Instead of the punches hurting him they seemed to make him angrier. He reached up, grabbed my shirt and tried to throw me off. I wasn't good enough in Jiu-Jitsu to instinctively fall into an arm bar so I resisted keeping the mount and could hear my t-shirt ripping. As my t-shirt ripped he continued his turn, turning his back to me, so I automatically put in my hooks and sunk in a rear naked choke. He jumped back and was kicking and bucking like a fish out of water. He was also clawing and scratching at my face so I just tucked my head in close against his head and squeezed the choke harder. He was going so crazy that, despite his landing on the sidewalk when I flipped him, we were now in the middle of the street.

Up until now I never choked anyone unconscious so I began to wonder if this sleeper choke I had learned and had him in actually worked. Then he grabbed my arm and began to twitch. The twitching indicated that he was unconscious and just as I was about to release the choke Egan arrived and was hysterically shouting, "Choke him! Hold him! Kill him! Kill him!" Egan's excitement got me all crazy, so instead of releasing the choke I squeezed it again hard. Then after what felt like eternity and I was sure he was out cold, I let go the choke and kicked his limp body off of me. He was heavy and after I kicked him off he ended up face down and was not moving. In fear of him waking up and attacking us again, we ran to our car, jumped in and sped off. As we were taking the turn I looked back through the rear window and noticed he was still face down and not moving. Our hearts were pounding and we didn't know what to do.

I don't know what happened to that irate guy but for me it was a confirmation that Gracie Jiu-Jitsu really works. Egan was so impressed that the next day after we got back from Hawaii he began training Gracie Jiu-Jitsu too. Guy thanked me for saving his life and I thanked Relson Gracie for teaching me so well. To my surprise, when I shared my experience with Relson and my other training partners, Relson gave me a degree on my blue belt. I was stoked.

Sitting back and reflecting on that auspicious day in Seattle, I'm so glad that I trained so persistently in Gracie Jiu-Jitsu. For if I didn't, only the Good Lord knows what would have happened to us on that night out in downtown Seattle.

Chapter 9

JAPAN – THE BEGINNING OF MY NEW LIFE

Because I was now back in school and fully committed to GJJ, I rarely played racquetball. However, because Egan was still on the pro tour, he had to decline an invitation to play in the All Japan Racquetball Tournament since the date clashed with his pro tour schedule. He had won the year before and they really wanted him back so they were very disappointed. Then, to my surprise, they went to their next best option, Egan's younger brother, me.

Egan asked me if I would like to go play in a racquetball tournament in Japan and I was hesitant. I didn't want to miss even a single day of GJJ. However, on a second thought, the chance to see the country of my roots on a fully paid trip was worth missing a couple of days of GJJ. It was scheduled to be a one-week trip and I had one month to train for it.

I had heard that the level of Japanese racquetball wasn't so good so I expected to win the tournament with just one month of training. To my surprise, the level was better than I had expected and I lost in the finals, taking second. I was bummed to lose but happy to be able to get back to Hawaii and my GJJ classes.

A month later I got a call again from the same Japanese club owner, Mr. Kaneko, who had flown me in for the last tournament, inviting me to another all Japan tournament, The Bashamichi Classic. I wanted so bad

to redeem myself, so I jumped to the chance even though I knew I was
going to be missing more GJJ classes.

The weird thing was that when I told Relson I was going to Japan to play
in another racquetball tournament he had a weird insecure reaction. He
practically begged me not to go. He said, "I know, if you go, you not
coming back!" I thought that was crazy. I couldn't imagine not returning
to Hawaii. Not only did I live for GJJ, I loved Hawaii! The weather, my
family, my friends, and the beach! I was an island boy in and out and I
could never leave the islands... so I thought. My objective on my second
trip to Japan was to redeem myself. I was to properly train and to take
home the Bashamichi Cup. All the players who entered in the last tournament that I had placed second, including the Japanese player who beat
me, Junichi Yoshida would be participating. This time I had more time
to prepare and this time I was not taking it easy.

I had a good three months to prepare and I was ready to take it all. The
tournament went well and I made it to the finals. It wasn't a cakewalk
though. In fact, I struggled. I barely made it to the finals, squeaking by
Junichi in the semi-finals. In the finals I played the number three-ranked
Japanese player and won in straight sets. I had redeemed myself. I was
happy and ready to get back to Hawaii and my GJJ classes. Then a couple
of days before I was supposed to return to Hawaii, Mr. Kaneko asked me
if I could extend my trip for a month and tour Japan doing racquetball
seminars.

I really wanted to get back home but I figured that this is my chance to
see Japan and I really didn't know when I was actually going to have this
chance again so I agreed. Mr. Kaneko put me up in a hotel and gave me
spending money for food and entertainment. I missed Hawaii and GJJ
but I was so impressed with this new country. I traveled all over Japan
doing seminars and about a week before I was supposed to go back to
Hawaii, I had an idea. If I stayed in Japan and learned to speak the language well, it would open up a lot of doors for jobs in Hawaii since there
were a lot of Japanese visitors every year.

So I decided that I was going to stay as long as I could until my money ran out. When I expressed my desire to stay in Japan, a member at the racquetball sports club that I was training at, Mr. Komiya, offered to let me stay at his parent's house. I was grateful because I couldn't afford to stay in the hotel so I packed my bags and took him up on his offer.

Another problem I faced was my girlfriend of four years, Reana Hayashi was waiting for me in Hawaii and the longer I stayed in Japan the more distant we became. Our plan was to be in Japan together but instead of going together and both struggling with a visa we decided that she would come later after I got set up. I finally called her and we discussed the situation, deciding that it was to our best interest to end the relationship. Amazingly, she took the separation in stride. I wasn't hit with sadness but instead was a bit relieved to be able to just concentrate on what was happening in Japan.

After staying at Mr. Komiya's parent's house for two weeks he then told me there was an apartment nearby that was empty and I could stay there for free. There was no furniture, but it had running water and electricity. I accepted and made another move.

The move into the apartment was not what I expected. It was nice to have my own place, but the loneliness hit me. I slept on the ground with no furniture and I didn't even have an icebox. I bought little speakers to plug into my Walkman so I had music and I began doing jigsaw puzzles, something I had no interest in prior to my trip to Japan. Money was running out so I began selling my own racquets. I had five and sold them one by one for $300 each until I only had two left. Then Mr. Kaneko asked me if I could do one more seminar up in North Japan for a small pay and because I was running out of money, I jumped at the chance.

This seminar was in a small city called Koriyama in north Japan and when the club members gathered for the seminar I noticed a familiar face in the crowd. It was Eric Texidor. Eric was a notorious hot head baseball coach for one of the top high schools in a Hawaii. He had a scary reputation of beating up his own players when they made errors and attacking umpires when they made bad calls so I was hesitant to talk to him.

However, as soon as he saw me, with a big grin on his face, he said, "Hey Enson! How you been?" as he walked towards me, with his hand stretched out to shake my hand. I was partially in shock that Eric Texidor was so friendly, but I didn't show it and shook his hand firmly. He then pulled me towards him and gave me a big hug and that's the first time I felt the warmness in this feared man. He had a beautiful wife, Toyoko, who owned an English School and she also greeted me with a warm hug. We chatted for a moment and before the seminar started, they invited me out for dinner after the seminar was done. I accepted and felt almost like a part of Hawaii was here with me.

At dinner we talked about the past and Eric told me interesting stories about his move to Japan. I then casually mentioned that I wanted to try to stay in Japan for at least a year or so and I was looking for a job. Instantly, Eric looked at his wife and said, "He can work for us at our English School yeah, Toyo?" Toyoko seemed to be taken by surprise and came straight out with some questions. Her friendly demeanor instantly changed as she asked me in her cute broken English, "You have any experience teach English before?" I didn't and the look on her face told me that she wasn't interested. Then Eric blurts out, "Come on Toyo, he can follow me to classes until he gets the hang of it and then, maybe, begin with some kids classes." Toyo still seemed dissatisfied, but to my surprise she agreed to give me a shot. Eric and Toyoko also agreed to take me in and let me share a room in their apartment with their son Mikio. I was happy and very grateful.

Chapter 10

SCARED AND CONFUSED – RENEWING MY VISA

By this time, my three-month tourist visa was running out so I had to apply for an extension, which required me to leave the country. The closest place was Korea and luckily, the cost of the flight was cheap. I didn't have the money so Eric loaned me the money for the plane ticket and a good friend I had made at the racquetball club, Mashiko, slid me some cash to get some food and a room during my short three day trip. I got my ticket and left on the plane without making any hotel reservations. Mashiko told me to just jump in a taxi and tell them to take you to Itaewon where there was a lot of shopping, restaurants, and hotels. I thought, "piece of cake" so I packed a small bag and off I went to Korea.

It was nice that the flight was only three hours long. However, little did I know that my problems were imminent. As soon as I tried to leave the airport, I got in a taxi and the driver spoke no English. I told him to take me to Itaewon and he gave me a frustrated look like "What?!" I repeated "I-tae-won" over and over to no avail. I decided to change taxis and the same problem occurred, until the fourth taxi understood what I was saying. I was relieved and was on my way.

The drive to Itaewon was about 35 minutes from the airport and I was shocked that halfway there my taxi driver was pulling over to other possible customers until one of them actually got in. "WTF?!" I thought to myself. Why is my taxi picking up other customers when he hasn't even dropped me off yet? I couldn't believe what was going on as the new passenger took a seat in the front like it was a normal thing and it was as I found out later.

I finally reached Itaewon without having a place to stay so I had the taxi driver take me to The Hamilton Hotel which was recommended by Mashiko. To my surprise, it was much too expensive so I decided to take a stroll around the town to see if there was a cheaper priced room. The Hamilton Hotel was about $100 a night and being a simple person, I didn't need a plush place to stay. As long as I had a bed and a roof over my head I was fine. I wandered the back streets and found a place for $25 a night and decided to stay there. It was busted up and dirty and the bed was hard like wood, but it was enough. I put my luggage in the dark room and decided to check out the town a bit more.

It was getting dark and the bars were opening and I suddenly found myself in the red light district. I was surprised that most of the girls outside the little bars spoke English. I decided to go in to have a drink at this one particular bar that seemed safe. I've had experiences before in Hawaii with the Korean hostesses trying to make you spend money buying drinks, so I made sure the girl understood that I was only buying one drink for myself before I decided to go in. I walked in the bar and the lights were down low. It had a gloomy atmosphere and I instantly began feeling uncomfortable when I realized that I was the only customer in the bar. Then it made me feel even more uncomfortable when three girls came and sat with me at my little table. They asked me what I wanted to drink and so I ordered a Coke. As soon as my Coke was served, they began asking me to buy them drinks too, despite the understanding that I was only buying only one drink. I reminded the girl that I spoke to earlier that I was only buying one drink, and she said something in Korean that I didn't understand, but by the expression on her face I could tell she was pissed. I downed my Coke just so I could get out of there, when suddenly a scary looking Korean guy came out from the back and he began screaming to me in Korean while pointing at my drink so just to simmer down the tension of the situation, I agreed to buy the girls a drink.

However, one of the girls told me, "Too late!" Those two words made my heart start to race as I began looking at the door and wondered how I would get out safely. The door was close by, but the problem was getting out of the table I was sitting at because I was blocked in, sitting in the seat furthest in. I had a plan to go to the bathroom and make a break from there so I asked them if I could go to the restroom. They seemed okay with it as they scooted out of the booth we were in to let me out. As soon as I got out of the booth, thoughts of making a break for the door whirled through my head but for some reason I couldn't get myself to make a break. I decided to go to the restroom and figure out a way to get out. When I got to the urinal to take a half ass pee I was caught off guard when the guy walked in too.

I finished peeing and felt very uneasy when the guy got right behind me as I washed my hands. I imagined him jumping me from the back or even stabbing me in the back with a knife. Seconds felt like minutes as I washed my hands trying to think of what to do.

Fear began taking over my body as the images of me getting attacked by this guy changed to me hurting this guy before he hurt me.

Suddenly I reacted. I turned around, grabbed the guy by the neck and slammed his face in the mirror. There was a big crack when his face shattered the mirror and I noticed blood beginning to trickle from his face as he slumped to the ground.

This was my chance! I darted out of the restroom and headed for the door. Apparently, all the girls in the bar heard the commotion for all three of them had formed a barricade across the front door. I headed their way in full sprint but these girls seemingly had no intention to move. I was in "life and death" mode and I was ready to do whatever I had to do to get out of the bar so I went full speed towards the door and I ran right through them like a fullback running for a touchdown as they were knocked out of my way like bowling pins. I burst through the door and began running down the street to my hotel, glancing back only once. No one was pursing me but I stayed at full speed all the way to my hotel.

When I got back to my room it was then that I realized that I didn't even pay for my Coke. I went to my room, locked the door and lay on my hard bed trying to bring my heartbeat down for it felt as though it was going to pop out of my chest from beating so hard.

My favorite GJJ sweater was splattered with blood and I reluctantly threw it away in the trash. It was only my first day and I wasn't flying out for another two days. I didn't know what to do because I feared they would be looking for me to get revenge. I thought of just staying put in my room but finally decided leave the room walking in the opposite direction from the area of the bar. The next two days passed without incident and I was so happy to be in a taxi headed back to the airport.

I was now back in Japan with a working visa and ready to begin a new chapter in my life as an English teacher. Japan was definitely a different place, much different from Hawaii. Although I was a fourth generation Japanese-American, and my parents held on to many customs of the Japanese, there was still a lot of customs I had to get accustomed to. The problem was, I am 100% Japanese blood so physically I looked exactly like a Japanese national, so it came with an expectation that I behave according to the standards of Japanese etiquette. Japan has a lot of verbal etiquette rules. For example, after finishing a meal they say, "Gochisousama deshita" which is giving thanks for a meal, "Itadakimasu" which you say before a meal, "Otsukaresama deshita" which is said at the end of a day of work, etc. These were the behaviors I was expected to practice and when I didn't, I was frowned upon and considered rude or arrogant. On the other hand, if I had had blond hair and was obviously a foreigner, there would have been more leniency and understanding.

The adjustment to Japan eventually became a lot smoother because of some of the customs and values my family instilled in me because of their Japanese ancestry. However, it was still not quite up to par to the expectations of the Japanese of Japan. Fortunately, Toyoko and Eric helped guide me on living the Japanese way but there was another big problem I had to deal with and it was the language.

As far as I can remember, in my lifetime communication was never a problem. I don't remember having difficulty with understanding the English language so being in Japan and not being able to understand a single word of Japanese was something very new to me. I would go on dates carrying an English-Japanese dictionary and communicate using the dictionary for every word. It became frustrating so I decided to take some action to learn the language. I made flash cards and memorized hundreds of words a week. My progress in Japanese seemed impossible but to my surprise I was getting better.

After my first month in Japan, my grandparents visited me and I was amazed at my grandparents' ability to communicate in Japanese. When we rode the trains, went to a restaurant to eat, or checked in at the hotel, they were able to communicate well in Japanese. I remember envying their ability and thinking that I would be satisfied just to be able to communicate like they did someday. How I wished I paid attention and took my Japanese classes more seriously when I was in high school.

However, there was no giving up. Fortunately, Fukushima, where I lived was in the countryside. There were no English speakers and everything I did, from going to the bank to buying groceries required me to speak in Japanese. Six months passed and my grandparents paid me another visit and this time, I found myself being relied on to communicate for them for I had noticed that their Japanese was not up to the standard of the Japanese in Japan. I even noticed them stumbling with the words and was not fully understood by the Japanese. I had not noticed this on their first visit but on this visit, it told me that without realizing it, my grasp for the Japanese language surpassed their ability and I was stoked! This motivated me to study my Japanese even more so I studied the language even harder.

Teaching English was an amazing experience. Eric and Toyoko taught me some techniques and I was slowly getting the hang of it. I taught private adult lessons, kids, big companies, and even went to a kindergarten to teach. One rule was that we were to never speak Japanese and that was no problem for me. During this experience, I realized that English is a hard language. There were actually times that I couldn't answer my students' questions., as when to use "a" and when to use "the." Never in my life did I ever think I was going to be in Japan, teaching English.

Now, I just played racquetball, snowboarded, and taught English.

Chapter 11

CULTURE SHOCK – I'M NOT JAPANESE???

The culture shock was very subtle because of my Japanese upbringing in Hawaii. My parents had pride in being Japanese and tried to hang on to the Japanese culture as much as they could. My biggest shock moving to Japan wasn't the food or the customs. My biggest shock was that I realized that I was not "Japanese". Growing up in Hawaii I always considered myself a Japanese. Whenever I was asked what nationality I was, I always answered "Japanese". However, when I moved to Japan, I realized that all I had that was Japanese was my blood.

The language I spoke was English and more importantly, the passport I carried was American. I was also called "Gaijin" which literally meant "outside person". I couldn't work or stay in Japan for longer than 90 days without a Visa. When I bought a car, it had to be in a Japanese person's name and when I bought a house, a Japanese person had to own at least 51% of it. When I moved to Japan, it was the first time that I ever called myself an American. Japan was my homeland, my roots and yet, it was a very shocking experience. It wasn't a warm welcome back to where my bloodline started but instead a very rude awakening that I wasn't considered a Japanese.

During my second year in Japan, my brother Egan realized I was going to be there for a while, so one day he called me and asked if I was interested in being part of the Japan division of his racquetball company, E-Force. Egan felt that I was someone he could trust and because I was now the current All Japan National Racquetball champion, I would be a great asset to the sales of his E-Force racquets. Up until then, for the past two years he was letting a man by the name of Mr. Kaneko run the sales out of his sports club. I thought it would be a great opportunity, so I set up a meeting with Mr. Kaneko and sat down to discuss with him how we could begin working together. He seemed a bit caught off guard and definitely was uneasy about the new set up. I felt the meeting went well and I told him that I'd be back in a week and we said our goodbyes.

The next day, Egan called me and was upset. After our meeting, Mr. Kaneko had called Egan and told Egan, "If I have to work with Enson I don't want to do this at all. I work alone or I don't want to do this at all." Egan felt that he was out of line so he put me in charge of the sales of E-Force racquets in Japan.

The only problem was my Japanese wasn't good enough to be able to comfortably converse, especially in a business type of conversation. So I asked Toyoko, Eric's wife, if she could help me and she agreed. Her help was tremendous and it helped increase the sales of E-Force racquets.

I was doing seminars throughout Japan while competing and winning the All Japan National Tournaments. Things were going smooth for a while until Toyoko and I began to have some differences in opinion about the company to a point, where some friction developed in our relationship. I also realized that it was taking much of Toyoko's time that I felt it might have been hampering the growth of her English school. I finally made a decision, a very big one, that I really did not give enough thought to, suggesting to Toyoko that I would take E-Force off her hands and try to run it all by myself. Until this day, I'm not sure if she was angry or hurt but she promptly answered "Okay" and suddenly turned everything over to me. I was hoping it would be a more gradual change but I got everything "dumped" on me. I had to transport all the stock to my small apartment and had to do everything from orders, faxes, taxes, and deliveries in my very limited Japanese.

I had to send a letters in Japanese which took me about five hours to compose, explaining the change and that everything from orders to questions would be done by fax. I felt that doing everything by fax would prevent miscommunication and allow me to be able to decipher the faxes at my pace since my Japanese wasn't yet good enough to communicate properly. Trying to do both was taking a toll on me. I would get home from my English teaching job at around 9 or 10 p.m. and then would begin going through the faxes of orders and questions about the product.

Figuring out each fax and breaking down each Japanese kanji took long hard hours. There were nights where I could barely get two hours of sleep before having to get up and get ready to go to my English job. I would fall asleep in the middle of a student's reading exercise and even brought my E-Force work into my English job. I would bring the faxes I got from sports clubs and have my students do translations for an exercise. Honestly, I wasn't sure if it was all translated perfectly so all I did was correct the grammar and made sure that I could grasp the meaning from their translation. I tried for months to make it work but I felt drained and knew that I was spreading myself out too thinly to do a good job for both. I finally decided to concentrate on one job in order to do it well. Since I felt there was a better future in doing E-Force, I decided to discontinue my English teaching job so I could concentrate 100% on E-Force.

Thus, I made numerous trips to Korea to manufacture a line of racquetball gloves I named "The Partner." I also started my own line of racquets and thought of the name "Purebred" because the word purebred brings animals to one's mind and because there were an endless list of animals, I felt that I could find an animal to address the various lines of racquets, namely the low, medium and high, and also, further names of animals to address the four to eight different models of racquets. In addition, anything that was purebred, like a dog or a horse, was always considered elite and this connoted a classy and quality product.

Chapter 12
A Man's Dying Wish

Everything was going well, especially when my girlfriend of three years, Chiyoko Kasahara made the move to relocate and move in with me to help me with the company. Chiyoko was tremendous help and sales began to pick up. We had three good years and even talked about marriage in our future.

I first met Chiyoko when I first came to Japan. I was invited to participate in the racquetball tournament by Mr. Kaneko, who owned a sports club in Yokohama called Viva Sports Club. While in Japan I trained and hung out every day at Viva and got to know the staff very well. Chiyoko was one of the staff at Viva Sports and she stood out. She was a very simple quiet girl who caught my attention with her innocence and sweet personality. In time we became good friends and eventually we saw each other more than friends to a point where we called and kept in touch with each other, even though I moved hundreds of miles away up North to teach English.

After only about six short months after Chiyoko moved up north with me, her father was diagnosed with cancer. I got along very well with her whole family, especially her father who kept implying that he wanted Chiyoko and I to tie the knot. His battle with cancer lasted about a year and I visited him about three times a month only to see him getting weaker and weaker, thinner and thinner with each visit. Then about a month before he died, Chiyoko asked me if we could just get married on paper just so she could show her father to make him happy before he passed. I agreed and it was my first marriage. This marriage was totally just on paper to please her dying father so Chiyoko and I just continued as we were. A year later I felt my love for her change into a sister kind of love so we agreed to break up and just be friends. We quietly signed and filed the divorce papers and like leaves that drop off the branches of a tree in the fall, my first marriage came and went. We no longer communicated and have been out of contact for over a decade. She is now remarried. I hope she is happy and that all her dreams came true.

I also hired another fellow racquetball player, Shoichi Sakai, who was someone I felt I could trust to take over E-Force while I made my move back home to Hawaii. Yes, for the past four years that I was in Japan my heart longed to get back to the beaches, the warm weather, and the place where my whole family was, Hawaii, the place my heart called home.

However, God had other plans for me. Little did I know I was on my way to enter the ring to become a professional fighter. I didn't see it coming but everything fell into place like a puzzle and the ring was to become my new home.

Chapter 13

CONTROLLING THE FIRE WITHIN

In my childhood I had always been active in sports and at the very young age of five, I started playing Little League baseball and basketball. When I was in elementary school, I started track and field and Pop Warner Football in addition to baseball and basketball. My mother allowed me to play only a year of football because it was "too dangerous." In high school I was a four-sport varsity player making the varsity team for baseball, basketball, volleyball, and track...while on the side pursuing racquetball. When I graduated from high school, baseball and racquetball were the two sports I decided to concentrate on, eventually singling it out to just racquetball.

Training MMA for me was never about getting in the ring; it was a part of survival for the streets. It just was a good way to channel my energy and learn to defend myself and my pride on the streets.

I remember way back, when I was only about 12 or 13 years old, I saw a documentary in which a family was shown driving along a mountain highway. The father, who was driving, lost control of the car and it went off a cliff. When the car settled on the bank below, it caught fire and burst into flames. The father managed to escape and knew he had to get his family out before the car was engulfed in fire. However, he couldn't think straight being in a state of panic and as a result, he struggled with opening the car door, something that was so simple and basic.

He grabbed the door handle, pulled it and shook it but seemingly had forgotten how to open it. He couldn't do a simple task like open his own car door because being in a state of panic just jumbled up everything in his head. The fire eventually got to the gas tank, there was an explosion and his whole family died.

When I saw this documentary, I realized that, as a man, I must be able to protect and take care of my loved ones at all times. So in order to be capable of doing that, I must be able to keep a level head and be in control of my emotions no matter what situation I'm in. I always visualize myself in that type of situation and I pray to God that if that day comes I can keep my fears in control, keep my cool and save my loved ones.

I relate this way of thinking to sports because no matter how well you can execute a shot in practice, your nerves and emotions could interfere with your consistency. In racquetball, for instance, if there was a shot I could hit perfectly 99% of the time in practice but that percentage could drop to about 40% from the lack of control of my nerves during a big tournament. Simple things like footwork would get complicated but of course, this was no comparison to saving my family out of a burning car, but it was a start and would be connected.

Controlling my nerves in a racquetball tournament was a start to eventually taking control of my nerves in a life and death situation if it ever were to occur. Four years of playing racquetball all over the world helped me slowly but steadily take control of my nerves to a point where my movement and shots in a tournament could be executed with the same consistency and accuracy that I had in practice. This proved to me that I was getting better at staying calm and thinking straight in a situation where my emotions could disrupt my train of thought, affecting my capability to execute things to the best of my ability.

I got further practice through television interviews and appearances. Something as simple as speaking made me nervous. My voice would shake and the words just wouldn't come out right. As the years went by, I became relaxed and calm in tournaments and television interviews. But still, I wasn't satisfied. I knew I was still a long way from controlling my emotions in a life and death situation.

Then, I found a way to take this to the next level. It was 1994 and Rickson Gracie was coming to Japan to participate in Japan's first big mixed martial arts event, The Vale Tudo Japan. Rickson and I became personal friends., due to having trained with Rickson's older brother Relson for four years.

When Rickson was fighting I found myself losing control of my emotions.

I was standing in my seat, screaming and cheering out loud like something had taken over my body. Then it clicked in my head that if I could not control myself when my friend is fighting in the ring then what would happen if I myself were fighting in the ring? I knew the jitters I felt just watching, would be magnified 10 times if I were fighting.

Now I'm a pretty quiet person when cheering for friends, but for some reason, because it was a fighting event it was a bit different from a normal sporting event. It was something about fighting that boiled a different hot blood in me. If it were baseball, the objective of the game would be to hit the ball and run around the bases to score runs. If it were basketball, the objective would be to put the ball in the hoop. Even a rough sport like football, the objective is to get the ball across the line. But in fighting, the objective is to render your opponent unconscious or hurt him so bad that he gives up or can't continue.

After the fight, a Karate friend, Mr. Shigematsu, told me he was interested in fighting in MMA, so he asked if I could show him some ground techniques. I agreed and we drove to a kickboxing gym he trained at, Watanabe Gym. When we entered, the owner of the gym, Watanabe Sensei, walked up, greeted me and asked me if I was a fighter. I said no, but I did train as a hobby. One of his eyes was white, dead with nerve damage from boxing. He looked at me with a big smirk on his face, as if he were going to burst out laughing any minute.

We entered the ring sparred and I had no problem taking Mr. Shigematsu down and submitting him on the ground. After the training, Watanabe Sensei shook my hand and said, "If you ever want to train. Come here anytime." I nodded and was a little humbled by this man's confidence and straight forwardness.

The more I thought about it, the more obsessed I became to make the move to the ring. However, I was currently the fourth time reigning Japan racquetball champion and I knew I couldn't do both. I knew the ring was a dangerous place so I wanted to give it my all, my 110%. I knew a loss in the ring could result in a serious injury, so I wanted to use all my free time to prepare for the ring. In the past, I trained martial arts as a hobby and for the streets and never in my wildest dreams did I ever think I would someday be getting in a professional ring.

So I decided to hang up my racquet and go full time in martial arts. Don't get me wrong; I didn't get into the ring because I wanted to be the best fighter in the world or to make money. It was my chance to grow as a man, because to me, it was definitely not a sport. I started off by calling all the fighting associations like Pancrase, Rings, UWF, and Shooto. All but Shooto asked me to send in pictures and a resume and told me I had to wait for a preliminary test. Only Shooto didn't seem to have a set procedure and instead, they told me to come down so they could take a look at me.

The next morning I jumped on a bullet train and headed one hour south to a town called Omiya. When I arrived in Omiya I caught a taxi to the Super Tiger Gym. At this time a good childhood friend, Craig Haga was visiting me so he came with me when I first went down to the Shooto Gym. When I entered the gym, I was greeted by a friendly overweight man, whom I later found out was the legendary first Tiger Mask pro wrestler, Sayama Satoru. We talked a bit, then off to the mats we went. When we got to the mats there was a young small Japanese fighter, Nakai Yuki, stretching and getting ready to train. Sayama asked me to grapple with him, so I did for about 15 minutes. In the 15 minutes, I had total control of him and must have put him in every position in the book. I mounted him, took his back and only felt really uncomfortable whenever he began attacking my legs. It was obvious he understood nothing about ground position and when we were done Sayama looked really excited.

We sat on the mat with Sayama and he looked over to Nakai and said, "We can use him." Nakai replied, "Yes, we sure can!"

We later went to dinner and Sayama asked me if I could make my pro debut in two and a half months. That caught me off guard and I quickly answered, "Pro??? No! Amateur is fine." Then Sayama said, "Don't worry. You'll be okay at pro." So I thought, get in the ring, feel it, then win or lose, in control or out of control, that was it. I wanted just one fight to get the experience. I had no desire to fight as a professional and Hawaii was my home and that is where I needed to return. But I accepted Sayama's offer for the experience and began training for my very first professional martial arts debut.

Chapter 14
MY DEBUT INTO MMA –
SHIGETA SHINGO

To train for my debut, I decided to drop everything in Koriyama and move to Omiya. I even stopped cold turkey competing in racquetball tournaments so I could prepare for my ring debut. To me, this wasn't a sport but a regulated fight. How could you even consider this a sport when the objective is to hurt your opponent?

I lived in one of the private rooms in the gym and trained daily with the 4th Tiger Mask, Yamazaki. As I frequented the gym, I came to learn how famous Nakai was. When they made me spar with him, I thought I was sparring with one of the members but little did I know I sparred with one of the toughest and best Shooto fighters. I then decided to take Nakai under my wing and teach him the proper ground positioning. He didn't understand a single thing about the ground positioning of Brazilian Jiu-Jitsu but he was a very fast learner. For my personal preparation, every day it was always just me and Yamazaki.

I was about 185 pounds and he was only about 165 pounds so I consistently beat him up . It seemed like he always had a bleeding nose or a swollen ear. My debut date was getting closer so I was getting nervous while Sayama was making some changes to the Shooto rules to adapt to my style. Sayama had created a whole new rule he named Freestyle to adapt to my Jiu-Jitsu background. For instance, before I came onboard the Shooto rules prohibited all ground punching.so to address my style, he created a new rule that would allow ground punching. Sayama created this set of new rules he called Freestyle and then referred to the old rules as General style.

As I was showing Sayama a lot of the Ju-Jitsu techniques, I noticed he was featured on television and in magazines showing these techniques saying that he figured them out. Numerous times he would tell me that I am a secret weapon and that's why he never mentioned me. I didn't care and just let it go.

This was going to be just the second time these Freestyle rules were going to be used in Shooto and Sayama expected the media to go crazy. As the fight drew nearer, I was working more and more on my takedowns because my stand-up game sucked. As for my ground, I was a solid purple belt and felt confident if the fight went to the ground.

Before I knew it, it was the night before the fight. I was physically 110% ready but emotionally I was a wreck. I couldn't stop my mind from imagining what it would be like getting into the ring and I was so nervous about it that I couldn't get much sleep. The strategy for the fight was to play with my jab and pretend like I felt comfortable on my feet but I was to be ready for the opening to take my opponent down and bring the fight to the mat.

It was fight day! I was 27 years old and all my fellow racquetball players came to see how I would fare in my new venture. For the last four years, I had been the top racquetball player in Japan and I just disappeared from the racquetball world, giving no warning to properly prepare myself for my ring debut. This was just a one-time thing for me just to see if I would be able to control my emotions. I knew it would be nearly impossible but I felt that the more experience I got now, the better I would be prepared when a real test were to come in a life and death situation.

My element was on the ground because of my Jiu-Jitsu background. For my ring entrance song, I decided to go with a Hawaiian group because I was really proud of my Hawaiian roots. My ring entrance consisted of two songs: the first one by Bu La'ia called "Day Old Poi" and the second by a Hawaiian group named Ho'oaikane. For my fight trunks, I chose red, white, and blue tights to represent my true nationality, American. For my corner I had my brother Egan, my sparring partner Yamazaki, and Nakai.

I remember walking into the ring and looking over at my opponent, Shigeta, only to see him glaring at me like he hated me. So I glared back at him feeling my heart churn. I felt the urge to smash his face growing stronger and stronger within me. My feet didn't feel like my own and I felt as if I were floating and walking on clouds. In other words, I was so nervous that a simple thing like walking became a foreign thing to me. On the other side of the ring, Shigeta was continuously staring at me like he wanted to fuck me up and that stirred up mixed and strong emotions in me. I felt a bit of fear, which triggered the urge to hurt him bad, and the anxiety to get the fight started ASAP.

MMA debut – Japan, 1995.

Every fighter feels fear – it's totally normal. What makes the difference between a man and a warrior is what he does with the fear. Some people have the misunderstanding that a warrior fears nothing but I believe otherwise. I believe a warrior feels fear like any other man but doesn't let it conquer and control him. He conquers it to a point where the fear becomes his friend. If fear conquers you it becomes your enemy. However if you can feel it, prevent it from conquering you and then control it, it will turn into incredible power for you. I'm not going to sit here writing this book and pretend to all of you that I had no fear in the ring, because I did. But never once did fear ever get the best of me, ever.

Then the gong rang. I felt like I was walking on clouds as we approached each other in the center of the ring. I threw a few jabs, just waiting for a chance to shoot in for a tackle but he never committed. This flustered me and I was wondering what I was going to do if he never committed to attack.

Just when I was getting antsy, he committed with a low leg kick and that was my chance. I got ahold of his leg, easily took him to the ground and went straight to the mount. He had absolutely no knowledge of ground positioning and was lost in a state of panic. Although my ground punching was horrible, I rained down punches, expecting for the fight to be stopped soon, but to my surprise, it was much harder, than I thought, to finish with mount punches I was actually getting tired and winded. I began getting a bit worried but sucked it up and continued punching.

It finally came to a point where Shigeta was grunting and groaning in pain with every punch that hit him and the referee moved in closer to get a closer look. I knew the end was near so I delivered a few more hard shots to the back of his neck until the referee finally stepped in and stopped the fight. I felt angry and wanted to continue hitting him, but with the stern pull on my arm from the referee I snapped out of the semi trance I was in and realized that I had won the fight.

What I found very interesting was during the fight, I felt like an animal instead of a fighter. I didn't want to just win but I wanted to break my opponent. When I was in the mount I had numerous chances to take his arm and finish with an arm bar, but I chose another route. I instinctively didn't want to just win, but rather, found myself wanting to break him.

Instead of having him tap because his arm was going to break, I wanted to make him tap because he thought he was going to die. I felt an animal part of me come alive and I loved the feeling. When the referee pulled me off, I could still feel the adrenaline running through my body, keeping me in a dream state, aware that my emotions had totally taken control of me. Damn, I still had a lot to learn but was so glad I finally got this ring experience under my belt.

That's all I wanted, I was done and ready to move back home to Hawaii. However, Sayama had other plans. He wanted me to fight again, even though I had told him from the beginning that I just wanted one fight.

Chapter 15
BAD RULES – RENE ROOZE

I wasn't sure if getting in just once made me prepared for a real life and death situation, but I felt that it was definitely better than never feeling it. I got the experience and was ready to move on with my life. I came out of it alive and I was done. I didn't want to fight again but to be honest I was actually enjoying the rush I got in the ring and the little fame I was starting to get. I was relieved that I walked away without injury and was stoked that I finally got to experience what I felt would be uncontrollable emotions. However, the media covered the event like I was already some famous fighter. My fight was only the 2nd fight of the night, which usually gets only the results printed in small print, but my fight, for some reason, was treated totally different. It got a full-page color picture with the headline, "Birth of a Japanese Monster!" With the brand new "anything goes" rules and the fact that Gracie Jiu-Jitsu was the talk of the Martial arts scene, my fight hit the spotlight. The timing of my debut was just perfect. The Japanese media found someone of Japanese descendant who was a Gracie Jiu-Jitsu practitioner and they just jumped all over it.

It was so funny how I was considered an outsider or a "Gaijin" all these years and the moment I got the spotlight, they wanted to consider me Japanese. I resented that, because I felt I was being used just for their benefit. All these years in Japan as a "nobody", my life was made two times more difficult because I was a foreigner. I needed a visa to work and stay in Japan. Even with a visa I couldn't be the sole owner of a car, house, or a company.

I was offended but decided to go with the flow because the write-up in the magazines was full of praise in a positive light. I wasn't sure what to do: whether to do as I planned and end it with one fight, or to go with the flow and take advantage of the publicity I was getting. The next morning at the gym, Sayama sensei called me into his office and asked me if I wanted to fight again in April, in the Vale Tudo Japan Tournament, three months away.

I was baffled because just a year ago in the 1994 Vale Tudo, I was in the stands cheering Rickson. I asked who was going to be in the tournament, and he said he wasn't certain, but he wanted to have Rickson back to defend his title. I instantly declined his offer because, Rickson was a personal friend of mine and is the younger brother of Relson who was my Jiu-Jitsu teacher/brother. To me, because fighting is not a sport, I wouldn't even consider fighting someone I called a friend. When I fight, I go in with the mentality to hurt or kill my opponent, and ready to die in the ring if I have to. To me, thinking of hurting a friend, especially someone like Rickson whom I admired, was beyond me. I also didn't consider myself even near Rickson's level and remembered that I was only in this for the experience.

When I declined the offer, because my debut fight had such a big impact on the fighting world in Japan, Sayama insisted I participate in the event even if it wasn't in the tournament. After all the time he gave me training me for my debut fight, I felt the least I could do for him was to fight one more time for him. I confirmed with Sayama that if there was no chance that I'd be fighting Rickson, I'd be more than happy to participate in the event for him. He then asked me to participate in a special single fight, and I accepted.

Two weeks later, Sayama again called me into his office to inform me that they had decided on my opponent. It was going to be a Dutch fighter by the name of Rene Rooze, known as a very dirty fighter. He was 6 ft., 7 in. tall, an established fighter with almost no ground skills. All I had to do was take the fight to the ground and he would be all mine. However, I felt most uncomfortable with the rule that allowed the fighters to grab the ropes to prevent themselves from going to the ground. I didn't like this rule because takedowns take a lot of stamina, and if your opponent grabs on to the ropes, it would make it three times harder to take him down. My wrestling sucked and I figured I had no chance with Rene if it were kickboxing, so there was no recourse. I just had to get the fight to the ground.

I was training very hard for this fight, and I decided to wear the same fight shorts I wore for my debut fight. The tights were red, white, and blue tights with a Gracie triangle and a Super Tiger Gym logo on it because I considered myself a Gracie practitioner and was also grateful for all the training Sayama was giving me. I wore my red, white, and blue tights because I wanted to emphasize the fact that I was American. During the four years I was playing racquetball in Japan, I experienced so much prejudice that reminded me that I was American and not Japanese.

Rickson Gracie and I.

The day before the fight at the rules meeting, I went to talk to Rickson about my uneasiness of the rule that you could hold on to the ropes.

Rickson just chuckled and said, "If he holds the ropes with his right arm, you hit him on the right side. If he holds the ropes on the left, you hit him on the left. It's simple, my friend." Rickson was someone I really looked up to, so his calm demeanor and simple explanation wiped my worries away immediately.

When fight day came, I had the 6th fight of the night, so I was relaxing in my room watching the fights on my television monitor. Two fights before my fight was Rickson vs. Yamamoto, the first round of the tournament. As I watched the fight, as expected, Yamamoto respected Rickson's ground technique and began holding on to the ropes to prevent himself from going to the ground. As I watched, everything wasn't as simple as Rickson had said. He couldn't get Yamamoto to the ground, and was taking a lot of hard punches. At one point in the fight, Yamamoto even got Rickson in a tight guillotine, and cranked Rickson's neck. Rickson was in a battle and the rope-holding rule was the only reason Yamamoto ever even had a chance. As the fight went on, you could tell Rickson was feeling the punishment and I thought, "Holy shit...what am I going to do?" If Rickson couldn't get his opponent to the ground, what am I going to do? Egan and I began brainstorming and that's when Egan came up with foot stomping. It was soon my turn to fight so I got psyched up and mentally prepared for war.

This time my ring entrance song consisted of two songs. The first song, I again used Bu La'ia's song "Day Old Poi" and for my second song I used Queen's, "We Will Rock You". My entrance songs pumped me up and I was ready for war but for some reason I felt more nervous than my debut fight. I guess the mixture of the rope holding rule and the arena being10 times bigger than where I fought my debut didn't help. My debut was held at Korakuen Hall that had a capacity of about 2,000 people and this fight with Rene Rooze was at the Nihon Budokan with a capacity of 50,000.

I felt very uneasy and nervous but there was no turning back now, so I had to psych myself up and prepare for battle. When I finally got into the ring and was staring Rene down, only then did I realize how tall he was.

He was 6 feet 7 inches, a good 10 inches taller than me. However, his height didn't worry me much because I was confident that I would get him to the ground, and on the ground height didn't matter.

Then the gong sounded and we were off! Surprisingly, he didn't come out attacking me like he did in all of his past fights that I saw on the videos. Instead, he just sat back and waited for me to make the first move. This worried me because all the months of preparation were spent preparing for a fighter that was going to attack me right off the bell. He didn't and all my plans went out the window. I knew I was in a bind but just had to go with the flow.

We circled each other and waited for each other to make a move. I was trying everything I could think of to lure him in to attack me. I glared at him, got close and pointed to my chin like, "hit me here" and even began stomping my feet pretending to attempt a tackle. However, he was patient and didn't bite the bait so I decided to make the first move and close the distance one step at a time. I slowly closed the gap until I was in range and then shot for a tackle. Luckily, I timed it right, got ahold of him without taking a single punch, then set up for my takedown.

However, as expected, before I could take him down he ran back to the ropes and wrapped his arms around it. He was so much taller than me that my punches had a hard time reaching him, and even if they did they really weren't hurting him but I was really feeling the elbows and punches he was dropping down on me. It was a nightmare. I was taking a lot of punishment and I just couldn't get him to the ground. He was dropping elbows and punches down on my shoulders and head that was rocking me with every shot. He caught me with some hard knees that knocked my wind out and he was heeling the back of my calves so much that they both had contusions. Although I caught him with some solid foot stomps, he was getting the upper hand and I was taking a beating.

Then an idea just popped into my head out of nowhere. If he can use the ropes, I thought, then so can I. My first thought was to climb up on the first ropes to eliminate the height difference, which would take away the leverage of the punches and elbows he was dropping down on me. Then as I was trying to jockey myself between the ropes, I saw an opening as he was trying to hang on to the ropes with both hands. I put my head under one of his arms and suddenly I ended up between the ropes with Rene's back facing me. I then instinctively used the ropes like a ladder, climbed up on his back and sunk in a choke from the back. I couldn't get it in that deep, but I felt it was deep enough so I locked in the choke hard and squeezed the choke tight. He then panicked and tried to jump out of the ring with me on his back.

The choke was in tight and I wasn't going to let go unless he tapped or went unconscious. As he tried to fall out of the ring, I just hung on and got ready for the fall. Luckily, the referees were on the ball and grabbed ahold of our legs, as we were about to fall out of the ring. They pulled us back into the ring with me attached to his back and we fell to the mat. I still had the choke locked in good and as soon as we hit the mat, he began tapping frantically on the mat, signifying he was giving up. I then released the choke, got up, and raised my hands in victory. I could feel my calves tightening up so I quickly left the ring so all the fans and Rene wouldn't see that he hurt me.

As soon as I got to my locker room I began icing my calves and approximately an hour later, my calves swelled up to twice their normal size. About five hours after my fight and for the next four days I had to hobble and walk like a penguin. God must have been watching over me because. I was taking a beating and climbing the ropes to get to his back was just done by chance.

Now I was 2-0 and wondering if I should actually get into the ring for the third time or count my blessings and be grateful that I climbed into the ring twice and was still healthy and alive to tell about it.

When I got back to the gym, Sayama was ecstatic. He was talking about when my next fight would be and naming different fighters he thought would be good for me to fight.

Chapter 16

ARM BAR, I'LL BREAK IT — ED DE KRUIJF

I was ready to move on, chalking up my two fights as growth to becoming a true man. I never imagined in my wildest dreams that I would be in the professional fighting ring and being recognized as a professional fighter. Getting into the ring was just on my path to becoming a true man. Never once did I think of it as being a career. Even my martial arts training was to be able to defend myself on the streets, not to get in the ring.

Now here I was, 2-0 and ready to put this behind me, when a week after my fight with Rene Rooze, Sayama came to me and asked me to fight in an event he was producing in Omiya. After all he has done for me and the time he has spent on me, I felt that fighting for him just one more time was the least I could do for him. I accepted again telling myself that this time for sure it was my last fight. The opponent Sayama chose for me was the European Cage Fighting Champion, Ed De Kruijf. When I saw the videos of his past fights I noticed he was a very well rounded fighter with his striking being his weakest point.

However, my striking also sucked so even though he had a wrestling base, my strategy was to get him to the ground and let my Jiu-Jitsu do the work. Another concern I had was the infamous dirty Dutch fighter Gerard Gordeau was going to be in his corner. Gordeau was famous for gauging welterweight Shoot Fighter Nakai's eye, destroying all the nerves in his right eye, killing his eye and causing him to have to retire from MMA. I flew home to Hawaii to train for this fight, working my ground and cardio with Egan.

I did so much conditioning on the beach in the deep sand that my weight dropped to 202 lbs. but I felt fast, strong, and ready to go.

Fight night came and we were the co-main event in the dark, hot skate center they turned into a fight arena. The arena was packed and the ring we were fighting in was a poorly made Octagon/Ring with net between the bottom ropes and the ring. The lights were also too low and too strong, which created a sauna effect in the ring. All of the early fights went smoothly except for the controversial disqualification loss my buddy/training partner, Carl Franks, suffered.

Then my turn came up. The nervousness was still strong but much less than in my first two fights. Again, like my debut fight, I started out circling my opponent throwing jabs, waiting for the right time to shoot in and take him down. We both sucked at our standing technique and it seemed neither of us wanted to commit to a heavy punch or kick. Then suddenly on a lazy jab, one of his fingers poked my eye. The pain from his finger going into my eye caused me to start blinking and rubbing my eye trying to regain my vision. I tried to keep my distance, hoping my vision would come back quickly, and I wondered if it was done on purpose or it was just an accident. He noticed that I was having a hard time seeing with one of my eyes so he became a lot more aggressive.

When he came in for a kick, I saw an opening so I grabbed his leg. I had a good grasp of it so I lifted him up off the mat and threw him down. As soon as we hit the ground, he put me in a headlock and began to squeeze my head. The fact that he was squeezing my head so hard just showed his lack of knowledge of submissions because there was no way he was going to submit someone just by squeezing a headlock.

I knew the more persistent he was with squeezing my head the more time I was going to have to slide to his back. In the brief scuffle, we ended up on the edge of the ring when the referee yelled, "Stop! Don't move!"

Instinctively, before the three referees got into the ring to drag us to the center of the ring, I grabbed the ropes and slid my body a little bit to the side for better position. That enabled me to get my foot hook in deeper which enabled me to promptly get to his back as soon as the fight was restarted. You could say I cheated but it was done instinctively and the referees let it go so you could also say otherwise. What was funny about the whole thing was that instead of his corner being aware of me adjusting my body into a better position when the referee told us not to move, Gordeau screamed something in Dutch which triggered Ed to begin to squeeze my head harder. I think he thought that he was going to hurt me by getting in a longer squeeze without the referee knowing. However all this did was show me his lack of understanding of submissions making me a bit agitated.

We were reset in the center and when the referee yelled, "Ready? Go!" I instantly based up with my right hand, popped my head out from the headlock he had me in, and quickly took his back. From there I could tell he was lost and had no idea how to get me off his back. I then just took my time and picked my punches.

To get me off his back he was trying to pull my head down, hoping that I would slide off but I had my hooks securely in so I was safe. However, because the lights in the arena were so low and so hot, we were sweating profusely and I could feel myself beginning to slip. He also could feel me beginning to slip, but was still on all fours, so he stood up on his feet with his arms stretched out to the mat. That's when I saw my chance. I let myself slide down to his left and positioned my body into a perfect inverted arm bar. I then grabbed a good hold of his wrist so he couldn't twist his arm out and then I began hyperextending his arm. I could hear his ligaments in his arm popping but he didn't tap so I torqued his arm to the other side and more ligaments began to pop.

Finally, the referee stepped in and stopped the fight. Ed and Gordeau began complaining and protesting that he didn't tap and they felt cheated. I also was at the verge of hurting his arm badly so in a way I felt the same way too. I wished the referee didn't stop me because I would have damaged Ed's arm so bad it would have given him a big lesson on how dangerous arm bars were. It was apparent that their lack of understanding of the dangers of an arm bar made them feel cheated. What they failed to realize is that the referee saved Ed's arm and possibly his career. I circled over to where Gordeau was standing and glared at him, hoping he would give me a reason to punch him in the face, but he avoided eye contact with me. I still felt animosity for what he did to Nakai's eye and wanted a reason to hit him.

Wow. My third win in a row, one technical knockout and two tap outs. Three wins a row, but I was certain I was done and ready to move on. However, an amazing thing happened. In the August issue of the biggest fighting magazine in Japan, I got front cover! I really wanted to call it quits but damn, I was on the cover of the biggest fighting magazine in the country, so again, I felt an obligation to fight one more fight. Sayama was excited and I didn't want to pop his bubble so I again told him that I would do just one more fight.

Note: After this fight I got a call from Relson Gracie telling me that Rorion wanted me to take the Gracie triangle off my fight shorts. I was surprised because I only put the logo on to show appreciation for all Relson has taught me. It really disappointed me but I respected their wishes and took the logo off.

Chapter 17

Wow I Might Actually be Good at This – Andre Mannaart

In Japan K-1 was the biggest and most respected event and for my next opponent, Sayama picked the Dutch K-1 fighter, Andre Mannaart. Of course, because Andre was a respected K-1 fighter and my standing still sucked, I had no intentions of trading punches and kicks with him. His punches and kicks were far superior to mine and this was by far the biggest challenge for me. I was anxious to see what this next fight had in store for me and my strategy was the same as my last fight so my training didn't change much which was a lot of conditioning, takedowns, and grappling.

I also decided to make sure I kept my guard up and slowly but steadily continued to move forward and close the distance. He was either going to keep moving backward or he would have to commit with an attack, which is when I could close in for a takedown. Just the fact that he was a K-1 fighter, meant that everyone was considering this to be my true test. Little did anyone realize that K-1 was not MMA... in fact, it was far from it. It is like comparing racquetball to tennis just because both use a racquet or like comparing a dog and a cat. I had my insecurities but knew that if I trained hard and smart, I would be okay. Leading up to the fight I could feel doubt in the interviewers questioning and on fight day, there was a buzz in the crowd, anxious to see how a respected K-1 fighter would do in MMA rules.

When the gong rang, I stuck to the game plan. I kept my guard up high and began to constantly move forward. Mannaart backed up until he was against the ropes and then he did exactly what I expected. He came in with a punch. Then with perfect timing, I shot in, grabbed his legs, lifted him up, and slammed him on the mat. I stabilized my side control and waited patiently until I saw the opening when he bridged to try to turn me over. I made the instant transition to the mount. I easily secured my position and, because he was strictly a kick boxer, he didn't have a clue on what to do to get out.

I took my time and just softened him up, one punch at a time, waiting for my corner men to give me the 30-second call at which time, I was going to start forcing a submission without being too concerned with keeping position because time would be up soon. I connected with only a few punches, but I guess the referee saw that it was a done deal because he stepped in and stopped the fight before I got the 30 second call.

I personally think the stoppage was much too fast but Andre was a class act and took the loss graciously and congratulated me like a gentleman. He did, however, ask me to fight him again in the old Shooto General rules, where there was no ground punching and a lot of breaks to start the fight standing. I was reluctant, but felt it would only be fair. However, Sayama wanted to move on, so this rematch never materialized.

Before this fight, I had decided that this was really going to be my last fight. But being 4-0 with all four of my opponents never making it past the first round was an accomplishment. Especially now, after beating a legit K-1 fighter, the Japanese media was going crazy on me being the next big star for the Japanese people. All the hype got me thinking and although I did this only to gain control of my emotions and fears, I seriously began to wonder if I actually had a future in this. How good was I? Could I be one of the best in the world? I sat down, thought it out thoroughly, talked it over with Egan and made up my mind. I was not going to fight just one more but instead I was going to readjust myself and seriously make a run at being a professional fighter.

There were moments in those days of pondering my future that I couldn't believe what I was deciding and second-guessed myself a lot. I knew that

I was a man and when my mind was made up, I would give my all, 110%, and no one and nothing could change my mind. In a few days after my victory over Andre, my life took a drastic turn.

I was not only never going to move back to Hawaii, my home, the place I loved with all my heart, but I was now in full gear to try to become the best fighter I could possibly be. Hawaii was still in my heart and Japan was still a foreign country to me but it was like I was blindsided. Becoming a respected fighter in the world and fighting the world's best suddenly became a dream that I was going to give my all and make whatever sacrifices I had to make to attain this goal. In my heart, I was now a "Professional Fighter".

At this moment, I realized, over a decade ago, the shot I had missed in the racquetball court and believed as the worst thing that happened in my life, was actually a blessing in disguise. For if I didn't miss that shot, I would have never retired from racquetball and therefore, I would have never went back to school where I found GJJ . Also, because Egan was still on the pro tour, he had to decline the invitation to play in Japan, allowing me to play in his place. To make a long story short, if I didn't miss that racquetball shot I would not have been available to come to Japan. Undoubtedly, it turned out to be the best thing that ever happened to me.

Everything happens for a reason and if we can keep the faith, keep our heads up and continue to move forward, the reason will eventually be revealed. As human beings, whenever we think something bad happens to us in our life, the first thing we ask is "why?" Our impatience as human beings makes us want to know the reason immediately but unfortunately, God has a plan and it will be revealed in due time. With faith and perseverance, one will see in time that, everything... yes everything happens for a reason.

Chapter 18

CATCHING A ROBBER

My popularity was growing as I won more fights. Although I did do a lot of bad things when I was in Hawaii, I felt a small change coming about inside of me. Episodes that were happening in my life and the choices I was making in the episodes made me realize that there was a change taking place.

One of these episodes was on one of my off days. It was a nice calm day and I was killing time in Chiba. I had a lot of free time so I decided to try my luck at Pachinko. Pachinko is a pinball type of gambling game popular in Japan that you rarely win at, but if you get lucky and pick the right machine, you could win a lot. This day I got lucky and my machine hit a jackpot after only putting in about $20. My machine dumped for about an hour and when I felt it was getting cold, I cashed out $280, making a profit of $260. Not bad for an hour of fun and excitement but little did I know that the real excitement was about to start.

I was content and proudly stuffing my earnings in my pocket as I walked back to the train station when I suddenly heard, "Burglar! Burglar!" coming from a small side alley. I looked over to where I heard the screams and I saw a guy in his mid-30's come scampering out of a pawnshop and dash down the street. Seconds later, an older gentleman burst out of the pawn shop and ran after the younger man who was already far down the street. The older man was weak from his old age and as he ran in the direction the younger man ran, he suddenly stumbled and fell because of his weary, aged legs.

Seeing the commotion, I approached the old man, helped him up from the ground, and asked him what happened and if he was okay. He was out of breath but managed to say, "That guy stole jewelry from my shop! Oh no, what am I going to do?" He then ran back into his shop and got on the phone. I then looked down the street where the burglar ran and he was nowhere in sight. I didn't think it would be any use to run down the street after him so I figured that I continue on my way to the station and just keep my eyes open for the younger guy who was wearing a green jacket. Then, as I was walking down a narrow alley, a few streets away from the station, I heard footsteps coming up from behind me. I turned around to see who it was and lo and behold, it was the guy with the green jacket running towards me.

"Holy shit!", I thought. It felt like there was a typhoon whirling in my head as my mind raced, debating what I was going to do. Do I just let him run by and mind my own business or should I grab him and call the police? As I was deciding on what I should do, I could hear his footsteps getting closer and I knew I only had seconds left to make my decision. Then when the burglar came running up beside me, even though I still hadn't decided on what I was going to do, I just reacted. I turned towards where he was coming from, stuck my arm out, grabbed his neck, and took him to the ground.

I proceeded to instinctively mount him to hold him down. He seemed like he was trying to get his hands in his pocket, so just in case he was reaching for some kind of weapon, I held the hand that he was trying to put in his pocket. As soon as I put one of my knees on his throat he then began screaming, "It hurts! It hurts! Stop hurting me!" I really didn't care because I feared he was trying to get a weapon so I didn't let up until I noticed that dangling out of his hand was a thick gold necklace. He threw the necklace in the bushes next to us and just to be safe I kept the pressure a bit longer. He continued screaming, "You're hurting me! Take me to the police! I'd rather go to the police than be here with you!"

When he finally stopped struggling so much I eased off on the pressure and asked him why he did what he did. The reason why I asked him is because if it was for food for his family or if he did what he did because he was in a big financial bind, I was actually considering taking the necklace from him so I could return it to the shop and let him free.

However, he was in a panic and all he could say was, "I didn't do anything, I didn't do anything!" I felt that it was no use in talking to someone who was set on lying, so took out my cell phone, called the police and asked them to come as soon as possible. About 10 minutes later four police officers came and to my surprise they thought the guy I had mounted was the victim. "Get off of him! Let him go!" I turned to the police officers and explained to them that this guy was the perpetrator and I was the one who called them. They looked confused for a moment but finally realized who was who and quickly came and handcuffed the guy I was mounted on. I then got off the mount walked over to the bushes and retrieved the gold necklace from the bush. The police then asked me to come down to the police station to fill out a report. After the report was filed, the storeowner thanked me and the Police Department gave me an honorary certificate of appreciation.

Filing the report took approximately four hours and the storeowner's thank you just didn't seem sincere at all and honestly, it seemed like it just wasn't worth my time. However, I didn't do what I did to please the store owner nor because the storeowner was a friend. I did it because my instinct told me that it was the right thing to do. Just not being appreciated was very disappointing but if it happened again, I would do it all over again simply because it was the right thing to do.

The article in the paper about the incident.

Funny how back in the day when I was growing up in Hawaii, the roles would have been different. I would be the one running and I would have never imagined that someday the roles would be reversed.

Chapter 19
RUDE AWAKENING – JOE ESTES I

Wow. I'm now a professional fighter, ready to do whatever it takes to become one of the best fighters in the world. I had to make some adjustments in my life that definitely included some major sacrifices. One was moving out of the North and relocating to Omiya. I loved Koriyama and had so many friends there, but there was no training facilities available and besides Sayama Sensei was in Omiya. Second, I wasn't about to make the same mistake I did in my past and give only 50%. I wanted to give 110%.

In the past, I split my time between baseball and racquetball and performed very mediocre in both. I also didn't train as hard as I could. Egan trained hard and literally trained 5 times harder than I ever did. He made more sacrifices and never missed a workout. I, on the other hand, slept in occasionally, cut workouts short, and sometimes gave myself a day off because I was in pain from the previous days workout. Egan stopped playing baseball and went full time into racquetball; I on the other hand did both. So this time, instead of pursuing both racquetball and fighting at the same time, I decided to choose just one. So after being the #1 racquetball player in Japan for the past four years, I decided to hang up my racquet and give 110% to my fight training. Also, the girl I was seeing at the time was against my fighting. She gave me an ultimatum that if I decided to fight I was on my own and I had already made up my mind that I was going to fight so I was suddenly single, which helped me dedicate myself to my new dream, Mixed Martial Arts.

I bought a van for transportation and spent every day gearing to become the best fighter I could possibly be. I had a little apartment where I basically just stored all of my luggage and washed my clothes. I would sleep and shower out of my van and stop by my small apartment just to wash clothes and fill the water tank I used to shower. I flattened all the seats in my van so the back of my van became a big bed. I bought a battery-operated hose I could insert into the water tank for my shower. Oh, and of course my loyal beloved Pit Bull, Shooto, was always with me by my side. Even if I were to get lucky, and score a hot hostess she would end up sleeping in Hotel Toyota, my Toyota van. I had no shame for fighting was now my dream and the new founded mission I was chasing with all my heart.

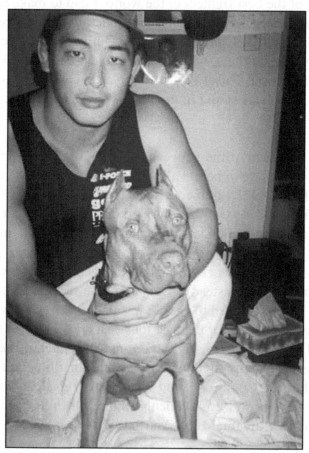

Me and my boy Shooto.

I felt comfortable at 202 pounds so I didn't feel the need to put on more weight and spent more time increasing my stamina and speed. My next opponent, Joe Estes, was an ex-football player who weighed about 253 pounds, outweighing me by about 50 pounds. I wasn't too concerned because when I use to train in Hawaii, there were guys just as big as Joe and I never really had problems grappling with the extra weight. I took the fight and was ready to up my fight record to 5-0. Joe was training out of AMC and being trained by a very respected fighter/trainer Matt Hume so I knew Joe was going to be prepared.

The stare down before the fight was intense because Joe was staring me down like he wanted to punk me and I wasn't backing down an inch. When the fight began, at first contact I could feel the power and weight Joe had. I felt that Joe was too big to take down to take top position so instead I pulled him to the ground and put him in my guard.

Up until this fight I still had my head in Jiu-Jitsu mode and in Jiu-Jitsu the bottom position, when my opponent was in my guard was considered an advantageous position. Little did I know that today I was going to get a wakeup call that MMA and BJJ were not the same. I felt my technique was better than Joe's, but every time I was positioning myself for a submission or an attack, I could hear Matt's voice giving him the perfect advice to stop my attack or counter it. It was frustrating.

There was nothing Joe was doing to me that I felt, put me in danger, but the fact that I couldn't do shit to him, made me feel helpless. The fight was three boring rounds of Joe in my guard, controlling me and defending all my submission and sweep attempts. Finally, the gong to end the fight sounded and the decision was made. Joe Estes was the winner by majority decision 3-0. I was devastated. I felt so lost and frustrated. I knew I had to reevaluate my training and needed to up my game drastically. I needed to work on my striking and put on more weight.

Although I just suffered my first loss, the focus on my goal of becoming one of the best fighters in the world didn't waiver one bit. My face was swollen and marked-up. My pride was hurt but I was far from being broken. Not for a split second did I feel like quitting, but instead I was determined to train harder and go back to the drawing boards, ready to crush any obstacle in the way of my dream.

Chapter 20

THE END – IGOR ZINOVIEV

My next fight came up before I knew it. I was trying to put on weight but putting on quality weight was harder than I had imagined. I was also incorporating a lot of cardio in my workout, which made it that much harder to put on weight. My next opponent was going to be a Russian fighter by the name of Igor Zinoviev. My striking was getting a lot better but I didn't have the confidence that I could execute it properly in a fight. So again, my strategy was to avoid the standing and take him to the ground. I knew virtually nothing about Igor, so it created a little bit of uneasiness in me. I was a bit insecure because of my last loss to Joe Estes, but I went back to Hawaii to train with Egan and I trained so hard that all my insecurities were wiped out. I busted my ass day after day doing everything I needed to and doing it 110%.

The fight with Igor was almost like a replay of my last fight. I took him down with ease except this time Igor was better prepared and he put me in a tight guillotine. I wasn't ready for it, but as I felt him squeeze, I wasn't too worried about it. However, I underestimated his power. From the bottom, he cranked the guillotine, and the pressure was so tight on my neck that I had to give up the top position and put him in my guard. I don't remember much after that, except Egan was in the ring asking me if I was ok. I asked Egan, "What happened?" Egan replied that I got knocked out from ground punches. I couldn't believe it.

That was two consecutive defeats and I was crushed. I trained so hard for the fight, and it was all over in 44 seconds. I was devastated by the loss and I felt like something was squeezing the life out of my heart. For the first time in my life, I doubted the strength of my heart and my decision to dedicate everything I had to this sport. Also, as we were walking back to the locker room, Egan suggested I hang up the gloves and channel my energy towards Jiu-Jitsu. He felt there was just too much to cover in MMA and in the mist of my disappointment, Egan's idea actually was a bit appealing but I decided to toss it around for a few more days.

Chapter 21

I'm Not Just Finished Just Yet – Mushtaq Abdullah

I was so devastated by my 44 second KO by Igor that the weakness in my heart caused me to look for a way out. I thought Egan's suggestion to hang up my MMA gloves and pursue Jiu-Jitsu instead might have been the answer. I decided to think it over thoroughly, but I was so disappointed. My disappointment was not just because I lost, and not just because I got knocked out, but because I trained so hard and dedicated so much to a fight that only lasted a mere 44 seconds. I was teeter-tottering 50/50 and it scares me now to think how close I was to hanging up my MMA gloves for good. I hated to think I was a quitter, but instead I looked at it as making a possible career change.

Like baseball, you get three strikes, so to be fair to myself I decided to give my all for one more fight and see what happens. I thought that if I lost again for the third time, it would be my last fight. It wasn't about just pulling out a victory: it was about truly testing my ability as a fighter for the last time. Sayama and most of the people around me suggested I take an easy fight to get the win, but I had different ideas. I wanted to see what I was made of and if I still had what it took to be a great fighter. I wasn't looking for someone I knew I could beat, but rather someone I thought could beat me. Someone with ferocity and intensity that would make most people run away. I didn't want to prolong anything. If I wasn't cut out for this fighting stuff, I wanted to find out as soon as possible.

The one I had in mind was a fighter from Iran, a wrestler named Mushtaq Abdullah who had destroyed Sanae Kikuta in the same ring that I lost to Igor in. Mushtaq showed no pain when he fought Kikuta. Sucking up the pain of a knee bar, pounding his way out of a near fight-ending hold, breaking Kikuta's spirit in a TKO victory. Yes, that's whom I wanted to fight to decide my fate in my life as a MMA fighter. I felt that if I could beat a monster like Mushtaq, then I earned the right to call myself a MMA fighter and continue my career; if I couldn't then I was done.

I was working hard on my striking at Watanabe Gym and was excited to try my striking out, but at the same time a bit scared that this may be my last fight. I weighed only 204 pounds while Mushtaq weighed in at a solid 215 pounds. I was going into this fight ready to be on my feet or on the ground, but because Mushtaq was a wrestler and my wrestling sucked, I was training a lot of fighting off my back. His wrestling was probably a lot better than mine so I planned to fight him standing until he wanted to take it to the ground. I knew absolutely nothing about him except that he was Iranian and had a wrestling background. There were no videos of his past fights so all I had to go by was what I saw in his fight with Kikuta and that made me a bit uneasy but I was ready for war.

As soon as the starting gong sounded, I took the initiative and checked him with an inside low leg kick. Then before he could get set I stepped in with a big right cross and "Bam!" it hit it's mark and he went down. I wanted to step in and finish him off but before I could, I noticed him tapping the mat frantically, signaling that he quit. As soon as I noticed that, I assumed it was over so I abandoned my attack and raised my hands in victory. I then walked to one of the corners, stepped up on the first ropes proclaiming my victory towards the cheering crowd.

As I turned around I noticed the referee was counting and Mushtaq was getting back on his feet. What?! It's not over? I turned to the referee and while gesturing with my hand, I said, "He tapped." The referee looked at me like he didn't understand what I was saying so instead of repeating myself and giving Mushtaq more time to recover, I turned back to Mushtaq and quickly resumed the fight. He tried to take me down but I stopped him. He then threw a big roundhouse haymaker at me. I ducked under it, got my feet set, and "Bam" landed another solid right. As soon as he hit the ground, again, I saw him begin to tap the mat. But this time, instead of letting the referee give him another chance, I jumped on him and prepared to pound him. Suddenly the referee jumped in and called the fight.

When I realized I had officially won the fight, I felt this overwhelming surge inside as if all the blood in my body had been set on fire. I raised my hands in the air, looked up to the heavens, closed my eyes, and suddenly all my muscles in my body flexed as if they were giving out a big scream. That's when I realized the amount of worry and insecurity I had about the fight. All the fear and insecurity that a fighter has about a fight shows in the celebration after the victory. Either I was too focused on the fight, or I made myself ignore it, but I was a lot more worried and insecure about this fight than I had imagined. Well, that all didn't matter now because I was now back and here to stay.

After having to beat Mushtaq twice I came to a conclusion that my job in the ring was never to stop fighting on my own power when I see my opponent tap. My job was to beat my opponent, smash him, and annihilate him until the referee stops me. As a fighter I can't worry about the jobs of the ring doctor, judges, or referee. I must just concentrate on doing my job to the best of my ability, which is to hurt my opponent, break him until one of the officials stop me. Never again will I play the role of the referee and stop fighting on my own power. I will focus on one thing and one thing only... to break the man standing opposite of me who is there to break me too. Kill or be killed!

Chapter 22

SLAPPED IN THE FACE BY JIU-JITSU – REI ZULU

After the Mushtaq fight I took five months off to concentrate on putting on more weight. I definitely wanted to fight in the unlimited weight class and 205 lbs. was much too light to be fighting 250 pounders. I was determined to put on only quality muscle and without drugs or excess fat. Six pounds was the best I could do. I was now a solid 211 lbs. and I was offered a fight in the biggest most prestigious show, The Ultimate Fighting Championships (UFC). The UFC's rules were a bit different from the Shooto rules which I was used to, so I asked Sayama if I could fight a tune up fight in Shooto with UFC rules. Sayama could get the rules changed to suit the UFC rules better but not 100%. He managed to get the rules to allow elbows but couldn't get the bare fist rules passed.

Oh well, better than nothing, I thought. Sayama agreed and began to search for an opponent for me to fight. Ironically, the fighter that he found was the infamous Brazilian wild man, Rei Zulu. What was really amazing was the primary reason I started training Jiu-Jitsu was because of a video I saw of Rickson Gracie and Rei Zulu in Brazil. No one in Brazil wanted to fight Rickson except the so-called crazy man named Zulu. Rickson ended up choking out the bigger Zulu and that's when I got hooked on Gracie Jiu-Jitsu. However, never in my wildest dreams did I think that I would be fighting that wild man Zulu about 10 years later.

For this fight I wanted to concentrate on my standup, because Zulu was a very unorthodox fighter and I personally thought that his striking was very sloppy. Although my standing was just average, I felt my standing was good enough to take him. Before the fight I noticed that in Zulu's corner there was a very well-known Brazilian Jiu-jitsu practitioner, John Alberto. I was shocked!!! BJJ always had a fierce rivalry with Luta Livre and I considered myself 100% a BJJ guy and to see a senior BJJ guy in the corner of a rival, a Luta Livre guy, was beyond comprehension for me. Was it because he was a Brazilian too? I had so much love for BJJ that I felt betrayed. Could it be just because I wasn't Brazilian??? Then as if it wasn't enough, just before the fight started, John Alberto began complaining to the referee about the way I taped my hands. I was infuriated with John Alberto and in the middle of my wrath and anger stood Zulu. I wanted to erupt; I wanted to hurt someone so bad.

This was the first time I felt personal anger before a fight and I didn't know how it was going to affect my performance. John Alberto's meaningless complaints about the way my hands were taped caused about a five-minute delay to begin the fight. It bothered me so much and being upset, I had a hard time waiting for the starting gong to ring. Finally the gong sounded and I went straight for Zulu. I first checked him with a solid inside leg kick; then, just like what I did to Mushtaq, I unleashed a straight right that hit right on his chin. Down he went and, to be sure I didn't make the same mistake as my fight with Mushtaq, I didn't let up and continued the assault.

I was on him instantly to finish the kill only to be stopped by the referee who gave him a standing eight count. After he got the standing eight, I was again on him catching him with another right cross. He staggered and crumpled to the ground so I put in my hooks and took his back to prepare to put an end to the fight. As soon as my hooks were set in I noticed he was haphazardly tapping the mat, signifying his defeat but I wasn't going to make the same mistake as I did in my last fight so I took advantage of the revised rules and rained down elbows on the back of his head until the referee stepped in and called the fight. My mindset was set on "kill" mode and my adrenaline was pumping so much that when the referee came in to stop the fight I instinctively pushed the referee away and gave Zulu one more punch.

I really don't know why I did that, because I had nothing against Zulu and I didn't want to hurt him knowing that the fight was already over. When I got his back and was raining elbows down on his head I felt like it was the finale of a fireworks display, where the last 30 seconds is a nonstop flurry of flash and light and before silence took the scene I felt like it needed to drop just one final bang. The last punch I dropped was more like a slap than a punch as I got off of Zulu's back.

Then it finally sunk in to me that I had just won and I was victorious over the infamous Rei Zulu. As Zulu was staggering to get back on his feet John Alberto's betrayal suddenly popped into my head and I felt a rush of fury take over my body. Then instead of being satisfied and happy with my win, feeling betrayed was all that filled my mind. I then tried to make my way to where John Alberto was, only to be corralled in the far corner by Egan, like I was an out-of-control wild beast.

I was physically restrained so instead I lashed out verbally. I screamed, "Are you Jiu-Jitsu? Are you Jiu-Jitsu?" I was 100% loyal to Jiu-Jitsu and it really hurt me to be betrayed, just because I wasn't Brazilian. First, I proudly displayed the Gracie triangle to show my appreciation for all the Gracie's taught me only to be asked to remove the logo from my fight trunks, then this. Was I not truly accepted by the Gracie family as an important person in the clan? I wasn't angry; I was more disheartened and disappointed. This is the first time I wondered if I was really a BJJ fighter. Yes, that was my beginnings of feeling like an outsider. I was confused.

Chapter 23
SHOOTO MEETING

I only had seven fights but I was already establishing my fighting style. I had this kill or be killed style and gave everything I had in every fight. I began attracting a lot of fans, most being gangsters or Yakuzas. I had nothing against underworld figures so I befriended many of them just as I would anyone else. However, the Shooto Association got wind of my relations with them and called me in for a meeting. I had no clue what this meeting was for so I went to it accompanied by my manager/ friend Sakai. When we walked in I noticed two referees, Suzuki and Ogawa with another man I never met. I also noticed that the commissioner, Urata and the founder Sayama weren't present.

I was curious as to what this meeting was about as I took a seat in the middle of the table. Suzuki began to talk as he expressed concern with my relationship with the Yakuza. He said that I was representing the Shooto Association and that they were concerned that my relations with the Yakuza would hurt Shooto's reputation. Then suddenly the man I never met before took control. I've seen him sitting ringside at the Shooto events although I was never introduced to him. He started off wrong by referring to me as "Omae" a very rude way to address someone. The word alone lit a little fire inside of me but I did my best to keep cool. He went on to say that I needed to cut all ties with anyone who is Yakuza speaking down to me in a disrespectful way. By this time, the little fire became a big fire to a point I no longer could control it.

I pounded the table and looked at this unfamiliar face and said, "Who the fuck are you? Who do you think you are to talk to me with so much disrespect? I don't even know your name!" He responded by telling me his name was Sato and he is an ex-cop that specialized in tracking down Yakuza and that he'd helped out the Shooto commissioner Urata, in the past.

I was boiling by now so I lashed back saying, "I don't give a fuck who you are! You have no right to speak to me with so much disrespect!" I went on to say, "Cut my friends just because they are Yakuza? Are you guys fucking kidding me?" I paused and took a deep breath. I glared into Sato's eyes and said, "In all honesty I have Yakuza friends that I can trust more and have more honor than anyone in this room, so you guys can fuck off!" I then stood up and walked out of the room. My manager Sakai ran after me in tears begging me not to leave but I'd had enough and left.

I felt they had no right telling me whom I could and could not be friends with in my personal time. And to top it off, they stepped over the line talking down to me as if I was one of their servants. Respect is given to those who deserve it and to those who give me respect.

I left the meeting fuming and on a mission to find out who this Sato guy was! I called all my sources and found out some very disturbing facts about Sato. It was true he was an ex-cop that was a specialist in Yakuza, but what he failed to tell me was that he was fired from the police for working with the Yakuza and making a big amount of illegal cash from it. I couldn't believe it!!! He was in no position to tell me not to associate with Yakuza when he personally did himself. I was pissed and planned never to talk to this asshole ever again.

Months passed before they had another Shooto event. As usual I went to attend and again Sato was sitting next to Urata. I ignored him until he saw me and I was confused when I saw him walking in my direction. I pretended not to see him and before I knew it he was right in front of me. He stretched out his hand and said, "Hey Enson. How have you been?"

I couldn't believe my ears and my first instinct was to slap his hand away from me. Although we were in the middle of the Shooto event I didn't care. I blurted out in a loud voice, "I did research on you! You are 10 times dirtier than me. I know you got fired from the police force because you did illegal things with the Yakuza! You have nerve telling me not to associate with them when you yourself did!!! More than me, a Shooto fighter giving Shooto a bad name by associating with Yakuza, YOU sitting ringside after what you did is worse for Shooto's reputation!"

His jaw dropped as he started muttering something I was too upset to hear. I told him, "You are a disgrace to Shooto and don't you dare ever come talk to me again." Then I walked away. All the fans along with the Shooto officials saw what I did but no one came up to stop me. I had a feeling the Shooto officials knew and were shocked that I found out and revealed it to everyone. It must have been true, because at the very next Shooto event, Sato was no longer sitting at ringside.

Chapter 24

Problem with Relson Gracie – Ridiculous Ultimatum

From the day I began training GJJ I had a loyalty to it that I felt would never die. My loyalty for the art, GJJ and to Relson Gracie as my instructor was strong in my heart. However, with the mixture of the strict rules, of not ever training anywhere else, not showing anyone GJJ techniques, and their fear of teaching an outsider of the Gracie Family was confusing to me. The art they had was supposedly so untouchable, yet they were so insecure about it. I was always at Relson's house watching videos and hanging out. I practically lived there. He was like a brother to me and because I was always at his house, I got to know all his brothers well.

Rickson, Royler, and Royce Gracie would come over often and knew how close Relson and I were. There was a time when Royce Gracie came over from Brazil to visit and I asked him to show me some technique and he was more than happy to do so. We went to Relson's garage and we lightly rolled as he began showing me new moves. It was awesome and going well, when suddenly Rorion Gracie popped in and began telling Royce something in Portuguese. Then to my surprise Royce turned to me and with a chuckle he said, "That's all for today my friend, I can't teach you too much." I was a bit bummed, but more grateful to him for showing me what he did. I then knew that no matter how close Relson and I got, I would never be considered real family.

That was actually an incident that was the beginning of the break between Relson and I. Relson's English was still minimal and hard to understand, so whenever we ran seminars and exhibitions in Hawaii I would be
the one speaking and running it. We went to school dorms, martial arts
events and even shopping centers. I printed the first Honolulu, Hawaii
GJJ t-shirts and even gave Relson one of my old cars. We were like brothers and I was willing to do almost anything for Relson and GJJ.

The first sign of instability between Relson and I was when he began
putting me between a rock and a hard place, by putting pressure on me
to keep my brother Egan at a distance when it came to GJJ. At one of
the seminars we did in Hawaii, where Relson's brother Rickson was in
attendance, there was a problem when Egan videotaped the seminar only
to be stopped. However, Egan was able to continue by promising them
that he was taping it for them and would turn the video over to them after
the seminar was over. I found it strange that they didn't trust Egan who
was my blood brother and that they were so insecure about their incredible art.

The problem began when Relson claimed that Egan took too long to turn
over the video. After the seminar was over it took Egan about 2-3 hours
to bring the video to Relson's house. The Gracies were pissed and accused Egan of copying the video against their wishes before bringing it
to Relson's house. Until this day I really don't know if Egan actually did
that, but I had a feeling he did. Relson was furious and I had mixed feelings. I was bummed that Egan might have broken his promise to them
and more bummed that Relson would react so drastically to my own
brother as if he were an enemy.

At the next class, after the incident, Relson pulled me to the side and told
me of his disappointment with Egan. He then forbade me to teach, or
even talk to Egan about anything related to GJJ. I was in a tough situation
and at this time, I wasn't strong enough to be straight up with Relson. In
fact, I was showing half-ass loyalty to both sides. I was being untrue to
Relson because I was still teaching and showing Egan techniques while

PROBLEM WITH RELSON GRACIE – RIDICULOUS ULTIMATUM

at the same time not being true to Egan by avoiding a lot of discussions of GJJ with Egan. I felt weak and didn't like the situation Relson put me in.

My move to Japan just created more distance between Relson and I, and although the awkward situation between Egan and Relson lingered, whenever I came home to Hawaii I would train in Relson's class. This all came to an end when I went to train with Relson after one of my trips back home to Hawaii. I remember it vividly as if it happened yesterday.

I walked into the studio at the University of Hawaii and was approached by Relson near the door just as I stepped on the mat. In his broken English he came straight to the point: "You need to choose between your brother Egan and myself." I was baffled!!! I thought I was hearing things. However, Relson kept a straight face and waited for my answer. I didn't know what to say. Relson, who I considered my brother, was giving me a ridiculous ultimatum by making me pick between himself and Egan!

He could have asked me for any other favor and I probably would have done it but what made this so different was, he wasn't just asking me to make a ridiculous choice, he was showing he doubted my loyalty and really didn't care for me like I did for him. No matter what kind of problem I had with any of his brothers, I would NEVER ask him to choose between myself and one of them.

I looked Relson in the eye just to confirm the authenticity of his demand and I could see it in his eyes that he was dead serious. A mixture of sadness and anger rushed through my body and I looked Relson in the eyes and replied, "You give me no choice." I turned around and began walking out the door. The 10 feet to the door seemed like one mile as I left the studio without Relson saying a word. I couldn't believe what was happening and knew that I had just lost something dear to my heart.

Losing Relson as a brother/friend was hard for me. I missed his company and his guidance, but most of all I missed just hanging out with him, sharing smiles and laughs.

Chapter 25
Pan American BJJ Riot

As if losing a dear friend wasn't painful enough, having that friend turn on you doubled the pain. This was a sad day in my life. It was a nice sunny day and I was back in Hawaii to watch my brother fight in the Brazilian Jiu-Jitsu Pan American event. He was entered in the brown belt division and his opponent was one of Rickson Gracie's brown belt, Bruno.

Egan's match was scheduled for noon and it was weird because it was already 11:30 a.m. and Bruno was nowhere in sight. Nobody had seen him since that morning and we were getting worried he might not show up. As noon approached, Egan walked up to the tournament desk and asked if his match was on time and they said yes and told him to get warmed up. He began to stretch and 30 minutes later his match was called. He walked to the mat a bit bewildered because there was still no sign of Bruno. Then just as he got to the mat the referee told him that his match was going to be postponed to a later time.

Egan was a bit confused but walked off the mat and went back to sit in the bleachers with the rest of his team. The same routine happened three more times within the next five hours when Bruno finally came walking in the gymnasium at about 5 p.m. What made everything worse was that Bruno didn't seem like he was in any kind of rush. He just strutted into the gym with his gi slung over his shoulder and was even greeting friends as he strolled over to the tournament desk. Finally at a little before 6 p.m. their match was to begin. As the referee began to do the routine gi check of Egan and Bruno's gis I went to the side of the mat to root Egan on.

Out of the blue, the referee signaled to Egan that his gi sleeves were too short and he had to get another gi to fight in. This was impossible because this was the same gi the Egan used at the World Championships a few months ago and at the Worlds, they do a complete thorough check of the competitors gis.

So Egan disrobed and walked up the bleachers to his bag where he kept his extra gi. However to our surprise, he just picked up his bag and began to walk straight for the exit to leave the gymnasium. I was confused and a bit bewildered when Egan left the gym so I ran after him to see what was going on. When I finally caught sight of Egan he was walking towards the parking lot and his belt was just thrown on the ground in the middle of the walkway about 50 feet behind him. As he reached the parking lot I yelled to him, "Egan! Where are you going?"

He screamed back to me, "I'm tired of their bullshit, tell them to go fuck themselves!"

Seeing Egan so upset and having watched all the bullshit that went on, my blood began to boil. Tell them to go fuck themselves??? Hell yeah I can do that and maybe a bit more. I turned back to the gymnasium and began a full sprint back. I planned to return to the arena, go to the officials at the tournament desk, tell them to fuck themselves, and then flip over the tournament desk! As I was running back to the gymnasium I could hear Egan yell, "No Enson!!! Somebody stop him!"

About 100 feet from the gymnasium I ran into a childhood friend, Carey Higaki. Carey saw my face and my demeanor and he knew I was out of control. He tried to tackle me but I managed to get by Carey. As I got passed him he also began to yell, "Stop him! Stop him!" My next obstacle was my Father. He is a bit overweight and out of shape so I managed to juke by him too. After getting by Carey and my Father I had a clear path straight to the wide open gymnasium doors. As I approached the gymnasium doors, two 300 pound plus security guards suddenly appeared at the door blocking the doors as I approached. Apparently they heard Carey's screams and were prepared to stop me from getting in.

These security guards were so big that just the two of them standing at the door blocked the double doorway where there was little or no space to get in. From my rage I decided to try to run right through them. I was so angry that my thinking was clouded, so I thought 190 pound me could bowl over the 300-pound plus security guard. I ran full speed, put my head down and tried to run right though one of them. I imagined bowling this security guard on his ass but when I ran into him it felt like I ran into a brick wall and all I did was make him take a few steps back. On impact, I could feel it was mission impossible as I tried to hit and roll around him.

Unfortunately, a desk they were using to sell t-shirts was in the way and I ran into the desk knocking down the desk and the t-shirts. Then the other 300 pound plus security guard grabbed me and I was stuck. Then as my Father approached the ruckus, two other security guards jumped on him knocking him to the ground. Then as if everything wasn't crazy enough, along came Egan. As Egan approached the first thing he saw was me getting held down by three guys and the next thing he saw was my father being held down by two guys with one choking him. Egan then went into "save his family" mode and went ballistic. He began throwing punches dropping guys left and right. Then Kekumu and another one of Egan's students jumped in and more bodies began to fall. As for me, as much as I struggled, I had three guys on me, so all I could do was watch. The fact that the riot was at the doorway and because of the rush of people, no one from the inside could get out and no one from the outside could get in.

Eventually Egan was also restrained by three guys and pulled back about 20 feet from the door against a wall. At the same, time I was also being restrained side by side with Egan by about three guys too.

Then out of nowhere, Relson Gracie stands up onto a table so we could see each other and began to taunt us. He made faces at us and motioned with his hands as he gawked at us saying, "Here I am, come and get me!"

"What an idiot", I thought. No one is holding him back and he can see that we have three guys on each of, us so it would be impossible for us to get to him. Then I realized that Relson was just taunting us and in reality he wanted no part of Egan and I. Instead of standing far away on a table in safety, if he really wanted to get us he could have just walked over to us without a problem.

Then while we were being dragged back into the parking lot, I suddenly heard a woman's voice screaming, "You people should be ashamed of yourself..." I instantly recognized that voice and it was no other than my dear mother. Both my father and mother were right in the middle of the mix. My father mixing it with the security and my mother ripping Relson hard with her mouth! They are true fighters, and with their upbring-ing, the "Don't take shit from anyone" belief is probably where I got my Yamatodamashii, my fighting spirit.

When we finally reached the parking lot there were about five police cars arriving, so to be safe and avoid getting arrested we promptly jumped into our cars and went home.

At the time of this riot, Egan and I were both brown belts under the Machado's and I was stoked to see John Machado standing by our side through the whole riot. However, Egan made a decision that surprised me when he decided to break away from the Machado's and find a new group to train under. I supported Egan 100% because when I heard his reasoning it made sense. The reason why he decided to no longer stand under the Machado flag was because he didn't want to cause any more problems for the Machados. Bottom line was that they are the blood cousins of the Gracies; and the feud with the Gracies and us was just put-ting them in between a rock and a hard place. The Machados understood and we shook hands. They gave us their blessings and we thanked them for all they have done for us. We wished each other luck and went our separate ways.

Relson Gracie went as far as getting Temporary Restraining Orders out on both Egan and I. I then knew Reslon had turned on me. I was living in Japan and there was no sense in trying to get a restraining order on me except in spite.

Currently I have no beef with Relson. At an event called "Shogun" in Hawaii I approached Relson and told him I was willing to bury the past and wished him luck. He agreed and we shook hands and this feud that has been going on for years had finally been ended.

Chapter 26

UNEXPECTED CHANGE -
SAYAMA FIRED

After the ties with Relson and GJJ were severed, I was now a legit Professional Shooto fighter. I was so proud that when I got my first tattoo I put the kanji mark of Shooto "修斗" on the back of my left shoulder. I was training at Sayama Satoru's Super Tiger Gym and was surprised when suddenly the owner/financial backer of the gym wanted to talk to me. When we met, he informed me that the founder of Shooto, Sayama Satoru who has the title of The First Tiger Mask recipient, was getting fired because he was spending too much money, 3 million dollars in five years, which had put the company in the red.

They were getting rid of Sayama and if I didn't want to take over the gym, they were going to close it down. I didn't know what to say at first because all I had was a small racquetball company, E-Force Japan, and wasn't sure if I was ready to run the gym. I conferred with my manager at the time and decided to put the gym under my company and try my best at running the gym. The fact of the matter was, that if I didn't take it over, they were going to straight up close down the gym.

The second part to this problem was really a big problem for the whole Shooto association. This is a very long story that was kept undercover for the longest time. I believe this is something Shooto doesn't want to be exposed but to be fair I believe everyone has the right to know what happened.

A group called Ryusha Group was being threatened by their bank, that if they didn't get rid of Shooto, the bank would have to drop Ryusha Group completely. Ryusha Group was a multi-million dollar company that ran health centers, pachinko parlors, funeral homes, and a food service center. Instead of letting all of their businesses go down, they decided to just cut off the Shooto Association which meant discontinuing Shooto events which would result in the end of Shooto. Mr. Nakamura, the head of Ryusha Group, called a big meeting with everyone involved in Shooto.

He explained the problem and asked if anyone was willing to take over Shooto, which meant running Shooto events. He asked Kawaguchi of Yokohama Shooto Gym, Sakurada of Gutsman Gym, Nakai from Parestra, Sakamoto from Sustain, all the big dogs but no one was willing to take the chance.

I thought about it and wondered if putting my racquetball company on the line by adding Shooto, a company in the red, to the company. However, my whole life is an adventure and taking a gamble like this was not out of the ordinary so I raised my hand and told Mr. Nakamura that I was willing to take a chance and take over Shooto. No one would take the gamble except me. All the other gyms sat back and watched to see if I would succeed or flop and when I succeeded, all of a sudden they all wanted to get on board. I wasn't trying to monopolize Shooto, so I agreed to join up with all the other ones who wanted to promote and we all split the promotion within the year.

No one else was willing to take the chance, only me. They all know that if I didn't take the chance, Shooto would have been finished. My racquetball company, E-Force Japan, became the sole promoter of Shooto events. So E-Force applied and was issued a promoter's license, which enabled us to promote Shooto events.

However, instead of appreciating this, through good times and bad, when I had a problem with the law they took away my promoters license, only because two years had passed and there were three other gyms participating in the promotion of Shooto events. These three other gyms who joined in promoting Shooto events didn't want to do so at the beginning until they saw me run a few. After I ran a few successful events, then they wanted to give it a shot. Let it be known to the public today that if I didn't take the gamble, no other Shooto associate would have and there would be no Shooto today. I know this just as well as all the top people involved with Shooto, who like to pretend this never happened. Well, now let it be known.

I was now fighting under my own gym, which I decided to name after my new line of racquetball racquets called Purebred. Officially, "Super Tiger Gym Omiya" was renamed, "Purebred Omiya".

Chapter 27

BIRTH OF YAMATODAMASHII – THE SPIRIT OF THE SAMURAI

With eight fights behind me, my fighting style was established. I fought to finish my opponent in any way I could. Whether it was physically, mentally, or emotionally, it didn't matter. I wasn't interested in winning on points and I never wanted to leave it in the hands of the judges. It was literally, I had to hurt him before he hurt me.

One thing I am known for is, even though I faced some of the best fighters in the world, never once did I give up or "tap out". This is a very misunderstood thing; in all honesty, it has nothing to do with how tough I am. A lot of people come up to me and say that they don't understand how I don't tap but it's actually not that hard to explain.

You see, when someone sees an arm breaking, it is not the same to me as hearing my own arm popping because of the mindset I go into a fight with when I am in total control with what I'm feeling inside. Your two different mindsets can make the same situation look very different.

Your whole life is about options. When you're driving a car and a person jumps in front of you, you either hit the person or swerve left or right. There's always an option. When you're getting your arm broken or when a fighter is in any critical type of situation in a fight, there are also options.

For most fighters in a normal mindset, there will be options throughout the fight that pop up into their heads. Usually two options will pop into their heads if they are caught in an arm bar: my arm is going to break or I need to tap. Fighters train hard, fighters experience fear. They train to the point of exhausting themselves so much in training, that they feel like falling down because they cannot do another rep or sparring so intensely they think they might really be hurt.

A lot of fighters don't take it in the right way. They don't absorb it deep enough to change the person that they are. If a fighter applies all the trials and experiences he goes through as a fighter it will help him grow as a person.

For me, I've tried to apply all that I've learned in fighting to my daily life so I don't just grow as a fighter but as a person too. The discipline of diet and sacrifice before a fight, the perseverance to get up and train consistently, and the strength to push harder even though your body is screaming in pain are the things I took with me in my personal life too.

The more I can absorb, the more I can take with me into my daily life after my fighting days are over, will make me a better man. I try to live my life the Yamatodamashii way, where you give everything you've got until the very end. The only time you know you can't do it anymore is when you absolutely have no more options.

Basically, when I'm getting in an arm bar and can hear my arm popping, because of my mindset, the two options that come to my mind are: your arm is going to break or you need to get the fuck out of the arm bar. In the heat of the moment when you only have a split decision to make that choice, the only thing you can choose from are the options that pop up into your head.

There is no time to reason or analyze. It pops into my head, get out or get your arm broken. I don't want my arm broken so I'm going to get out. As I'm getting out, I'm never going to know when my arm breaks. I don't ever want to wonder what would have happened if I didn't tap.

BIRTH OF YAMATODAMASHII – THE SPIRIT OF THE SAMURAI

Would I have gotten out, or would my opponent have given up and moved to another hold? Only God knows when my arm will break. It's like how you go to sleep when you get choked. Only God knows when you go to sleep from a choke. Who am I to decide and play God and decide when my arm is going to break or when I go unconscious? All these people come and pay millions of dollars to watch the fights. I get paid six figures to fight. I'm there to entertain, give 110%, to leave everything in the ring. That's all I do. It's nothing special or extraordinarily tough.

Fans pay a lot of money to see me fight. The promoter pays me, kisses my ass, flies two corner men to my fight, puts us up in hotels, gives us food money, gets me on TV and in magazines, etc. People are going to come from all over to watch me fight and some even cry when they watch my fight. I heard of many that cry when I walk to the ring. It's that big of a thing and to me it's more than just a sport. Therefore, I definitely give all I have!

I'm not going to anticipate when my arm will break or when I will pass out. There's a referee, ring doctors, and your corner men; so I just trust them and concentrate on doing everything in my power to keep fighting. Think about it... in the last 20 years of MMA I can only think of three instances where although they knew their arm was going to break, the anticipation of it didn't cause them to tap.. Renzo Gracie, Miesha Tate, and Minotauro Noguiera. 99%of the fighters will give up before their arm breaks. 99% of the fighters will give up before they go to sleep.

Why... because of fear and because they are not in the right mindset, fear is controlling them to a point that it is making them anticipate the outcome. They are assuming that their arm is going to break. However, because I am in the Yamatodamashii type of mindset I will assume that I'm going to get out and keep your mind focused on that. My thinking is really different. It all depends on what your mind is focusing on. I'm focusing on finishing an opponent. If he hits me hard enough to wobble me, I'm focusing enough that I hit him right back with the same kind of punch or to avoid being hit again so I can recover.

If I get caught in an arm lock and I can hear the ligaments pop, I'm thinking -- That mother fucker, before he breaks it, I'm going to hit him or kick him, anything that might create a way to escape the situation. It depends on your mindset and what you're focusing on. If a fighter is focusing on the penalties of failure, as his arm getting broken or getting choked unconscious, the fear of a horrible outcome will usually allow "tapping out" to become an option.

Fear is inevitable, but depending on your mindset when fear sets in, your choices will differ. With my mindset, my fear is going to make me stronger. My fear is going to make me want to get out before he breaks my arm. My fear is going to give me adrenaline to punch, even if I am too tired, to stand up straight, or hit him with my free arm even as I hear my arm popping.

When I was younger Egan and I always went to a sports psychologist for racquetball and I will always remember this certain psychologist that came and talked to Egan and I. This guy told us that you're either going to focus on the penalties of failure or the rewards of success. That is the exact situation you are in when your arm is going to break during a fight. In that situation, what I mean by rewards of success is getting my arm out and eventually stomping on my opponent's face. Penalties of failure would include getting my arm broken or being choked unconscious. Which one you are going to focus is determined by what you choose.

For example, imagine if I were to put a plank of steel about a foot wide and about 10 feet long on the mat, a soft cushioned mat, the same kind of mat you can find probably in most MMA and BJJ schools. Then I put a $100 bill on one end and tell you if you walk from one end to the other without touching the mat, and you can pick up the money without stepping off the plank, you can keep the $100 bill. What would you do? I bet, without a second of hesitation you're going to get up, walk the plank and pick up the $100 bill.

However, what if the situation was a little bit different? What if I was to put the same $100 bill on the same plank but instead stretched it across to the other side of an adjacent 10-story building. What are you going to do? If you even decide to take the challenge, you're definitely not going to be able to walk normally with the same confidence. You're probably going to shimmy across the plank inch-by-inch taking 10 times longer than you did when the plank was on the mat. It's the same plank, the same money with the same objective but with the small change of where the plank is placed, your focus changes.

When the plank is lying on the mat, the only thing your mind is focused on is getting the $100 bill. There are no penalties to failure. You're not going to really lose anything and you are definitely not going to lose your life. Your mind starts focusing on when you get to the other side and pick up the cash and what you are going to do with that $100 bill.

However, when I put the plank on the top floor of a 10 story building, the fear changes your focus. All of a sudden, instead of focusing on the rewards of success, your focus is going to be on the fact that it's 10 stories high and what will happen if you fall. Right there, you're not even thinking of the $100 bill; you're worried about falling 10 stories.

I believe every fighter has fear, whether it begins as soon as he accepts a fight, at the beginning of the fight, or when he's hearing his arm pop. What is important is what you do with the fear and how you look at it. If your focus is weak and fear takes over, you're going to tap. If your focus is strong and the fear you still feel is in control it, then you can make it work for you.

Everyone says Enson is so tough, so brave, a warrior, but people don't usually look at the big picture. I did not become a warrior because of what I do in every situation as it comes, but because of the way I live my life and the way I live my life creates the mindset I live with. The reason why those two options that comes to my mind in critical situations are so different is that when I live my life, whether it's fighting, training, working, or just living everyday life, I'm always giving all I got until the very end. I'll try to negotiate a business deal until I run out of options, just like I'm willing to fight until I die. I will not ever quit in a situation whether it is in everyday life or fighting. Quitting is never an option. Because of this mindset I go into every fight with everything I have, willing to fight until the very end.

I still remember in an interview I had with a major fight magazine in Japan before going into fight in the UFC, the reporter, Mr. Mitsugi asked, "Have you heard of the word Yamatodamashii?"

My reply was, "Yamatodamashii? What is that?"

He replied, "It is the word that comes to mind when I see you fight and when I read your interviews." Little did I know that at this moment, it was the birth of a word that the Japanese people would refer to me until this day and possibly even after I die.

Yamatodamashii literally means "The Japanese Spirit" but it was a word that was used mainly in the days of the samurai so it usually is interpreted as, "The Spirit of the Samurai".

A STRONG MAN feels no pain...
but A MAN OF YAMATODAMASHII feels pain but goes on and endures the pain moving forward step by step.

A STRONG MAN has no fears...
but A MAN OF YAMATODAMASHII has fears, but controls them and makes them become an asset

A STRONG MAN controls the less fortunate and conquers the weak...
but A MAN OF YAMATODAMASHII helps the less fortunate and protects the weak.

A STRONG MAN is feared and terrorizes others...
but A MAN OF YAMATODAMASHII is respected and gives inspiration to others.

Chapter 28
YAMATODAMASHII T-SHIRT DEBUT

The funny thing is, I didn't really understand how deep and strong the meaning of Yamatodamashii was until many years after I was introduced to the word. By chance, I began using the word on my t-shirts and slowly throughout the years, I learned the true meaning of the word and how lucky I was to be labeled it.

After the reporter, Mr. Mitsugi, told me that I reminded him of Yamatodamashii I practically forgot about the word until I was contracted to fight in UFC 13 in Augusta, Georgia. I would be representing the Japanese Shooto association so I wanted to make a t-shirt with Japanese kanji on the front. I thought of "Ichiban" which meant number one and "Nihon" which meant Japan. However, I didn't think these kanji looked cool.

Then "Yamatodamashii" came to mind and I was curious on how it looked written in kanji. Then when I saw the kanji to it, it was perfect! However in all the preparations for the fight, I never got around to doing anything and nothing came out of it. My preparation for my fight took everything I had and my appearance when I entered the ring was the last thing I was concerned about. Fortunately, Egan took the liberty and printed a dozen t-shirts and brought them to my fight… and the birth of Yamatodamashii had begun.

Chapter 29

Journey to Augusta, Georgia – UFC 13

In my career as a fighter, I've always fought in the unlimited weight class, but for the UFC, I was offered a fight in the 200 lbs. class. Now for the first time I had to cut weight, a total of 11 lbs. Since the fight was all the way in Georgia, near the east coast of the Untied States, I decided to break up the travel and instead of going straight from Japan to Georgia, I stopped in Los Angeles for a few days. In Los Angeles I trained with a good friend and fellow martial artist, Burton Richardson. He helped me with some strategies and touched up my striking.

After getting a few good days of training in, I headed off to Augusta, Georgia. When I got there I was still 2 lbs. overweight, and because I wasn't used to dropping weight, even 2 lbs. was a big task. Two days before the weigh-ins I didn't eat or drink anything. The day of the weight check I was still worried about my weight, so I just sat in my room with my sweats on, under the covers, with the heater in my room set on high. Then, two hours before weigh-in time, I went downstairs to the training room with my brother and hit the pads and sparred for another 40 minutes.

Finally, it was time to check my weight. I guess I was so worried about my weight and wanted to be safe that I actually dropped too much weight. I was 2 lbs. under, and my official weigh-in was at 198 lbs. I was drained but very relieved that I had made the weight. After weigh-ins, there was no time to rest. We went straight to the press interviews and picture taking. All the interviews were revolved around Royce Alger, and I got the feeling that I was already counted out, with everyone assuming Royce was going to be the champion. I was in a four-man tournament that consisted of a judo expert, Christophe Leninger; a Pancration fighter, Guy Mezger; NCAA wrestling champion, Royce Alger; and myself, a Shooto fighter.

The alternate was a street fighter with a wrestling base named Tito Ortiz. At this time in the MMA scene, the wrestlers were dominant so that is why Royce was a heavy favorite. He was also Mark Coleman's boy and Coleman was the reigning UFC heavyweight champion. Royce also had some Golden Gloves boxing experience in his past, so he was a very well rounded fighter.

Everything leading up to the fight in the press conferences, interviews, and commercials was Royce Alger this, Royce Alger that. In the pre-fight interview, I was asked, "How does it feel to be going up against some-one of Royce Alger's caliber?" Yes Royce was a well-respected class A wrestler but this was MMA! My answer was, "I hear Royce is one of Dan Gable's most ferocious wrestlers, so I look forward to meeting his feroc-ity and aggression head on head."

When we got in the arena, I was in awe at the set-up, and still had a hard time comprehending that I was going to be fighting in the pioneer event of MMA, the UFC. Two fights before Royce and I were going to fight, we were called to be on stand-by in a warm-up area where there was a small mat area.. What was very awkward was across the way from my warm up area, I could see over to Royce's warm up area.

I wasn't interested in seeing Royce before the fight so I tried not to look over there, and just focused on my warm ups. However, even though I avoided eye contact, what Mark Coleman was screaming to Royce was hard to block out. I could hear Mark screaming like a mad man saying, "Fuck him up! Fuck him up! Fuck him up so bad that he will have to show his own mother an I.D. to get into his own house." Hearing this just pissed me off and fueled the fire in my heart three times bigger than it was already burning. I thought to myself, "Okay, we'll see about that... Yeah, try and come fuck me up. We'll see. We'll see."

Our time was up and it was our time to go to war. I was called first to the Octagon and when I stepped in, something was different. All my previous fights before were in a ring surrounded by ropes. This was the first time I was in an Octagon with no ropes, but instead, a chain link fence like a cage used to barricade animals. The moment I stepped into the Octagon, I can't pinpoint what it was, but I felt something change inside of me. I wondered to myself if this is how a pit bull felt when he was thrown into a pit about to fight to the death. What added to the animal-like atmosphere was the fact that this event, UFC 13, was the last event in the United States that allowed the fighters to fight bare knuckled. In fact my fight with Royce was THE last bareknuckle fight in the history of the UFC.

When my name was announced to enter the ring, there were very few cheers with a trickle of booing mixed in. When Royce's name was announced, he was greeted with cheers like he was a national hero. I didn't give a shit because once you step into the Octagon, you're on your own, just you and your opponent. No amount of fans or cheers was going to help you win the fight. When the gong sounded, we were like two predators ready to pounce at any given moment. I respected Royce for his superior wrestling and decided to see how he would react if I came in with a right feint.

To my surprise, he was a lot more intimidated with my striking than I thought he would be. He shot in for a tackle, the moment he saw my feint. I threw the feint to lure him in to shoot for a tackle but because his tackle was so quick and covered so much ground, he almost got in deep enough to take me down. He had one arm stretched out between my legs as I sprawled on him and flattened him to the mat. While keeping control of him, I then swiveled my body over to the side and locked him up in a crucifix. Instead of rolling over and putting him on his back, I mistakenly decided to drop elbows onto his head.

However, because he was such a good wrestler, soon after the first elbow hit, he dumped me to the mat and suddenly, I found myself in the bottom position. We were exchanging strikes back and forth, me from the bottom and him from the top, when I saw a chance. I swiveled my hips over and slapped on a deep arm lock from the bottom. I locked my leg deep on his neck and set his elbow in, deep by my crotch. It was in deep and his arm was all mine. I then began arching my back hard, knowing his arm couldn't come close to matching the power of my hips. As I was arching I could feel his arm slowly but steadily beginning to straighten.

Then like a gift from the gods, he made the most basic mistake... trying to pull his arm out, which lifted me off the mat. With him lifting me, the mat was no longer restricting my hips from getting full extension so like a pendulum my body swung into an inverted position. With the power of my hips and the momentum from the swing, instead of popping the ligaments and feeling small pops in his arm, there was one big pop. It was like nothing I'd ever felt before. He instantly fell face first to the mat tapping the mat in a panic with his legs thrashing like a fish out of water. Although I knew he was done I kept the tension on his arm, keeping it fully extended.

Then Big John McCarthy stepped in and put a stop to the fight at 1 minute 36 seconds of the 1st round. His arm was broken and I proved the so-called "experts" wrong. I had just beat Royce Alger and I didn't feel it in me to do much of a celebration because I felt that only half my work was done. For this was a tournament and I still had one more fight before my work was done. I also knew in my heart that I could beat Royce so the feeling in me wasn't, "Oh my God, I won, I won!", instead it was like, "See everyone, I knew I could beat him." After I was officially announced the victor, I quickly returned to my locker room to rest and get rejuvenated for the final. In the other semi-finals Guy Mezger beat Christophe Lenninger so the final was going to be Enson Inoue vs. Guy Mezger.

When I got back to the locker room and lay on the mat getting a massage from Egan, I felt a little trickle of blood running from my nose so I wanted to clear out my nose of the blood by blowing my nose. Little did I know I was about to learn a big lesson in fighting and that is, you should never ever blow your nose for 24 hours after a fight. As I blew my nose, instead of the air coming out of my nose, it filled up in my face and I felt a weird feeling like the air was going to push my eye out of its socket. I stopped blowing, placed my hand on my eye to make sure my eye wasn't going to pop out and turned to Egan and said, "Something's wrong with my eye, I feel like it's going to come out." As Egan slowly removed my hand from my eye, he took one look at it and ran out of the room to get the doctor. Now Egan was almost like a personal doctor and was very educated in all aspects of the human body so it worried me to see him take such immediate action.

Minutes later Egan returned with the doctor and the doctor took one look at me and said, "You can't continue." I couldn't believe what I was hearing! My first reaction was, "What!? Are you joking!?" I felt like my whole world was crashing down. I then looked at the doctor and explained to him that I felt fine and I could continue. I explained to him that I can still see clearly with my other eye and there's just one more fight left.

He just looked at me with a blank stare and shook his head saying that it was over for today. I wasn't about to just give up then so I put all my pride aside and began pleading with him. "Do you know how hard I trained and how many sacrifices I made to be here? You can't tell me I can't fight. I've felt more pain in training! I feel great. It's just my eye!" The doctor then explained to me that the reason why my eye puffed up was because somewhere in the paper-thin plate of bone in my face, there must be a crack in it.

The bone plate is there to keep all the air out from my face and with a crack in it, blowing your nose is not a good thing to do. He continued by explaining that the crack could be anywhere and the danger is that the crack may be on my cheekbone and if it's on my cheekbone and I take another solid shot there, it could cave in my whole face. So to prove him wrong I began pushing on my cheekbone telling him there is no pain so it can't be my cheekbone. He just shook his head and told me that it was too swollen and that I wouldn't be able to tell.

He then turned to Egan and said, "I'm pulling him out." My heart dropped and my spirit exploded! Tears began pouring out of my eyes, out of frustration of being stopped short of the mission I had set in my heart. I felt like a samurai being told to retreat to the hills because my sword was chipped. It wasn't like I couldn't see or I was in severe pain so it was so hard for me to understand. The alternate for this fight was Tito Ortiz so although my injury was unlucky for me, it was the birth of one of the most prominent figures in MMA.

In my fight with Royce, we wore the newly printed "Yamatodamashii" t-shirts into the ring and since we had some leftover shirts I brought them back to Japan with me to just give them away. Some of my Japanese fighters shied away from accepting the shirt saying they would be too embarrassed to wear them.

They were afraid that the kanji, Yamatodamashii, printed so big on the front of the shirt might be mistaken for a Right Wing Extremist group. I didn't quite agree but then, because my fight against Royce went so well we began getting calls from fans that wanted to purchase the shirts. The demand was so big that there weren't enough leftover shirts, so I decided to print out a bunch to put on sale. This was the birth of my "Yamatodamashii" t-shirt line.

Chapter 30

PAIN IS TEMPORARY, PRIDE IS FOREVER – KAWANA

It was a day like any other day. We were waiting in front of the Yokohama Arena to attend a K-1 event. As we were standing outside the arena we noticed that to the left of us there was a big commotion, consisting of a bunch of men all in black suits. There were a whole lot of them making a barrier like they were barricading the little scuffle that was going on in the middle of it. It was obvious that it wasn't just an ordinary problem. This was definitely a Yakuza problem.

In Japan, people tend to ignore problems, especially Yakuza ones, acting as though nothing were happening even though it was happening right in front of their eyes. It was absolutely forbidden to get involved in any type of Yakuza problem. Even if you were involved, the rule was to get uninvolved. I knew the safest thing to do was to pretend like nothing was happening and look the other way, but my curiosity got the best of me. I couldn't help but glance over to see exactly what was happening.

When I looked I noticed that in the middle of the human barrier there were two more men in black suits that were beating a guy in regular street clothes. This guy didn't fight back but just took the hits, getting back up only to be hit and dropped again.

Suddenly I realized that the guy being beaten up was a good friend of mine named Kawana. My first reaction was, "Holy Shit! It's Kawana! I have to do something!"

Kawana and I go way back when I first I met him in 1996. He was still one of the leaders of the notorious bike gang in Tokyo, the Kanto Rengo. The Kanto Rengo is a feared motorcycle gang that you did not want to have problems with. They were a powerful gang, numbering close to 1,000 members. Kawana was the boss, and like all gangsters and Yakuza, the Kanto Rengo loved fighting.

I didn't even remember my first meeting with Kawana, but he remembers it, clear as day. We were supposedly introduced at a party by a Yakuza that we were both friends with. Our second meeting was at a K-1 event in Tokyo where our seats were just a row apart. As my friends and I were taking our seats, from the row behind, a dark scary looking gangster stood up, bowed, and then stuck his hand out to greet me. I didn't remember who he was, but to save the both of us any embarrassment I went along with it and pretended to remember him, shaking his hand saying, "Hissashiburi," which meant "long time no see," in Japanese.

We both then took our seats and began watching the K-1 fights. Then about after the third fight I turned around to glance at Kawana and he was out, head back, mouth wide open, fast asleep. I just couldn't resist the temptation, so I turned around, pulled out the antenna on my cell phone, and stuck it up his nostril. Before he opened his eyes I quickly turned around and pretended to be watching the fights. Seconds later he began dozing off again, so I got ready to do it again.

This time, as if he were waiting, as soon as the antenna touched his nose his eyes opened and he caught me red-handed. He smiled, I smiled, and then we both started laughing. Little did I know at the time that Kawana was one of the famous top gangsters in Tokyo, and it was unheard of that someone would play a prank like that on someone of his status.

Kawana loved me as a fighter and was entertained at the fact that I dared do something like that to him. He took out his cell phone, we exchanged numbers, and that was a start to a deep relationship that still goes on today.

Three years ago when I stuck my cell phone antenna up this Kawana's nose, little did I realize that I would be faced with a situation where I had to make a decision in seconds that could save his life. As I watched Kawana get hit repeatedly, the only thing that ran through my mind over and over was, "Shit! I've got to do something! I can't just watch!"

Now, I was absolutely NOT involved in whatever this problem was, and just being friends with Kawana was not even near enough of a reason to make it my business. As I was walking towards the closest opening of the barricade, like a whirlwind, all sorts of thoughts were racing through my head. "This is a Yakuza problem. I shouldn't get involved. I might get killed. I might have to leave Japan. I might get beaten too..."

Even with all these thoughts telling me not to do anything, one thought outweighed them all and kept me continuing on toward the barricade: "You can't just watch this happen to a friend I cared about."

Then I recalled Danny and that was when I knew, in that instant, that no pain the Yakuza would put me through could be worse than the pain I'd been feeling for 21 years from not standing up for Danny. Wow! God was giving me a second chance! I knew what I had to do, and something in me hoped that somehow doing the right thing this time might justify the choices I made with Danny and maybe, just maybe, even just a tad, it would ease the pain and guilt I'd felt for not backing up Danny 21 years ago.

As soon as I got close to the barricade, two Yakuza came to stop me from entering. I tried to walk around them only to be met by another Yakuza. The third Yakuza that came to stop me happened to be someone I'd met a year before through a mutual friend. His name was Bobby. He approached me a said, "Enson, stay out of this. Don't get involved with this sort of problem." So I replied, "But Kawana's my friend!" only to be surprised by his cowardly reply: "I know, he's my friend too, but don't get involved."

When I heard his reply, instead of second guessing my decision, I realized that all men are not made the same. Bobby was a gutless man, a disgrace, a man with NO honor. My disgust for Bobby made me push even harder to get to where Kawana was being beaten. All the commotion that was caused by the three Yakuza guys trying to hold me back got so big that the guy who was beating Kawana, Mr. Kobayashi, looked over to us and said, "What's going on? Who the fuck is that?"

Then Bobby said, "It's Enson Inoue, the fighter. The Shooto fighter." Mr. Kobayashi didn't seem to care and would have gone on with the beating, but the fact that someone was standing up against what the Yakuza was doing, something unheard of in Japan, interested him a bit and he began to walk towards me.

Shit! I thought, now I'm going to be beat up. Should I fight back? Why didn't Kawana even block Mr. Kobayashi's punches? I was frozen with these thoughts going through my head trying to look stern, confident, but respectful. My physical outer appearance stood up tall and strong while inside I felt scared and lost like a rabbit that was tossed in an alligator pen.

When Mr. Kobayashi got close enough to reach me, he stopped, looked into my eyes and asked, "Who are you and what is Kawana to you?" Being as respectful as possible I said, "My name is Enson Inoue and Kawana is my friend, and I couldn't just watch a friend getting beat up like that." Without even blinking Mr. Kobayashi said, "Even if he does wrong? Do you know what he did?"

As I told him I had no idea what the problem was, Kawana bleeding through the mouth, blurted out, "I didn't do it; I'll show you proof!!!" Mr. Kobayashi turned towards Kawana and said, "You better, before next weekend or I'm going to find you motherfucker."

He signaled to his guys to go and without saying a word, they began to leave. He took five steps away from me, stopped, and then turned around. When I saw him stop, I thought, "Oh shit, now what?"

Mr. Kobayashi walked up to me and asked, "What is your name?" I looked him straight in the eye and answered, "Enson." He looked at me up and down then said, "Hmmm," while slowly nodding his head up and down. He turned around and walked into the arena as if nothing had happened.

Kawana, still bleeding from the mouth, looked at me, shook his head, and said, "Don't ever do that again -- but thank you!" and gave me a hug. Later I found out that the Yakuza group Kawana was having problems with was called The Kobayashi Kai. They are a part of The Sumiyoshi Gumi, the second largest Yakuza Family in Japan. It dawned on me that this was Mr. Kobayashi from the Kobayashi Kai. The Oyabun, or Boss, of that family. The man himself! The guy the Family is named after. Holy Shit!

I was also later informed that most people that interfered in a Yakuza problem like that, especially one directly involving the Oyabun, pay with their life! I believe that the reason Mr. Kobayashi spared me was that, as offended as he was of my interference, he respected the courage and loyalty I had for my friends. That is probably why he asked my name before departing.

I knew what a close call this had been. I was aware that I got lucky when Mr. Kobayashi decided to stop beating Kawana, and that he could have easily beat me too. I was also aware that I almost jeopardized my existence in Japan, let alone my existence here on earth.

Sometimes sucking up your pride is another form of honor. Just letting your honor decide what you will do in pinch situations is not necessarily the best thing. At times, your pride and honor can shut down your mind and reactions, so that only later do you realize there was a better solution to the problem.

What I learned with this problem is that a man of honor needs to also use his head. Being stupid and reacting off one's ego is not necessarily being honorable. Whether it's in the ring or on the streets, keeping a level head will help me move better and ensure better decision-making. This time I wondered if I made the wrong choice. Now, reviewing the incident with a level head, it is very unlikely that Mr. Kobayashi would have killed Kawana in front of so many witnesses. But it was very likely that my interference might have angered Mr. Kobayashi more and caused him to hurt Kawana, more than he planned to, and then move on to hurting me.

Maybe I did jump the gun and unnecessarily endangered myself. Maybe I didn't. I just reacted to what my heart told me without filtering the incident through my mind. Keeping a level head in a fight and keeping a level head on the street work hand in hand. It will help you to make wiser decisions. I will never know if how I reacted to help Kawana was right or wrong, but deep down, something tells me I made the right choice. Adding another knot in my heart, like the Danny incident did, would have been unbearable.

This incident made me realize that the road of the Samurai and keeping the honor of a true man is something very hard to do. Just being brave and fearless doesn't necessarily equal honor. Being a crazy Kamikaze, putting your life on the line for every little situation is not honorable. Using your head and finding the best remedy is ideal, and if all that fails, then let your heart, your pride and your honor take over. Then, if you have to put your life on the line, so be it.

I have learned from my experience of watching Danny be humiliated in the park and from Kawana being beaten, that if it's for all the right reasons, I am willing to die today, and if the day I die, I can die as a man of honor who reacted in the best way he saw fit, I will welcome it with open arms. You can take my life and stop my body, but you can never ever take my honor and pride. My body may be conquered but what's deep in my heart will never die.

Chapter 31

REDEMPTION – JOE ESTES II

I still wasn't a legitimate heavyweight, but I refused to go down in weight because I wanted to fight the best in the world, no excuses. I made the decision to stay in the unlimited weight class although sometimes I knew was going to be outweighed by 50 lbs.,.

I guess my fights were making a good impact on the MMA scene in Japan because to my surprise Japan's biggest and newest association, Pride, was interested in having me fight in their ring. From what I heard the offered pay was $10,000. All these years I was fighting for Shooto at about $4,000 a fight and here I was getting an opportunity to fight in a major promotion that I would have fought for free in and they were offering me 10 G's!!! Unbelievable! Moving up in status by fighting in Pride and being paid more than twice as much... just like having my cake and eating it too. Rickson Gracie fought in Pride 1 and here I was getting an offer to fight in Pride 2.

However, Shooto was afraid to lose me. They stopped the offer from Pride and instead, they offered me a fight in Shooto. Shooto was still small and didn't have a big bank account so instead of bettering Pride's offer they offered me a World Title match. Wow! Being the first ever World Shooto Heavyweight Champion!? How could I turn that down? My opponent was going to be the man who gave me my first defeat, Joe Estez. As if having the chance to etch my name in the history books forever by becoming the first Shooto Heavyweight Champion wasn't enough, they offered me a chance for redemption!

They made the title match proposal and only after I agreed to take the fight did they tell me about the Pride offer. I was a little bit confused at why they would use such a tactic because after all, my loyalty was with Shooto. For me, I had my values and money would never outweigh loyalty.

I first fought Joe two years ago when I weighed in at a mere 202 lbs. But now I was 211 lbs. and I felt as strong as a beast! Training was going great until I got a call from Shooto where they informed me that Joe Estes just declined the fight demanding more money. Shooto said that Joe was insisting that he beat me once and would definitely beat me again so he should be paid more money than he was offered.

I don't know how much Shooto offered Joe but he wanted more. Shooto also didn't tell me how much Joe was demanding but they said that it was more than they could afford! He claimed that he was a much better fighter than me and that he should get paid much more than me. I was infuriated! Not only because he was talking big but because I sacrificed an opportunity to fight in Pride for this title match.

I was the #1 ranked heavyweight and Joe was #2 ranked so the only way this could be a title match was if Joe and I fought. My chance to fight in Pride had passed and now it didn't look like I was getting a title match anymore. I was desperate. So I called Shooto and told them to do whatever they need to do to get him here. Even if they had to pay him out of my fight money and that's just what they did. I wanted the title really bad and now I also wanted Joe's neck. Training was going perfectly and the image of breaking Joe's heart and wrapping the championship belt around my waist helped me through the hard training days. I felt like a finely tuned fighting machine and I was angry. I wanted Joe's neck so bad I could taste it!

On fight day I avoided any contact with Joe because I wanted to save it for the ring. Before I knew it the gong sounded and the fight was on. I walked across the ring straight to Joe to throw a big right but instead we clinched. I torqued my body to the right and threw Joe to the ground.

Joe felt really heavy because he weighed a good 260 lbs., approximately 50 lbs. heavier than me. I then immediately took his back and thought, "Yeah, now he's mine!" Seconds after taking his back I saw a chance to lock up his arm so, like I did in my fight with Ed De Kruijf, I pivoted over and set my body in place for an inverted arm bar. I shouldn't have been so hasty and should have kept his back for a while and soften him up with punches.

To my surprise, just at the right time he pulled his arm out and like a transition from heaven to hell, I was suddenly on the bottom. "Damn! The same position as the last fight" I thought, but this time I was determined to push the fight more than I did in our first fight. So instead of lying flat on my back and playing guard, I kept aggressing him, never giving him a chance to set himself. Since our last fight I drilled many reversals and one of them that worked really well for me in practice was the hip throw. Then, at about a minute into the fight, I saw an opening for a hip throw. I sat up into position and, just like I imagined many times in my head, I executed a perfect throw that landed me in the mount.

Then it was like I was releasing all the built up tension. I began to rain down a flurry of punches. In the flurry I landed numerous punches that landed flush on his face and I noticed that there was a noticeable swelling starting on his left cheekbone. His cheekbone must have had a fracture because of the quickness and the size of the swelling but I still went in for the kill. I felt like a predator sensing injury in its prey and setting up for the kill. But before I could release my fury, he began to tap. When I saw him tapping I felt a surge of anger rush, take over my spirit that took control of my body.

"What!? You're tapping!? You need to walk the walk after talking the talk!!!", is what went through my mind at that moment. "You said you were a better fighter enough to take fight money from my pocket and you're tapping already!?!? Fuck this shit!!! Just one more...punch!" Then before I knew it, the referee was tackling me and rolling me off of Joe. Then my brother and the rest of my corner were in the ring dragging me to the furthest corner, trying to calm me down. It was a weird feeling because I felt possessed, and like I was being prevented from finishing off my kill. Egan was holding me in the corner as Burton, Peter, Big Ken. and Ed hovered around to make sure I didn't get loose. I looked over to Joe and he was still on his hands and knees. "Get up! I didn't even get to put the real pain on you yet so get the fuck up!!" I thought. The irritation of his weakness, of not walking the walk sent a rush of anger through my body again as I tried to break free so I could give him a reason to stay down but my corner had a good hold on me so luckily I couldn't get free. As I was trying to get free I thought, "You want to act hurt? I'll give you a reason to act hurt!"

Everyone who sees that fight just sees the surface of it all and they see a crazy guy who doesn't stop fighting when the referee says to stop, but they can't see all the inner frustration and they can't feel the adrenaline that flows through a fighter who is willing to fight to the death. Now, I wonder if everything Shooto was telling me about Joe was true? Maybe they were making Joe look like a bad guy to pump up the fight and to save some money on cutting my fight money. A few years after fighting Joe, I found out the true colors of Shooto. Their dishonesty and deception makes me look back on the past and wonder what was true and what was a lie, just to steer me where they wanted me.

Well, now I was the first ever World Heavyweight Shooto Champion, a title that will stay with me forever. It was a surreal feeling when the belt was put around my waist, something I will definitely cherish for the rest of my life!

Displaying my Shooto World Championship belt at my Kyoto Gym.

I would like to take this opportunity to apologize to all my fans for the animal-like lack of control I displayed after the fight. Even after you all read this explanation I know that it is still no excuse for carrying on the way I did. Last but not least, I would like to send my apologies to the AMC academy and to Joe Estes. I was out of line and one day when I can meet you in person I would like to tell you "I'm sorry", face to face.

Chapter 32

FOUNDED YAMATODAMASHII ICHIZOKU IT WILL BE MY HONOR TO DIE FOR YOU SOMEDAY

In 1998 I began to organize a group I call The Yamatodamashii Ichizoku. It is a group of friends that, although they have no blood relation to me, I call Family. Not the normal person's idea of family, but one that has deep meaning and is more important than life itself.

The Yamatodamashii Ichizoku crest.

Family... what is the definition of Family? Is it a group of people with the same bloodline that live together? Well, yes, in the dictionary of common people. But to me, more than that, it is a group of people who rejoice together in the good times and stand side by side in the bad; a group of people that care for each other more than they care for themselves and are willing to die for each other on any given day. I have a group of people from all over the world that I call Family or in Japanese, "Ichizoku." They, not only share the same beliefs that are written above, but they also understand, live, and respect the Yamatodamashii way. It is the way of the Samurai, which is doing what's right, no matter how hard it is to do and knowing what the consequences are: to protect the weak and to help the less fortunate; to have values of integrity, honesty, backed with courage and the willingness to die for what you believe is right.

Many of my brothers have marked themselves with the tattoo "Ichizoku" (一族) on the palms of our hands, the most painful place to get a tattoo. The reason why I chose to have it on the palm of my hand is because I believe clenching your fist is your first and last thing you could do in life. When a newborn baby is born, not able to talk or walk, you can put your finger in the palm of his hand and he will close it and squeeze. I've had many close people die of cancer and at the end of their life, when they've lost all of their power, the power to speak or the power to even open their eyes, I've seen a doctor put his fingers in the palm of their hands and tell them "If you can hear me, squeeze..." I believe that the first and last power you will ever have is clenching your fist. Therefore, the Ichizoku tattooed on the palms of our hands signifies that we will always hold and protect our family.

The Yamatodamashii Ichizoku stands strong and will never be broken or controlled by any one or group by fear. Not even the all-feared Yakuza families in Japan can intimidate the Yamatodamashii Ichizoku. The Yamatodamashii Ichizoku is one solid group that work as one family but consists of individuals from other families under one flag, the Yamatodamashii Ichizoku flag. The Yamatodamashii Ichizoku consists of brothers and sisters from around the world: Japan, Hawaii, Guam, The United Kingdom, Thailand, Canada, America (Vancouver, WA, San

Diego, CA), Guam, Saipan, Pompei, Ireland, Germany, New Zealand, and Australia. Yamatodamashii Ichizoku members include Yakuza's from many different families, students, lawyers, real estate agents, fighters, soldiers, teachers, doctors, police officers, etc., people from all walks of life. However, when we meet, all that goes out the window, and we stand as one, no matter where we come from.

In the Yakuza world you have the Yamaguchi Gumi and the Sumiyoshi Gumi. Gumi means group, a group of people. You have the Kobayashi Kai. Kai also means group. The reason why I call my group, *Yamatodamashii Ichizoku* is because we're a family; we'll do whatever we need to do, to help each other out.

Currently I am single and my choices in life do not lead me to getting married and having a family. I love kids and always dreamed of having my own, but children may not be in my destiny. I'm beginning to think that God has other plans for me. My life is an adventure and in any given time I may have to walk a fine line between life and death. There are things that I spontaneously do that I wouldn't do if I had a wife and children depending on me. If I lived a normal life, got married and had children, the only people I would be willing to risk my life for would be my direct blood like my mother, father, and my brother and my wife and kids.

However, without a wife and kids, I can die for my Ichizoku and any other human being that may need help. I imagine a house on fire and children trapped on the second floor of the house. The house is still accessible but not sturdy. If there were any possibility to save the children I would try even if I might die trying. I don't think I could live knowing that I watched them die and if I tried, I may have been able to save them. I, in no way want to be a hero, nor do I want any medals. I just want to be true to myself and do what I feel in my heart.

My *Yamatodamashii Ichizoku* has been growing slowly for the last 15 years and is currently 200+ and growing. Many people have messaged me saying they want to become a part of my *Yamatodamashii Ichizoku*. I've been asked questions like how do I become a part of the Family? What do I need to do to be accepted into the Family? The truth is, there are no rules or things you can do to become a part of the *Yamatodamashii Ichizoku*. It's a feeling in my heart and a feeling in the other *Yamatodamashii Ichizoku* member's hearts that makes someone a part of the Family. If I trust you with my life, feel that I can die for you at any moment and the feeling is mutual, you are a part of my *Yamatodamashii Ichizoku* Family. Meeting me and the other members, hanging out enough to get to know each other is the only way to be a part of the *Yamatodamashii Ichizoku*... the rest is all true feelings in the heart.

The mark of brothers for life. Ichizoku tattooed on our hands.

"Thou who shed his Blood with me...
Shall always be my Brother...
And thou who has become my Brother...
I will bleed for even if it meant bleeding to death."

Chapter 33

WAR9 LEAVING IT ALL IN THE RING – FRANK SHAMROCK

I was now the Shooto World Heavyweight Champion and my next fight was with Shooto's rival, Pancrase's King of Pancrase, Frank Shamrock. Shooto and Pancrase had a big grudge against each other, which gave this fight a lot of extra hype. I didn't give a shit about the Shooto/Pancrase bullshit. Frank was just a step on my way to being the best fighter in the world. Winning the Shooto World title was awesome, but to me, it was just one of my goals.

Another goal for me was getting the Ultimate Fighting Championships (UFC) belt. What everyone didn't know is that Frank and I had the same contract from the UFC that the winner of our fight gets to fight Kevin Jackson at the UFC Japan for the UFC belt. I had so much riding on this fight. Shooto vs. Pancrase, victory at Vale Tudo Japan, and now a UFC title shot! I knew Frank was one of the best in the world so as soon as the fight was signed I went into very intense training.

I did three sessions a day, anywhere from 6 to 9 hours of training daily. Two hours in the morning, two hours in the afternoon, and two to four hours at night for sparring. I was also living in my car, going back to my apartment only about 6 times a month just to wash clothes. I lived in the outskirts of Tokyo in a city called Omiya so time spent driving back to my apartment was turned into sleep time. I was training so hard; sleep was something I needed very much. I was showering using an electronic pump syphoning water from a 50-gallon tank of water. The vans

149

adjustable seats that flattened out into a bed allowed me to sleep comfortably in the car so all I really had to find was a secluded parking place to park at.

I got in the mode and everything I did was revolved around this fight. Train...eat...and sleep, that's all I did. I gave up my social life like going to parties and clubs but only when I had energy I would hook up with a hottie I was keeping in touch with. We would hook up for the night...no strings attached. Even the girls, no matter how rich or high class they were, would sleep in the car with me. Back then, I didn't think anything of it but now I would be embarrassed to date a hot hostess from a high class hostess club and have her sleep in my car. I guess back then nothing mattered to me but training and everything else had to adapt to my training.

A typical day would be like this. I would park my car at a park near the weight training gym. I'd wake up and go for a 50-minute run followed by sprints at the park. After my sprints I would head to the weight room and lift weights. After I lifted I would pick up something to eat and drive to Aoyama University to make the wrestling team's practice. I usually would get there early and get some sleep in the car until training time and allow my food to digest.

I would set my alarm to wake up to go to wrestling practice and after wrestling practice drive straight to Watanabe gym to train my kickboxing. I would again get to my next training destination early, get a bite to eat, and then take a short nap in the car until training time. When I was done with Watanabe gym's training I would head straight to Purebred Omiya to barely make it in time to catch the sparring with all the other pro fighters. When the sparring was done I would get dinner, then drive to wherever the next day's morning training was and sleep in the car so I could wake up at my next training spot. Everyday varied and the training location varied according to my opponent for my next fight. Sundays were usually my off days where I would just take a long, slow, one-hour jog.

Training for Frank's fight went great. I had two big sparring partners from New Zealand, Peter Leiatua and Anthony Netzler, and from my gym in

Guam, Melchor Manibusan. My sparring was always super hard-core. So hard that I couldn't keep sparring partners to stay with me for more than two fights. We would do MMA full sparring about three times a week and we would go about 85-90% intensity. Anthony and Peter were tough as nails and they were always there for me on call, any time of the night. Some days after training was over for the day, I would be lying in bed trying to sleep but the uneasiness of the sparring we had that day would not subside. I felt I needed a few more hard rounds so I would call Peter and Anthony and have them suit up and meet me at the gym for a few more rounds. Many times, these last minute extra sparring sessions would be at three in the morning. I would call them and we would meet up at my gym, beat the shit out of each other; then I would express my appreciation and be on my way. Like a typhoon coming in, the empty silent gym...going crazy for three or four rounds...being done in about 30 minutes leaving the gym silent again as if nothing happened.

I was so ready for Frank. I was probably in the best shape of my life and confident. I planned to come out hard and take it to Frank until he folded. The year before I had lost to Igor Zinoviev within a minute and I was determined to never ever let that happen again. I didn't plan to beat Frank on points but instead planned to go out like a pit bull and try to fuck him up before he fucked me up. Kill or be killed!!!

Now it was the day of the fight and I was lean and ripped at 93 kilograms. I was confident like a pit bull taking on a poodle, ready to take on anyone. I was ready for war, ready for anything that would come my way. Ready to absorb and fight through any type of pain and even ready to face death itself. I was planning to go in like a beast, give Frank more than he could take, break his spirit, take his soul, then go and take the UFC belt from Kevin Jackson.

Minutes before I made my ring entrance everything was perfect. I had confidence enough to feel I could break the devil himself, the shape and stamina to go 110% all 3 of the 8 minute rounds, and enough of a fan base to make me feel like I'm on my home turf. I felt like a beast, unstoppable and when I saw Frank in the ring staring at me like he wanted to fuck me up...instead of feeling fear or questioning my confidence, I thought, "I hope you're ready to walk the walk because I'm going to make you feel terror and a ferocity that you've never felt before."

Then the bell sounded and we were let loose. To my surprise Frank was tougher than nails and I realized right away that I was in for a war. However, I didn't have a problem with that because a war is what I prepared for and I wouldn't have accepted anything less. The first round he was basically in my guard and we both didn't do much. I kicked him in the face from my back and he caught me with a few solid punches from my guard. Nothing close to causing damage to affect us for the next round and nothing near to ending the fight. However, I told myself that in the second round I must take it to him harder.

As soon as the bell sounded I came out punching, only to find both of us tied up against the ropes, pummeling each other and jockeying for an advantageous tie up. Suddenly Frank tried a leg trip on me and his balance wavered. I was in better balance and took him down and took the top position. Rather than me creating the position, I just sort of took advantage of Frank's mistake. Then as if the angels were watching over me I not only took the top, I took one of the most advantageous positions in MMA, the mount position.

When I fell into the mount, I thought it was over. "Okay, I thought, it's just a matter of time before you break him, just take your time". I got the mount within one minute into the second round so I knew I had at least six more minutes to work. Six minutes may seem short to you but believe me when you're being mounted by someone that really wants to hurt you, six minutes can seem like eternity. I was now on top and I was ready to finish the fight by pummeling Frank into submission. Then to my surprise Frank's defense was a type of defense that I'd never experienced before. Up until that moment the mount was a 90% aggressive position that was near impossible to defend.

But Frank's defense was impeccable. He wrapped his arms around my back and pulled himself against my chest and because in the rules I couldn't elbow his head, I couldn't get any clean punches that would hurt him. There was a point in the fight that was interesting. It was when I was mounted on him that our eyes met and we both froze for a couple of seconds. Although the moment was very intense, just the way we froze when our eyes met made us both laugh. Then we went back into mode to finish each other off. I was getting frustrated and heard the timekeeper yell out "3 minutes remaining" and I didn't want this to go to a decision. I wanted to knockout Frank even though that meant him getting out of the mount.

So I decided to make more space hoping, that when he tried to get out I could get off some good punches and maybe end the fight. But Frank was explosive and when I posted my leg up he got out. Well, I lost the mount and he got back to his feet but I wasn't too worried because I was also fine with throwing down toe to toe with Frank. So then we went crazy. Swinging toe to toe literally trying to kill each other. We were both warriors and we threw blow for blow which even until today, after over a decade, this is still one of the best flurries MMA has ever seen. I knew the risk of standing toe to toe but I felt that I was going to hit him first before he got me.

Unfortunately for me, he caught me first. He got me with a solid knee to my face, then a right cross, then another punishing knee to send me down to the canvas. Out of all the excitement and adrenalin, Frank pounced on me to get in a few extra shots to finish me off. My brother Egan saw that and instinctively ran into the ring to stop Frank from continuing and that's when I was disqualified. I felt the knee and the right cross, but had absolutely no account of the last knee. DQ? Not in my eyes. In my heart I believe Frank earned a KO. I also hold nothing against him for trying to hit me when I was down because the fight was so heated that it is hard to stop yourself instantly.

Also in his book I saw that he stated that I was on steroids for our fight. I wondered why he said that because we never got tested so I conclude that he was probably on it or why else would he think I was? I also take that statement as a prop, instead of an insult for I must have felt that strong and in shape for him to think that. I trained for that fight with the will to die and it must have paid off for Frank to feel I was on something for our fight!

Although I lost, my fight with Frank changed me as a fighter. He brought out the best in me and he taught me that standing toe to toe isn't scary... in fact, it was a rush!!! I fought to the end and I gave 110%. To me that's what is important. Winning and losing is beyond the fighter's control so why worry about it and put extra pressure on yourself? What is in the fighter's control is fighting to the end and not giving up because you get controlled by fear and anticipate the end. Let the end come and trust that there are doctors, referees, and your corner men to stop the fight if it gets too dangerous. Giving 110% is also the choice of the fighter. But winning or losing... It's like driving to a crowded shopping mall and hoping to find a good parking space. Timing, luck, and chance are things you can't control and those are what will get you a win or a loss, or a good parking space.

My fight with Frank taught me a lot. It helped shape the warrior that I am today and if I could rewind the hands of time I wouldn't do anything different. Losing a fight is not necessarily bad. In every situation there is good and bad to it and you can choose which to dwell on. Winning or losing a fight will not decide whether the fight was good or bad for you. Just because you win a fight and your hand is raised in the end that doesn't necessarily mean it is a good thing. It is what you do with the win or the loss that will determine whether it was good or bad.

You can win a fight but if you don't learn anything from it, then it isn't good. You can also win a fight and get overconfident and it will be a bad thing. On the other hand, you can lose a fight but learn a lot to make you a better fighter and in the long run it will be just like a win. I lost to Frank because he was the better fighter that night. I didn't hang my head or sulk over the loss. Instead, I focused on the strength the fight gave me and learned from the things in that fight that I could have done better.

To me, winning or losing is not determined immediately after the fight when a fighter's hand is raised. After you analyze the fight tape and study your mistakes the true victory is whether or not you can enter the ring for your next fight a better fighter than you were in your last. Frank beat me but I have no bad feelings. He helped me learn and grow as a warrior. He also gave me a war that brought out the best in the both of us and gave the world one of the best fights ever, that will never be forgotten.

You are never really beat until you give up in your heart. So with that in mind, I'm still undefeated!

Chapter 34

NOTHING IS IMPOSSIBLE –
RANDY COUTURE

After losing to Frank Shamrock, I gathered myself and began training soon after. I decided I wanted to train harder and come back stronger. Shooto was having a hard time finding an affordable, famous, heavyweight fighter that would be qualified to fight for the title so I just waited and kept on training. I had no fight planned yet, but I had my heart set on fighting another big name as big or bigger than Frank. After beating me, Frank went on to fight Kevin Jackson and captured the UFC Middleweight title. So finding a name bigger or as big as Frank was very difficult for Shooto, especially when their funds were limited and a bigger the name meant a higher the cost.

I was slowly but steadily putting on weight and feeling a lot stronger. When I fought Frank I was 93 kilos and in six months I had put on 3 more kilos of solid muscle. I was now 96 kilos and itching to fight so I kept a strict regimen and waited. Then finally Shooto called! They couldn't find an opponent for a small event like Shooto, so instead they asked me if I could fight in the bigger Vale Tudo Japan event. I asked who they had in mind for my opponent and they said Dan "The Beast" Severn. Wow! The Beast!!! I was excited and eagerly accepted. Dan Severn was a UFC champion and was named the Beast because he attacked his opponent relentlessly with no mercy. I began to feel intrigued about how the aggression of the Beast would feel and if I was man enough to endure it or maybe even beat him.

As I was focused and setting my sights on Dan Severn, I got a sudden call from Shooto. Dan Severn had a prior commitment that he couldn't get out of and so he couldn't make the fight. I was bummed and asked if they had anyone else for me to fight and they replied yes. The name they put out in front of me was the infamous Randy Couture. My first reaction was to be blown away, because Randy was "The Man," an undisputed UFC champion with an undefeated record. Not only was he undefeated, but he dismantled the seemingly unstoppable Vitor Belfort by knockout and captured the belt from a devastating kick boxer, Maurice Smith. Okay, after the initial shock, the question was now, am I ready for the likes of Randy Couture?

Couture was the undefeated, undisputed world champion at the top of his game. Then something clicked in me. The idea of putting myself on the line in a seemingly impossible challenge began to intrigue me a bit. I thought, in the books, I'm not supposed to stand a chance against Randy and it would be a pretty accurate assessment to say I would get my ass kicked. So, what have I got to lose? I'm supposed to lose and the experience I would get by fighting "the best" would be priceless. So I picked up the phone the next day and accepted the fight.

It was still about four months away but I got into gear and began training hard for this seemingly "impossible feat". When this fight was finally announced, the Japanese press went crazy. The reason why this fight got so much press was because Randy was the UFC champion and I was the World Shooto Heavyweight Champion and the Japanese hope. I was flooded with television, magazine, and newspaper interviews. I was getting an interview practically every day and sometimes even three a day.

My training regimen was six to eight hours a day (two hours in the morning, two hours in the afternoon, and two to four hours at night) so juggling interviews was very difficult. It was frustrating because sometimes the interviews would inconvenience the training but I knew this came with the job so I did my best to cooperate. As if going out of my way wasn't frustrating enough, the negativity of the questioning was sometimes hard to bear. The interviews included questions like, "Are you ready for someone like Randy?", "Are you going to be alright?", "How do you plan to fight someone of Randy's caliber?". I got the feeling that they didn't think I had a chance to beat Randy and they were worried for my safety.

Now, I am a fighter, not a wimp, so instead of the interviews wavering my confidence, it fired me up instead. In fact, in one interview I got a little bit too irritated and I said, "Randy isn't superhuman. He's a human like me and everyone else, two arms and two legs. If I get him in an arm bar, his arm will snap like everyone else's and if I sink in a choke, he'll sleep like everyone else." Even my friends and training partners seemed worried, but this just made me more determined to not only climb the so-called un-climbable mountain but to climb it like a fierce lion, confident and determined, getting to the top and devouring the lamb at the summit. I had more fire than ever and trained harder than I ever trained before.

Then the unexpected happened. One day when I was doing my weight training circuit I felt my shoulder pop. When it popped I felt the power leave my arm but was determined to work through it and finished the grueling 40-minute full body regimen. It was just a month out from fight day so I couldn't take time off. I knew I had to train through the injury so every day before training I would tape my shoulder up so much that it felt like a cast. At first it was hard to move normally so we only did drills that I was able to do. Then day-by-day as the pain in my shoulder subsided we would tape it less and less until it didn't restrict my movement at all.

Going into any fight there are odds and the odds for my fight with Randy was definitely very much in favor of Randy. However, odds didn't matter to me. Even if Randy was favored 99-1, it was just numbers to me. So what if Randy has 99 roads to take to win the fight and I have only one. All I have to do is make sure we walk that one road to my favor. If there was 0% for me to win now that's a different story. If I could guide the fight to go on my one road, all of Randy's 99 roads would be useless.

So I decided that I would go out hard at Randy like a pit bull going for the kill. I wanted to start off the attack first to set the pace of the bout. So after talking it over with Egan, we decided to come out instantly with a hard kick to the inside of his front leg. Also, because Shooto had no rule on how much tape we could put on our legs, we decided to put one whole roll of white medical tape on each leg to make my kicks heavier therefore more painful. So Egan began taping my legs and when we were done it felt like I had casts on each leg without hindering my movement at all.

Then to test it out I tried kicking some of my corner men and one of them replied, "Holy shit... feels like a cast!" After hearing that I felt mission accomplished. I also heard that Randy was coming in at about 230 lbs. to my 210 lbs. so I decided to try to put on more weight. This was the biggest fight of my life and I was training really hard, so I was having a hard time keeping weight. So in order not to drop too much weight I began forcing myself to eat more and I was able to get myself up to 215 lbs.

The day of the fight I felt great and was getting more and more irritated with the behavior of the press. They didn't even give me a chance and it seems as though they already had their minds made up that I was going to get my ass kicked. At the weigh-ins when I finally saw Randy in person for the first time, he was much bigger than I thought. He was ripped and in great shape and calm as though he was about to take a stroll in the park. He was confident and very relaxed. All I wanted to do was hurry and get it on. The waiting was killing me.

This fight was perfect. They announced the fight as two World Champions squaring off. Randy as the Ultimate Fighting Championships (UFC) World Champion and me as the World Shooto Heavyweight Champion. For my ring entrance I came in to Fiji's "Chant of the Islands", a slow but confident sounding Maori song. As I entered the ring, I looked over at Randy standing on the other side. All I could think about was that first kick I was going to throw to the inside of his leg. The mental image I had repeated over and over in my head was his leg breaking with that first kick.

Finally, the gong sounded and off I went. Walking swiftly across the ring, I met Randy on his side and stepped in heavy, putting everything into the kick. As expected, it landed smack right in the inside of his thigh. To my surprise he took it in stride, grabbed ahold of my leg, and took me down. All I had in my mind was to attack. I not only wanted to beat him, I wanted to break him. Suddenly, before I knew it, I had him in a triangle. However, before I had a chance to set the triangle deep, I decided to hit him with a couple of lefts to soften him up. A big mistake I made was underestimating Randy's strength. Randy effortlessly stood up and lifted me off the mat causing me to lose my lock on the triangle I had on him. He was then standing over me looking down on me, looking for an opening to kick or attack me. I was on my back and 99% of the time the person on his back is in a defensive position, but not me. I was determined to be the aggressor no matter what position I was in, so I came off with a very hard kick from the bottom. I aimed for his head but only reached up to his shoulders. The kick landed flush and hard that it made a loud smacking sound. This kick landed so hard it practically threw Randy off balance and more importantly, it set the whole pace of the fight. I kicked him a few more times and he came off with a nice punch that landed but the overall movement was in my control.

Although I was definitely the aggressor, being on my back I wasn't able to apply as much pressure as I wanted to so I decided to take a chance and get back to my feet, allowing me to stand toe to toe and throw down with him. I waited for the right moment. When I thought the time was right I stood up only to find Randy ready and waiting.

He planted a nice straight right smack on my chin, which I felt, but was able to continue and get to my feet. We then flurried, stood blow for blow when he made the first initiative to tie up. He tried to shuck my head down a few times but all my wrestling practice had me ready. I wanted to avoid the dirty boxing skills he displayed in his win against Vitor Belfort so I got close to him and actually got lucky enough to tie him up, shucking his left arm high up and rendering it useless. I felt safe and waited for his next move to break away so I could begin throwing combinations again, but to my surprise he had other ideas.

My strength was my ground fighting and Randy's strength was to stay on his feet to wear me out. Then what Randy did next, caught me off guard. He took me down into my domain. When he took me down I was relaxed so I quickly put him in my guard and felt him grab the back of my head with his right arm, preparing to strike with his left. If he did begin to strike with his other hand this would make his arm around my head vulnerable to be arm-barred but I was sure Randy was aware of that. Was this a set up or was he unaware of what he was doing???

So instead of slapping the arm-bar on right away, I swiveled my hips over, climbed my legs up to his shoulder, stopping in the middle, waiting for his next move. If he released his left arm to strike I was already set in position to slap on an arm-bar in a split second. He let go to strike so I passed my leg over his face and set the arm-bar in deep! I had it in deep and began extending it and he did what his body instinctively told him to do... pull his arm out. However, I had his arm in so deep and locked in so tight, his arm was mine and I wasn't about to give it back unless he gave up or I broke it in two. As he tried to pull his arm out, I fell on his arm belly down and could hear his tendons popping as I arched my hips. I counted a total of four pops altogether and I was wondering if I was able to break his arm completely from my inverted position. Then, like I was dreaming, I felt tapping on my legs. It took a second to realize that I had just beaten the Undefeated UFC World Champion, Randy Couture.

As I planned before, I instructed one of my boys that if I win, he would run to my car, get my boy Shooto and bring him into the ring. NK Hall has never before had a dog enter their ring and I knew I would get a lot of shit for doing this. The year before, when I brought Shooto in the Korakuen Hall's ring, there was a big problem. However, through all my hard training and suffering, Shooto was the one that was with me through it all and I wanted Shooto in the ring with me to celebrate this victory. When Shooto came into the ring, I pulled him over to me, gave him a big hug and whispered in his ear, "We did it!"

Arm bar over Randy Couture, Vale Tudo Japan, 1998.

Those that didn't believe in me must have been in shock. Instead of jumping for joy, I stood up calmly, closed my eyes, raised my hands in the air and thought to myself, "See, it wasn't impossible to beat Randy!" The irritation of all the people who counted me out before the fight was built up ready to explode. It was still bothering me, so when I walked over to my corner, I told Egan that I wanted to get on the mic and tell all the doubters, fuck you!

Now Egan is an angel and I'm like the devil so, of course, Egan's reply was, "Nah, don't do that." However, all the irritation was built up over the months before the fight… so much that I just ignored Egan's reply and asked for the mike. When I finally got the mic, I waited for everyone to settle and the music to subside before I was able to finally express my feelings to the public. I planned to say, "To all of you who thought I was going to lose, in your face!" However, through all the excitement, "To all of you who thought I was going to lose, Fuck You!" came flowing out. Then I spiked the mic on the ring and without saying another word, exited the ring and returned to my locker room.

My victory against Randy was a big turning point in my career. Many good things happened to me. I was given my Brazilian Jiu-Jitsu black belt from John Lewis, got invited to Abu Dhabi's world submission event to fight the Super Fight against Mario Sperry, and last but not least, it opened the door to fight in Pride. In the post-fight interviews, the press asked me how it felt to beat a name like Randy Couture and I answered... "Awesome!" Then they asked me if I now considered myself the best in the world after beating Randy and I replied, "No. I was just lucky to have caught Randy in a mistake. If we were to fight again tomorrow there is a good chance that Randy might beat me. Tonight was just Enson Inoue's night."

Wow! I had just beaten Randy Couture and it was an unreal feeling to be even considered by some, to be one of the best fighters in the world.

Note: After beating Randy, John Lewis/Penederious gave Egan and I our black belts. Egan, for winning the worlds in brown and me, for beating Randy Couture.

Chapter 35

Taste of BJJ – 1999 Super Fight with Mario Sperry, Abu Dhabi

My win over Randy also opened a door for me, which was the opportunity to fight in Abu Dhabi! I got a call from my brother and he told me that the Prince of Abu Dhabi was inviting me to participate in the Abu Dhabi World Submission Championships to fight in a Super Fight with the prior year's champion, Mario Sperry. The fight money was $15,000 to show and another $15,000 to the winner of the fight. I excitedly accepted and I was on my way to a place beyond my imagination. When we got there, we were checked in to a very plush hotel and we were all taken to the grounds where the event was to be held. It was breathtaking. The gymnasium had an unreal weight facility with a big mat room for grappling, a horse racing track, bowling alleys, and a big arena. When we finished touring the facility we were taken to the arena where the weigh-ins were to take place.

As I was waiting to be weighed in, I looked around the arena and was amazed at what I saw. All in one arena there were some of the best grapplers in the world. Renzo and Ryan Gracie, Saulo, Amari Bittettii, Mark Kerr, Ricco Rodriguez, the Machado brothers, John Lewis, Ricadon, Rumina, Uno, Sakurai, Royler, and the list goes on. For me it was an honor just to be in the same room with all these elite grapplers, let alone be the one fighting in the super fight against the likes of Mario Sperry. In grappling, Mario is definitely a class above me and honestly, grappling-wise, I don't think I belong in the super fight with Mario. I guess my win over Randy had a really big impact on the Prince and the fighting world, enough to get me this special chance.

Nevertheless, I was here and I did have a chance. If Mario made one little mistake, I knew I trained hard enough that I would pounce all over his mistake. My match with Mario was the finale, the showcase fight called the "Super-fight". It was awesome watching all of the amazing dream like match ups. Then came along Egan vs. Renzo Gracie. It was a very close technical match with Egan squeaking out on top to out point Renzo and get the victory.

Everyone was applauding the match, when out of the blue Renzo's younger brother Ryan Gracie (may he rest in peace), was all riled up and began glaring at my brother like he was going to attack him. So I stood right by Egan's side and watched Ryan carefully. Like Egan and myself, the two brothers had two very different reputations. Renzo, like Egan, was considered the cooler, more level headed brother while Ryan, like me, was the crazy, uncontrollable, unpredictable one. Fortunately, everything ended up as just a heated stare down which left the arena buzzing, anticipating some kind of drama. Then when we returned to the room, the promoter Guy Nevins called our room and wanted to speak with us. When we met, he had a serious look on his face and said, "Here in Abu Dhabi if you fight, it doesn't matter who is right or wrong, you both go to jail. So if Ryan decides to hit you, by all means, don't hit him back.

I looked at Guy in astonishment and said, "If Ryan comes to fight and hits me, there is no way I'm not going to defend myself and I will fight back if I have to. So if you don't go talk to Ryan and settle everything you are going to lose your Super-fight. I'm not going to let someone attack me and not fight back, especially someone as dangerous as Ryan, and I don't want to go to jail here so maybe it is a good idea for me to jump on the next plane out of here."

Guy's face then tightened up and he said that he would talk to Renzo and take care of everything. Thirty minutes later we heard a knock at the door and it was Renzo and Ryan. We both apologized to each other for the commotion and we both decided to bury it. Renzo was always one of the nicest guys in the fighting world; while Ryan was like a time bomb, capable of exploding any second. Since the incident I've ran into Ryan in Japan and we always greeted each other with a friendly smile and a lot of respect. However, a few years ago Ryan met an untimely, shocking death. It was a sad day and a definite loss to the MMA world. May Ryan rest in peace.

Before I knew it, it was the day of the Super-fight. I was ready and expecting anything to happen. I began to focus and started warming up in a back room when Egan came in to the room with a excited look on his face. He had a t-shirt in his hand and he told me that the owner of this company will pay me $5,000 dollars if I wore the shirt into the Super-fight. $5,000? What? Just to wear the shirt??? I thought, hell yeah, and snatched the t-shirt from Egan and put it on.

When my name was finally called to enter the mat area the atmosphere in the arena was nothing like I ever felt before. There were guys in turbines beating tambourines and drums; chanting and dancing throughout the whole arena. It was a weird sensation and such a great experience that even until today I feel I was lucky to have.

The Super-fight was one round of 20 minutes with the first 10 minutes fought with no points. I didn't care and wasn't about to stall for the first 10 minutes so I came out hard from the opening bell and took the fight to Mario. Faking a shot, pushing his head, pulling his head down, while Mario played a really smart safe game wrestling more defensively. I was getting a bit frustrated so when we finally tied up I hastily tried to suplex him, underestimating his size. Mario was about 245 pounds and much too heavy to force a throw.

So I landed on my own back with Mario falling right on top of me. Then Mario began to play a boring but very smart game. Passing my guard getting points then letting me wrap up his leg again on purpose only to slide his leg out again, passing again and getting more points. He did that over and over again in the 20 minutes and racked up a double-digit point lead. He laid on me and stayed tight not allowing me any space for me to go on the offensive.

In the middle of the fight, I was being totally controlled so I began to talk to Mario and said to him, "You are so much better than me that if you don't move and try to submit me, I won't be able to move and the fight will stay just like this until the end." To my surprise Mario replied, "Yes, I know, but you are too dangerous my friend, you are too dangerous."

His reply was very frustrating but in a way it also very flattering for someone as good as Mario to consider me dangerous. Time was ticking and Mario wasn't taking any chances. At the 15-minute mark I tried to get him to be more aggressive by taunting him with gestures. As Mario was holding me tight in side control I purposely looked over to Carlson Gracie and then with my right hand, I made the gesture as if I were jacking myself off in the middle of the fight. However, Mario played it smart, kept his cool, and stayed close to me not allowing me any space to create any openings.

I then began to worry about the time. I positioned myself so I could make eye contact with Egan and pointed to my wrist indicating I wanted to know how much time was left. Then I heard Egan scream that there was only 5 minutes left so I knew I had to get going. I gathered all my energy up and exploded. With absolutely no technique involved with just brute strength, I incredibly managed to throw Mario off me from the side control he had.

I got up, backed up to where Egan was to confirm the remaining time, and because there was only a little more than three minutes left I went into desperation mode. I tried everything I could and at one point, I even dove for Mario's legs like I was a baseball player stealing second base. Then in the last seconds, I managed to get close by getting a firm hold on one of Mario's legs, only to be countered and end up on the bottom again. I was outclassed and lost the match by a big point margin.

Then as we were walking off the mat Egan looked at me, smiled, and said, "Welcome to the world of Jiu-Jitsu." I chuckled, shook my head, and replied, "Well, in that case, I never want to enter a Jiu-Jitsu match ever."...and I never did.

Chapter 36
GUAM – MY 2ND HOME

Although I love Japan, deep down in my heart I am an island boy. I missed Hawaii but most of all I missed the year round warm weather and the beaches. Traveling to Hawaii was always a chore because of its long plane ride and time difference which made jet lag a problem. However, little did I know there was a small chain of Micronesian Islands that were only three hours away and practically in the same time zone. One of my Japanese fighters got an offer to fight in Guam so I went as a corner man for his fight.

As the plane was descending into Guam I noticed it was a much smaller island than Oahu and I looked forward to walking its beaches. It looked so much like Hawaii, but even better, it looked like Hawaii 20 years ago, with less buildings and more greenery. When I got off the plane the heat was like Japan, a little muggy and humid. I was excited to be there and even more excited because I made my return ticket five days after the fight so I could sightsee and get a better feeling of the island.

The fight went well and Kato dominated his fight. The island boys on Guam had a fire in their hearts but their technique was still at a beginner's level. They were friendly as most islanders are well-mannered and polite. After Kato's fight the promoter, T.J. Thompson, was supposed to provide us rides from the arena back to our hotel but it seemed that he forgot to. So as I was watching the people at the arena dwindle I began wondering how I was going to get back into town. I'm not the panicking type of guy so as Kato and I just chilled in the waiting area one of the boys who fought asked us how we were getting back into town. I told

169

them that we came up with T.J. and he said, "What??? T.J. already left! Jump in with us. We'll drive you back."

Kato and I gladly accepted and we jumped in the back of a pick-up truck and headed home. As we were driving home, one of the boys, Roman, told me that they trained in the garage without proper instruction. That touched me, for that's how Relson Gracie started and that's also what Egan and I did to get extra training. I asked them when they were training again and that I would love to give them some training tips. They seemed surprised, as Roman said, "That would be cool but the truth is we don't have any money to pay you." A payment was the last thing on my mind as I answered, "Payment? I don't need a payment. I would just love to help you guys out."

Little did we know that a lifelong brotherhood had just been started. Over the years we created a bond and the boys of Guam became like my little brothers. As we got closer and we began training more, the people of Guam appreciated the friendship and love I showed the people of the island. With the connection from the boys we were offered a space to open up a gym. Now 15 years later, it has moved to a different location and is run by my brother Steven Roberto and it is still known as Purebred Guam. I funded the gym at the beginning by covering some small costs but most of the mats and equipment were donated or were on loan from other island people.

Guam became my second home as I traveled back as much as 8-10 times per year. In 1999 I was even given a certificate of recognition by the Governor of Guam showing that the people of Guam recognized me as one of them. It was a great honor for this was only the second time that this certificate has ever been awarded.

Visiting Guam, there was a little word that two of the boys, Pat Fleming and Roman Dela Cruz, brought to my attention. The word was Fokai. When I asked the meaning they said it was an abbreviation of "Fuck Eye", pertaining to someone getting their eye fucked up, like in a fist-fight. So if you were to get into a fight and you got the better of your opponent, you could say, "I Fokai'ed him." The term was also used more in surfing for when a guy carves a wave up with sharp cutbacks and turns; "I Fokai'ed that wave."

Roman was just starting small and had no store or stock but was just selling out of his bag to people who wanted the shirts. He was not rolling in cash so he printed only a small amount of shirts at a time. It touched me that, although he was barely breaking even, he would give me shirts as gifts every time I was in town. I was grateful and was more than happy to support my brothers in Guam so I put the Fokai logo on my BJJ gi and on my fight trunks trying to get that special 5 letter word out as much as I could.

As I was getting more famous so was Fokai. The word even matured to a much deeper meaning. It is like the Guam way of expressing Yamatodamashii. Everyone asked me, "What is that? What does Fokai mean?" and I still get asked that question time and time again. So to those who have that question, "It's a surfing/fighting brand out of Guam that stands for the undying spirit of Familia."

Today, the Fokai Familia has grown and is alive and strong in over a dozen countries. It's an affiliate of the Yamatodamashii Ichizoku, my brothers for life!

Chapter 37

Debut in the Big Show – Pride

After soundly beating Randy Couture there were many rankings that had me ranked in the top 5 in the world. Randy was the UFC Heavyweight Champion, undefeated, and I handed him his first loss. Now, the only other undefeated fighter was Mark Kerr. I was intrigued to fight Mark not only because he was undefeated but because of what I felt, after seeing him fight a tough Brazilian fighter named Hugo Duarte. Hugo had a very crazy reputation because he was the daring fighter, who dared to take on Rickson Gracie in the infamous beach fight video in Rio De Janeiro. In the video it is very hard to see exactly what is going on but it seems that in the beginning of the fight Hugo actually got the mount on Rickson.

Hugo came to Japan to fight Mark in a Pride event and to my surprise, Mark pummeled the heart out of Hugo. Mark's aggression and ferocity was too much for Hugo to handle. Mark ended up winning by disqualification because Hugo kept pulling himself out of the ring. When I saw what Mark did to Hugo I was in the stands and I thought, wow, the ferocity of Mark must be unbelievable for a beast like Hugo to be broken and run like a coward. I don't exactly know what happened inside of me, there was a sort of a magnet pulling me to put myself in that spot, imagining being on the other end of Mark's fury. It was like fear to avoid that situation, but at the same time a desire to feel that situation.

I was obsessed with wanting to feel that ferocity firsthand. I was intrigued to know what I would do with that kind of pressure if I were the one in the ring. Would my heart fold? Would my heart stay strong? So when

Pride contacted me to fight, I told them I wanted to fight Mark Kerr. I think I caught them off-guard because they asked me who I wanted to fight on three separate occasions and every time, I replied that I wanted to fight Mark. I guess it was also because I was considered a Japanese fighter and they wanted me to win for promotional purposes.

It was obvious that they didn't think I could beat Mark so they were trying to steer me away from that fight. The fight money was set at $30,000 and I was stoked because, not only was I fighting in the big show, I was getting 10 times more money than Shooto paid me.

However, my brother Egan took over the negotiations and got my fight money up to $80,000. I couldn't believe it. I was going to fight someone I was longing to fight and now getting paid almost 30 times more than I did in my past fights. Same four cornered ring, same 5-meter X 5-meter mat, but 30 times the money? Honestly, I would have fought for free to be able to get in the ring with Mark and have the chance to test the strength of my heart. Thanks to Egan, I was getting my cake and eating it too.

It was weird preparing for the fight with Mark, I had so many mixed feelings. Part of me was scared that I might turn into a coward like Hugo and another part of me was excited to feel Mark's power and ferocity in what may be a once in a lifetime chance. I began training like a beast, making many sacrifices, training three times a day or a total of 6-8 hours of training a day. I was even training so hard that I was having a hard time keeping my weight up. Mark was over 280 lbs. so I didn't want to come in too light. However, I was training so hard that I had a hard time staying over 200 lbs. That's approximately 80 lbs. lighter than Mark and, in my opinion, too much weight to be giving up.

Then like I was having a nightmare I got a call from Pride 10 days before fight day. They told me that Mark got hurt and the fight was off. The Vice President, for Pride, Mr. Sakakibara came to my Omiya gym and I was pissed! Ten days before the fight?? I start tapering my training 10 days before my fight!!! I sat with Mr. Sakakibara and explained to him that fight or no fight. I still expected to be paid 90% of my fight money.

He explained to me that it would be difficult if the fight doesn't take place but I strongly disagreed. I explained to him that the reason why I want to get 90% of my pay is because, as a fighter 90% of my work is done. The fight is only three rounds, merely 10% of my work. The fight was like a party compared to the three months of grueling training. All the sacrifices, blood, tears, and sweat that was dropped in training was the preparation for a party. Ten days before the fight all the work and the painful stuff is done. The fight is the easiest part of it all. He agreed and said he is going to find me another fighter for me to fight and when he does, he'll get back to me as soon as possible. We shook hands and when he left the gym something gave way in my heart. From all the frustration and disappointment of losing something I had my heart set on for so long, tears began to flow from my eyes.

Two days later I got a call from Pride telling me that they found a replacement fighter for me. His name was Soichi Nishida, a Byakuren Kiakan Karate fighter weighing in at an obese 360 lbs., about 150 lbs. heavier than me. I didn't really care because I was just excited to be fighting so I accepted.

Fight day came and I was anxious to put all the months of training to work. All the power and strength I accumulated through the three months of hard training was built up in me and now it was time to let it out, all at once in the ring. Nishida was the underdog so he was to make his ring entrance first. He walked cockily down the ramp playing up to the crowd and just as he was about to enter the ring at the final check, they found that he forgot to put on his groin cup. So, he had to run back to the locker room and it looked really comical, so everyone began to laugh. It upset me that Pride didn't catch this mistake sooner and that he and his corner men were so incompetent as to forget something as important as the groin cup. Here I am ready to go out and die in the ring, and because of Nishida's miss, the atmosphere was fucked and the crowd was laughing.

So when I finally made my ring entrance I was like a pit bull waiting to be released so I could throw down. The referee even had to hold me back once because I was so anxious to get it on. Then the gong sounded to start the round and I stepped in with a big right that connected. However, when the punch landed, on impact I heard a crack come from my hand. Nishida went down so I pounced on him, got the mount and hit him with a few more solid shots to the face. He turned his back and I sunk in the choke. As I tightened the choke I longed to release it and hit him into sub-mission but the throb in my hand made me opt to end the fight as soon as I could. He tapped out and the fight was over in seconds. I was happy with the win but I was concerned because my right hand was throbbing and felt weird.

After my win, although I knew it was prohibited to bring a dog in the ring, I brought Shooto Kun into the ring to join the celebration. Every day I train and commute in my van, Shooto Kun is always with me, greeting me even after training and accompanying me on my morning runs. Even when I had to sleep in my car, it was Shooto Kun that hung with me. So when I won, he is the one I want to give a big "We did it!" hug.

I then threw out Yamatodamashii t-shirts out to the crowd and with every shirt I threw out I could feel sharp pain shoot through my hand. That's when I began to really worry that my hand maybe badly broken.

I went straight to the doctor's room and, to my surprise, when he cut off the taping and slipped off my glove, the knuckle of my pointer finger was gone. Then I noticed that my knuckle was pushed an inch down my hand and that's when the doctor broke the news to me that I had a broken hand. This was supposed to be just a tune up for my fight with Mark, but now I had a broken hand. The doctor told me that I would be out for at least a month and I tried to stay positive that I would be back sooner than that. I hesitantly went in to see a doctor the next day and my biggest fear came true. They put me in a fucking cast from the base of my fingers to my elbow.

Chapter 38
Not Fully Healed – Pride 7

A month had passed since I had broken my hand on Nishida's head and my impatience just made the healing process much slower. I wasn't comfortable with my hand in a cast and within two weeks I decided to cut my cast off because I dreaded losing all my muscles in my forearm and my grip. I managed to make an incision in my cast so I could actually take it on and off. It was convenient because I could take it off once in a while to wash and do light forearm workouts.

However, when I went in to the hospital for my weekly checkup, the doctor freaked out when he found out what I had done. He told me that by taking off the cast and moving my hand around, I aggravated the injury, therefore slowing down the healing process. I must have really screwed up the healing process, because when Pride 7 came around, my hand wasn't ready to be used for a MMA fight. Pride was really insistent on me fighting so when I couldn't get clearance from the doctor, they asked me to just do a grappling submission match instead. I agreed, and my opponent was a fighter with Tongan origin named Tuli Kulipapa. He was an excellent boxer with almost zero ground although Pride announced him as the Tongan Jiu-Jitsu champion. Jiu-Jitsu in Tonga? What a joke.

When the fight started we squared off, got into a clinch where I easily shucked him to the ground. I then swept him, took the mount, and attempted to execute a choke using my own gi. The reason I chose to wear a gi in this match was because I knew a boxer wouldn't be able to use the gi to his advantage and it would add many more chokes and attacks to my repertoire. When I got the mount I could tell Tuli was very uncomfortable, because when I was attempting the gi choke he was grabbing and holding on so tight that it made it impossible for me to execute. I was afraid that the referee was going to break us and stand us up again so when he straightened his arm I fell into a perfect arm bar. I then arched my hips and began to hyperextend his arm until he tapped. It was an easy fight, grappling with a boxer and I was very happy with the easy $80,000 payday.

Pride 7. Walking off with the win over Tuli Kulipapa.

After the fight, I grabbed the mic to address the gossip magazine, The Shukan Post that was prosecuting me for roughing up one of their paparazzi reporters. What I said on the mic was to the point and harsh, "For all of you who are aware of the problem that I'm being prosecuted for, I'm sorry for disappointing all of you and getting bad press. But, if anyone, and I mean anyone, ever comes into my house again and does me wrong, I'm going to still grab you, kick you in the ass, and throw you out!" I said it in English so probably 90% of the fans had no clue what I said.

Then after seeing Mark Kerr's movie, "The Smashing Machine", it was clear to me that even Mark and the producers didn't know what I was talking about because in his movie he thought I was addressing him. They showed me like a shit talker making threats and going off on how I was going to hurt him. That is not my style and I didn't speak in any disrespect to Mark.

Now just for the record, I wasn't talking about Mark at all. I was addressing only The Shukan Post (covered in the next chapter). They came into my gym, fucked with me, and then prosecuted me in a court case that I was facing possible time. I wanted to express my feelings on the mic just to let them know that although they had me in a bind, if they ever tried the same shit again, I will not lay down for them, so beware.

To Mark Kerr, if you thought I was addressing you, I'm sorry for the misunderstanding, but I wasn't.

Chapter 39

The Year 2000 – Shukan Post Trouble

The Shukan Post problem all started when Norifumi, shot a Yakuza in the face with an air pistol. He got kicked out of the college he was attending in Yamanashi and got a one year suspension from being able to enter any wrestling competition from the Japan Wrestling Association. I was dating his sister Miyu at the time, so I suggested that while on suspension, he should train MMA since the movements were very similar to wrestling. That way his wrestling movement wouldn't decline much and maybe he would enjoy MMA. He liked the idea, moved into the apartment next door to me and eventually fell in love with MMA. I paid his rent, gave him a car to drive and he began training at my gym in Omiya. It seemed that the combination of Nori's Yakuza problem and the rumor of the affair between Miyu and I had the gossip magazines interested and they all wanted to get the story.

One of the biggest gossip magazines in Japan, the Shukan Post, began calling my Omiya gym, wanting to get an interview with me. My student who answered the phone told them that I wouldn't be in until the evening so to call back then. They agreed and hung up. I got to the gym at about 6 p.m. and since no call came I went about my business and began training. Sparring began at 7:30 p.m. and on this particular night, there was a full house.

Then all of a sudden, Miyu comes running into the gym, telling me that a guy grabbed her in the gym's parking lot asking her to do an interview.

He introduced himself as a reporter from the Shukan Post and gave her a business card. By the look on Miyu's face she was definitely startled and because I thought it was out of line, I got up in the middle of sparring, all sweaty and walked out into the parking lot looking for this rude reporter. I walked into the parking lot and saw him lurking in the dark, so I walked straight up to him and asked him who he was. He confirmed that he was with the Shukan Post, so I politely invited him into my gym.

However, the instant he set foot in my gym, I locked the door, grabbed him by the collar and led him to the back room. I asked him why he didn't properly call and make an appointment before coming and demanded he tell me what his reason for coming here was. He lied and said that he came here to write a story about my gym and my fighting career. I really found this hard to believe because this magazine was a total gossip magazine and a story with no controversy was too boring and unimaginable. So I asked him again and all I got was the same lie.

I was tired of playing his games so I grabbed a pair of Vale Tudo gloves, dragged him to the mat and told him, "You made a very big mistake coming here my friend. This is a Martial Arts Gym so anything on this mat is not considered assault, but instead it's just sparring. So if you don't stop telling me lies and come out with the truth, then you and I are going to begin sparring. I then asked him again why he was here and when I got the same bullshit, I grabbed his shirt, threw him to the mat, lifted my hand like I was about to strike him, and asked him one final time, "Are you going to tell me why you are here or does sparring have to start?"

He finally realized that he was in deep shit so he finally came out with the truth. He admitted that the purpose of his visit was to try and get a dual story on the affair between Miyu and I and the Yakuza problem with Nori. Since he was honest, I changed my whole tone, took off my Vale Tudo gloves, brushed off his clothes, and led him off the mat and back into the back office. I began to explain to him that if this story gets out, then it will be much more than an interesting story. Nori's father could possibly lose his job and Miyu could possibly lose custody of her son. He said he understood and apologized for his intentions and I also apologized for what I did. I then asked him if he was okay and he said he was fine, so I gave him my cell number and told him to call me if there was anything I could do for him other than the dual story. We shook hands and he left my gym.

Then late that night I got a call from an unknown number and when I answered it, it sounded like a Yakuza on the other side. "Hey you mother fucker! This is the Shukan Post! You fucked up a big story for us today, you asshole."

I was shocked. At first I was at a loss for words, I thought everything was fine until this.

"You mother fucker, we can't forgive you!", he continued. "Now you must grant us interviews with Miyu and Nori." I told him that because of the circumstances that wouldn't be possible and he got really upset. "Didn't you just have legal problems with the Naigai Times? Now wouldn't it be very bad for you to have another problem about roughing up another reporter?" It would be very bad for me so I answered yes but again declined his request to have the interviews. Then he exploded! "You dumb fuck! If you don't grant the interviews, then this whole article will become an article about you, a pro fighter, assaulting our reporter." I was shocked. At first I was at a loss for words; I thought everything was fine until this.

This was fucked up, because now he just gave me only one choice. There was no way I was going to sacrifice anyone I cared about to save my own ass. I would rather take the fall than have someone I cared about to take a fall. "Stupid piece of shit!" I thought. "You just fucked up, because now you will never get your story." So I calmly answered, "If that's the way it has to be, then so be it because I can't let you interview Miyu and Nori."

Then he blew his top and screamed, "After the story of your assault on our reporter comes out, we're going to take you to court and prosecute you! You're fucked!" Then he hung up the phone and a cold feeling ran through my body. I felt angry, confused, and scared but I knew I did the right thing so I was ready for whatever was coming. I have a belief I will

stand by to the death. It is that if I am in the right where I didn't do anything wrong, I will continue to do what my heart says is the right thing,
no matter what the consequences are. If the result was death or imprison-
ment, then I am ready to face it with my head held high. God has a reason
for everything that happens and sometimes the road he has destined for
you isn't pleasant, but it is the road you need to walk.

Sure enough, a week later in the Shukan Post magazine, there was a
two-page spread about me beating up their reporter. What made it worse
was in the write up there was a lot of bullshit and lies. They said I beat
him for 20 minutes... 20 minutes??? What a joke! He would be dead
if I beat him for 20 minutes. They also said that I kidnapped him and
brought him to my gym. They even claimed that the injuries the reporter
sustained kept him out of work for two weeks. Shit, that liar walked out
of my gym fine and even told me he was okay.

The screwed up thing about the Japanese system is that if you walk into
the hospital and claim pain in your neck or any part of your body, even if
the doctor can't find any injury, he will automatically tell you to rest for
a week. The story also said that the incident happened when the reporter
was in the midst of interviewing Miyu. They said that out of nowhere, I
suddenly intervened, stopped the interview, and began beating up the reporter. It was so full of shit, but there was nothing I could do for the power of the press is unreal. Then, about a month later, I had eight detectives
come over to my house at 7 a.m. to detain me for questioning, telling me
there were criminal assault charges filed against me by the Shukan Post
Magazine. I was questioned, released, and a trial date was set.

During my police interrogation and my trial I was 100% honest, thinking
that the courts knew what kind of dishonest, life-wrecking publication
the Shukan Post was, but it seems like this time, honesty screwed me.
However, until today, I don't feel I did anything wrong. I just did what
I had to do to protect myself and the people around me. When I find
myself in a difficult predicament, as long as I didn't do anything wrong,
whatever came my way - no matter how bad it may look; it wasn't punishment, but a way God guides you to certain paths. Even if I had to do

jail time, it wouldn't be punishment because God does things for a reason. Maybe He would be keeping me off the streets by putting me in jail because I was going to die in a car wreck or something.

I was tried, convicted, and my sentence was a six month suspended jail term with a two-year probation. That meant that if I stayed out of trouble for two years, then my record was cleared. But if I got in any kind of trouble with the law within the two-year period, I would automatically be serving a six-month prison sentence, no questions asked. I felt cheated and wondered why these low down people were allowed to get their way. Well, at least I was free and I was sure I didn't have to worry about any reporters coming to my gym to pull that kind of shit again.

This time, being honest seemed to have fried me, but I'm still positive that it was the right thing to do. Sometimes, on the outside, honesty gets you in deeper shit and helps a liar get away, but on the inside, deep in your soul, the merits are endless. Lying drains your soul. While being honest, especially at the roughest of times, builds your integrity and fuels your soul. Honesty helps you stand proud knowing you are taking the proper step to preparing your soul to be strong, for when you have to make the transition to heaven from earth.

Chapter 40

TOTALLY CONTROLLED –
MARK KERR

Finally, Mark Kerr. The fight took place in Pride's 1st Heavyweight Grand Prix Tournament. If they wanted me to participate in this tournament, I insisted that they give me Mark Kerr in the first round and if I won they would give me Royce Gracie next. To my surprise, they set it up and I was ready to go. I was very geared up for this fight because it has been over a year since I arm barred Randy Couture and I'd been seeking out a fight with Mark. I trained like a madman and was ready! Although my strength is ground fighting, I was working hard on my cardio and my kickboxing because I heard a rumor that Mark wanted to stand with me.

I planned to stand toe to toe with Mark in the center of the ring, throwing blow for blow. I even flew over to Seattle to train with Maurice Smith to work my standing with him and Kosaka. Again, because my training was so intense, I had a hard time keeping my weight up and came in too light again at a mere 202 lbs. I heard Mark was weighing in at a solid 280 lbs. so I was a bit concerned about dropping too much weight. Also, for this fight I decided to shave the kanji for "death" on the back of my head. Many people misinterpreted it as me sending a message to Mark that I was going to kill him but that's not my style. It was a message to myself signifying that I was ready to fight to the end and more importantly, prepared for death.

At this time, I thought of Mark as the best fighter in the world. That's why the moment after I beat Randy Couture, all my focus was chasing down Mark and mixing it with him in the ring. Mark was exactly what his nickname labeled him, "A Specimen." Ripped to shreds and built like a Greek god. The gong sounded and I wanted to set the mood of the fight by making an impression on Mark, so I just walked straight up to him with no guard and threw a big right. To my surprise, instead of trading blow for blow with me like I expected, he shot under my punch and easily took me down. Mark was heavy and strong like a beast and he was technical enough to control me and dish more damage on me than I could on him.

Every punch that Mark threw hurt and I must say Mark's punches were some of the heaviest punches I ever felt in my career. The only time I felt that I may have been able to turn the table was when Mark gave me enough space to up-kick him square in the jaw from the bottom. However, it wasn't enough and in the end, one judge had it a draw and the other two scored it for Mark. Physically Mark was just too strong and on that particular night, he was definitely the better fighter. However, what I was content with was that through the whole fight, my heart was nowhere near being broken or even hurt. I was happy that this beast that turned Hugo into a chicken couldn't waiver my heart, not one bit.

Chapter 41
READY TO DIE IN THE RING –
IGOR VOVCHANCHYN

Fans all over the world find this hard to believe, but taking the worst damage I ever did in a fight was one of the best things that ever happened to me for my growth as a man.

When Pride offered me this fight, I knew it was a very dangerous fight for me, but I did see it as a great opportunity to grow as a man. Before the fight everyone told me not to stand and trade with him, but instead to take him down, get on top of him, and let my forte, my ground fighting, go to work. I knew that was probably the best way to pull out a victory, but there was a crazy magnet pulling me to stand and throw down toe to toe with him. During my preparation for this fight I battled with my desire to stand and trade with him as I was preparing to do the logical thing, which was to get a take down and take the fight to the ground. I didn't want to give up too much weight, so I was trying to eat a lot and eventually came into the fight at my heaviest ever, 220 lbs.

I was ready for war, and more than that, I was ready to die. Rather than a sport, I saw this fight as a test of the growth of my manhood and a big stepping-stone in my life. There was a sort of fear mixed with excitement thinking about throwing down blow for blow, toe to toe with Igor, possibly the hardest hitter in MMA. In a split second, one blow could render me unconscious and end the night. I remember watching from ringside at Pride 8 where Igor fought a huge Brazilian fighter named Francisco Bueno and with one punch he knocked Francisco out cold as he was still standing.

With his eyes rolled back and his hands drooped limply by his side, he fell like a tree, taking a few more devastating blows on his way down to the canvas. It was one of the most brutal knockouts that I have ever seen.

It's very hard to explain but the fear of that happening to me seemed to somehow pull me towards it. I feared getting knocked out senseless like that, but deep down inside of me I wanted to put myself into such a fearful situation to see how my heart would react in the midst of the horror. I wondered if my heart would waiver even for a moment or would my heart stay strong until the very end.

In life, a strong man fears nothing, but the kind of man I long to be, a man with the undying spirit, Yamatodamashii, has many fears but never runs from them, instead facing them head on to the end, with an unbreakable heart through it all, even after the dust has settled. It is possible that the next time I faced such a scary life-threatening situation, it might be a matter of life and death for me, or for a loved one, and I want to be as ready as I can to handle it to the best of my abilities.

It would be a situation with no doctors at hand, no referees to jump in to put an instant stop to the situation, and no corner men to throw in a towel. I believed the strength, growth, and lesson my heart would learn stepping into the fire with Igor would only better prepare me, for when that time comes. With this test I would experience fighting Igor under my belt, I was positive that I would react better and be able to create a much better outcome. This could actually be a deciding factor about whether someone close to me lives or dies. How could I pass up a chance like this?

Because of the suggestion from the ring commentator, Stephen Quadros, I decided to wear my gi pants in the fight, to prevent Vovchanchyn from slipping out due to sweat if I put him in an arm bar or a triangle. Also, because I was set on testing the strength of my heart, I specifically told my corner men that no matter what, they should NOT throw in the towel.

The tension and nerves I felt before this fight were unlike any I'd ever felt before. I always walk into the ring ready to die, but for this fight, because of the power in Igor's punches, and because I knew how I was going to approach the fight, it was a bit different. As I wrote my farewell words to the people I care about, I felt a lot more emotional and my final words to some were much more difficult to write than usual.

When I entered the ring and looked across the way to Igor, I couldn't help but notice the thickness of his thighs and his girth, which helped me understand why he was considered one of the hardest punchers in MMA. I actually had a moment where my mind wandered, where I doubted whether standing toe to toe was what I really wanted to do.

Before I could figure out exactly what I wanted to do, the gong sounded. I faked a tackle and stepped in and threw a big right cross. The right cross clipped him on the cheek, and I instinctively grabbed and clinched with him. This is when I realized that this was going to really be a true test on my spirit, to see if my Yamatodamashii was imbedded deep enough in my soul or not.

You see, unless the situation you're faced with brings fear in your heart, it can't be a test of your Yamatodamashii. As scary as a situation may seem in the eyes of others, unless it brings fear to your heart personally, it isn't a Yamatodamashii test.

Yamatodamashii is not a situation; it's a feeling. I can have a Yamatodamashii experience hanging a hairpin turn driving an F-1 race-car but a professional F-1 racer wouldn't. This is simply because I'm not used taking sharp turns at 200 miles per hour, while it's something the F-1 trains to do every day. So the situation of taking a hairpin turn in an F-1 car at 200 mph can't be a Yamatodamashii experience for all. It really depends on the "feeling" inside the individual who is behind the wheel.

Because I'd had a bit of hesitation about throwing down toe to toe with Igor, by clinching with him after the first punch, I knew in my heart that I was being given a chance to test myself in a rare Yamatodamashii situation. I also knew that whatever I did in the next few seconds would determine whether I passed or failed this test of my Yamatodamashii.

He twisted and turned, trying to break away from me, but I hung on, staying close to him. It seemed as if everything was moving in slow motion and I could feel my Yamatodamashii grow from a flicker to an uncontrollable flame! Little did all those watching this fight know that they were witnessing a precious, all important growth and maturity of my spirit: A chance that comes very rarely in a man's life, to strengthen, stabilize, and carry the spirit to the next level.

Then to the surprise of all, especially Igor, I let go and unleashed a four-punch flurry consisting of a right, left, right, and another left. I knew I'd caught him by surprise because I had him moving backward as we stood toe-to-toe exchanging blow for blow. We were literally trying to knock each other's heads off and we got so caught up in the exchange that all our form and proper technique went out the window. At one point in the throw-down, we both missed huge rights, which threw us both so off balance that we actually bumped our backs against each other.

Then, as I was straightening up and looked towards him, I saw his face right in front of me with no guard. So instead of setting myself up for another right I instinctively slung my fist towards his face with a wild and ferocious backhand. Unfortunately, I was just two inches out of reach, but I knew that if that backhand connected, it would have been lights out for Igor. What I didn't know at the time was that, what I was going to experience from this point on is what makes this fight so dear to my manhood, and it would have never happened if that backhand landed. Weird as it may seem, missing that backhand was a blessing in disguise.

I then regained my balance and threw a big right that missed, and before I could regain my balance, he threw me to the ground jumping into my guard. I couldn't believe it, one of the most ferocious, dangerous punchers in MMA opted to go to ground rather than stand toe to toe with me? What the fuck? In a way, part of the battle was already won.

On the ground I quickly put him into my guard, and as I pulled him close to me, I could feel something warm dripping down the side of my face. At the time, what I thought I felt was my own blood running down my face. I didn't feel any throbbing on where I could possibly be cut so I began to wonder if I actually cut Igor in that crazy exchange.

When I looked up at Igor, I noticed a big cut about three inches long across his left cheek with blood trickling out of it. As he was pounding me from my guard, not for a moment did I go in defensive mode. Instead I was continuously attempting arm bars and continuously hacking and punching at his face from the bottom.

The small chops I was doing to his face weren't so much to hurt him, but to try to open the cut up and, more importantly, to show Igor that no matter how much he hit me, my spirit was alive and well. This would be much more damaging than any punch I could land from my back. I specifically remember one single blow that Igor connected to my left ear that, on impact, made a pop in my eardrum, and I began feeling a bit light headed with a faint buzz in my head. I knew there was some kind of damage done, but I didn't realize that at that moment, Igor had perforated my left eardrum.

I was being pounded throughout the whole ten-minute round, and as I look back on the video, there must have been two or three times where I may have lost consciousness for a moment only to recover before the referee could take notice. Igor's punches felt a lot different from Mark's. Unlike Mark's, I felt no damage on the surface from Igor's punches; instead, it felt like each and every one of Igor's punches that landed flush were piercing straight to my brain.

I also remember that at one point in the fight, after I was hit with a solid right, I purposely looked over to my corner and nodded to them, reassuring them that I was okay, even though I really wasn't sure if I was or not. I did that for two reasons: one was to lessen the concern my corner had for me from seeing me take too many hard shots; and two, to again play psychological games with Igor's head. It must have baffled Igor a bit, hitting me with punches that rendered most fighters unconscious or made them tap, and all I did was tell my corner I was okay.

Then at about the 7-minute mark of the fight one of the Pride, judges ran to my corner and screamed to my corner men that they throw in the towel. However, my corner knew that whenever I fought it wasn't for the sport or for a W, etched on my record. They knew I approached each fight, not just as a fight in a MMA ring, but as life battle, moments that bring spiritual growth in my life. And by no means were they about to take away one of the rare chances a man gets in his life, to build and strengthen his heart which feeds his samurai spirit. As painful as it was to watch, they knew it was just the beginning of a test to build my spirit, something that is far bigger than life, something my spirit will take with it for eternity!

I heard my corner scream, "One minute!" I knew I'd taken some damaging punishment during the first round, but instead of my mind worrying about that, all I could think of was that the second round would start with us on our feet again, and I would once again have a chance to throw blow for blow, toe to toe with the most ferocious puncher in MMA.

I don't remember much about the last minute, except that it felt like half an hour. I must have drifted in and out of consciousness and when the round ended instead of getting up right away, I needed to lie down for a while to regain my focus. "Whew" I thought, "that was a crazy last minute. Okay focus, get back to the corner and get ready for the second round," is what went through my mind. As I lay on my back trying to focus, my head was spinning. Then suddenly I remember my brother Egan was leaning over me and, with a concerned look on his face, he said, "That's enough! I'm going to stop the fight!"

I wanted to rest a bit longer, but because of the fear my beating instilled in Egan and my fear of Egan calling the fight, I felt I had to get up immediately to show Egan I was okay. I got up and began walking to my corner but something very strange was happening to me. Besides my head spinning, the beating I took must have done more damage than I thought. Something as simple as walking, putting one foot in front of the other, seemed like an impossible task. My brain was commanding my feet to step but my feet weren't responding. I literally had to be dragged back to my corner, so my corner couldn't get my stool under me, so I just sat on the ground in the corner. The moment I sat down, the doctor was in my face shining lights in my eyes.

Even though the doctor was standing right in front of me, his voice sounded like it was coming from a distance when I heard him say, "He can't continue, I'm going to stop it!" When I heard the words, "Stop it" come out of the doctor's mouth, an unexplainable rush overwhelmed my body. Suddenly all the three months of hard training and sacrifices I made in preparation for this fight flashed through my mind and then a strange feeling of fear overwhelmed me! Fear, not of the fight being stopped, but fear that an opportunity of a lifetime would slip out of my hands, the opportunity to mold and strengthen my spirit in the never-ending obsession to obtain true Yamatodamashii, fear of not being allowed to fight to the very end.

The first thing that came to my mind was, "NO!!!" I knew I had a two-minute interval between rounds, and I wanted to at least get my two minutes first before they made such a crucial decision to stop the fight. Of course I didn't know how badly damaged my body was at the time. All I knew was that my spirit was alive and well and wanted to go on!

Then I heard the doctor say in what seemed like an even more distant voice, "His eyes are dilated. The fight's over." Those words hit me deep in my soul. Suddenly, I could feel a rush fill my body. Like fire was filling up my soul and giving me this surge of energy I can't explain. Yes, my body was battered more than I imagined but my spirit was fresh, alive, and longing to continue this war even if it meant fighting to the death. My spirit and soul were roaring in distress while my body was battered beyond my imagination.

I had managed to accomplish something few have ever done. The fire in my spirit had outdone the limits of my human body. Then, like something took over my soul, I began screaming, "No!! No!! I'm okay! I still can fight! Nooooooo!" It was my soul screaming out. The fire in my spirit and soul was burning bright and ready for more, while my body had shut down, unable to go on, a victory in my soul far beyond any victory I could ever have in the ring.

Then in the distance I could hear the gong sounding, signifying that the fight had officially been stopped. I felt my soul fill with anger for a split second because it was still ready for battle and longed to begin the second round to stand toe to toe with Igor again. Then like letting the air out of a balloon, I felt my spirit subside as though it left my body. My soul took it hard and until the very end refused to see that my body was done, battered far beyond a two-minute rest interval.

My brother then helped me up to my feet, and as I tried to make my way to Igor's corner, for some reason my feet couldn't stay under me, and I found myself on the ground again. "What is wrong with me," I wondered. I couldn't even walk, let alone stand without having my head begin to spin. However, even in my critical state, I was determined to send a message to the spirit of a fellow fighter and friend, Andy Hug, before I left the ring.

I'd met Andy at a party a month before my fight. He wished me luck and said he would be there to watch. Little did we I know that he was not going to make it due to Sickle Cell Leukemia, which took his life a week before my fight.

As I was helped out of the ring, I realized that I faced one last challenging task: going down the walkway out of the arena on my own power. I had an agreement with myself that, by all means, I would walk in and out of the ring on my own power. The only time I would be carried out on a stretcher was if I were unconscious or if I were dead.

Although I thought I felt my spirit leave me, with the sudden task ahead, like a spark rekindled to a flame, it came back to me. As I shook off the hands of my corner men, they realized that I wanted to walk out 100% on my own power. It wasn't a macho thing, but rather, something I had to do for myself. My head was spinning and each and every step was grueling. I never thought that something as simple as walking could ever become so difficult.

The walkway out of the arena never looked so long, so I just concentrated on one step at a time. All I had in my heart was to get out of the view of all the spectators so I mustered up all the strength I had in me. It was a weird sensation because it seemed that the closer I got to the end of the walkway, the harder and harder each step became.

When I finally got out of view of all the spectators, I took three more steps and, as if someone had pulled the plug, all my power in my body suddenly left me and I collapsed. Then like I had blanked out for a moment, the next thing I remember was people asking me questions. They were all routine questions that seemed like a dream. I didn't bother answering and the only face I could see and the only voice seemed worth focusing on was my brother Egan. I could hear him asking me, "Enson., can you hear me?"

Before I could answer him, there was a big commotion about sliding a stretcher under me. To me, the stretcher is only a last resort and when I realized what they were trying to do I screamed to Egan, "No Egan! No stretcher!" Egan knew how I felt and quickly responded by pulling the stretcher out from under me. He pushed all the people away, somehow, picked me up in a bear hug, and carried me in to the doctors' room. By all means, if ever all my power expires and I can't finish the duty on my own, the only other option was to rely on nothing else but the power of my family.

When I arrived in the doctors' room, Egan laid me on a bed and the doctors immediately stuck me with two needles for intravenous feeding. I then began to feel sick and began throwing up. I knew that if someone had severe head trauma and they began throwing up, it was a very bad sign. That's when I began to realize that I was in pretty bad shape. There was a lot of commotion in the room and the next thing I remember hearing was sirens and a flashing red light. When I opened my eyes and looked around I saw men in white, that's when I realized that I was in an ambulance. Then I remember a strong but gentle touch on my leg as I heard Egan's voice saying, "Relax, Enson. You're going to be okay." I then must have faded out of consciousness because the next thing I remember was the paramedics putting me in some sort of space capsule to have my brain scanned. I must have passed out again, because suddenly I was in a private room with curtains all around me with 24-hour nurses on hand to watch me.

The next morning when I woke up, I was surprised to see Egan still there. Egan never stays longer in Japan than he has to. If there was a fight on Saturday he was heading back to Hawaii on Sunday. However, out of concern about my condition, he had postponed his flight home until I got better. I felt bad and told Egan that I was okay and not to worry, but Egan ignored me and continued questioning the doctors about what was in my intravenous.

I was bedridden for four days; many people came to see how I was doing. Everyone who came in seemed really concerned, but I assured them that I was fine. I couldn't understand why everyone was so concerned. Yes, I took a beating, but I was fine and my spirits were high. The only thing that made me uneasy was that every time I sat up in my bed, the room began to spin. I asked the nurse why and she told me that my left eardrum had been ruptured really badly, and because of that, my equilibrium was off. I had a hard time talking because my jaw was broken but everyone seemed to understand me or pretended to.

On the fifth day my dizziness subsided so I was allowed to go to the toilet on my own as long as I pushed my intravenous bag along with me. I got up to take a pee and when I washed my hands and looked into the mirror I was shocked to see what I looked like. My face and head were swollen and discolored so badly that I couldn't believe that it was me. I looked like I'd been in a massive car accident and it was only then that I began to realize why everyone who came to visit me was so worried. I myself even began to get a bit worried at how bad I looked.

When I got back to the room the doctor was waiting to inform me that he wanted to keep me a few more days. He said my brain was still a bit swollen and he wanted to keep me just a little while more until my brain returned back to its normal size. He wanted to make sure that there was no hemorrhaging in my brain and they wouldn't be 100% sure until my brain returned back to its normal size. He explained to me that when the brain is swollen, it compresses the veins, which clogs it, so until the brain returns to its normal size, you won't know if there is bleeding or not.

So I had a few more days of CAT scans and hospital food, which I actually thought tasted pretty good. He also said my liver count was 2000 times that of a normal person and he wouldn't consider releasing me until it dropped significantly. He informed me that if my liver count became too high, my liver would shut down, which could easily result in death. He continued, telling me I had a fractured left jaw, a broken right index finger, and a badly ruptured left eardrum.

Whoa!!! Damn, I didn't even realize that I was hurt to that extent and to think I was screaming at the ring doctor to let me have my two-minute rest interval, before deciding to stop the fight. Shit I needed more than two minutes; I needed a five-day interval to be able to fight the second round.

I had to smile then, because although I lost the fight, the lesson I learned about myself as a man was priceless. In this war with Igor, I knew my mind, my heart, and my spirit, actually overcame the power of my body. I felt really good about that because the majority of the fighters out there today give up, not because their body fails, but because their mind, spirit, or heart fails instead. Their mind anticipates a fearful outcome, which weakens their heart and their spirit, which in turn makes them give up. God actually makes the body very, very durable and strong, and most people don't ever realize this; because the fear in their minds, the weakness in their heart, and the underdevelopment of their spirit makes them quit before their body actually shuts down.

However, was this all worth it? For me, yes, because I am always on a mission to learn about my spirit and to develop myself as a man. I want to be a man of Yamatodamashii, to prepare for the day I finally face the most fearful test of dying. These kinds of experiences will only better prepare me to be able to deal with the most horrifying thing I will inevitably have to face, death. Whether I can face death as a man or not is one of the biggest fears that I have.

It took me more than three months to recover, and even before I made a full recovery, Pride was asking me when I could get back in the ring and fight again. As my fight career went on, my objective to get in the ring was slowly changing and taking on a much more honorable and deeper meaning. At first, getting in the ring was just to develop my skills in hand-to-hand combat so I could always be ready to protect myself and defend my loved ones in case I got in a dangerous street altercation. Then it changed to seeing how good I was compared to all the other fighters in the world by becoming a World Champion and obtaining title belts. Then, without me knowing, it eventually evolved into my ultimate objective, which was striving for inner growth to strengthen my heart and make my soul flourish.

This fight with Igor showed me that in the process of build my heart and soul as a man, there wasn't any more learning I could do in the ring. What I went through in my fight with Igor was by far the limit. Anything more would have definitely meant death and I decided that I wanted to move on. I felt that, in my obsession to be the best man I could be, there was no more that the ring could teach me. I couldn't imagine anything more dangerous and scary than what I'd gone through with Igor. I knew that it was time to hang up my gloves and it was time to move on.

However, I decided to get into the ring just one more time to show my fans that I was okay. I didn't want them to think that Igor had beaten me into retirement, because the truth was far from it. So I told Pride that I wanted to fight just one more time and that it would be my last fight. I fought Igor in Pride 10 and I felt I would be fully recovered and ready to go by Pride 12. So I gave Pride the green light and asked them to present me with fighters that I could choose from.

Chapter 42

MY SECRET RETIREMENT FIGHT –
HEATH HERRING

After I finally recovered from my fight with Igor, Pride gave me the choice to fight two fighters. One was Ken Shamrock and the other was Heath Herring. Ken was coming off a very disappointing loss to Fujita, but he was a pioneer and a legend in MMA so he was definitely an appealing opponent. Herring was a new, up and coming young fighter and what made me choose him over Ken was his convincing win over Tom Erickson. Heath's win over Tom was so appealing because Tom was a wrestler with inhuman strength and was supposed to be better than Randy Couture and Mark Kerr.

Heath fought and tapped out Tom, so Heath was my choice for my final fight. I decided that this was my retirement fight and another reason why I was retiring was because I planned to get married to Miyu. Every time I stepped into the ring I was prepared to die. So ready to die that I would wrote farewell letters to all the people close to my heart. I would tell one trustworthy student where the letters were and would instruct him to make sure everyone got their letter in case I died in the ring. Now that I was going to get married, I would have a wife and child, and in my heart, there was no way I could die in the ring and leave them alone. Therefore, I had to retire because fighting with the "Kill or be Killed" attitude was the only way I knew how to fight. Miyu had a son from her previous marriage named Erson and I loved him as my own. More than leaving Miyu without a husband, I couldn't imagine leaving Erson without a father.

My preparation for Heath was a bit difficult. I didn't think Heath had more ferocity and destructiveness than Igor, so there was no fear element to help me train hard. I decided to go to Thailand to hone my punching and kicking for a change of pace. I had no connections in Thailand at the time so I asked a friend, Yamaki Kaicho, if he could hook me up with somewhere to train. Yamaki Kaicho knew a retired Muay Thai champion, Sangtiennoi Sor Rungroj, who ran a gym in Pathum Thani. I flew to Bangkok, got a hotel room, called a taxi and rode 40 minutes to Sangtiennoi's gym. He was very soft spoken and spoke very good English and welcomed us with open arms. At Sangtiennoi's gym there was also an Australian fighter by the name of John Wayne Parr who spoke fluent Thai and he translated for me numerous times when Sangtiennoi couldn't understand me when detailed explanation was needed.

Training was great and the conditioning was harsh. In their daily routine they ran 10 kilometers in the morning and 5 kilometers in the afternoon. It was a struggle but reminding myself that this was my last fight gave me the drive to push myself and get in great shape. Two weeks before the fight I returned to Japan to finish off my training.

Then, a very unfortunate thing happened to me. I caught a highly contagious eye infection called Pink Eye, which caused a lot of tearing and prevented me from opening my eye fully for more than two seconds at a time. If I opened my eye up, even for a few seconds it would start burning, forcing me to squint. It eventually spread to my right eye.

When I went to the doctors and mentioned I had a fight in a week, they told me that it would be impossible for me to fight. In my heart, there was no way they were canceling my fight and I began to treat the infection at home. Needless to say my training never faltered because for me there was no doubt in my mind, the show would go on.

Pride had no connections with the doctors that I went to see, so they had no idea what kind of shape I was in. To avoid Pride officials from seeing my condition and possibly canceling my fight, I skipped the rules meeting, press conferences and the photo shoot. When fight day finally came, my eyes were still swollen but if I squinted, I could see so I concluded that my condition would not affect my ability to fight. However, I still had one last big hurdle to clear... the final doctors check before the fight. When I got to the arena, I wore dark shades so no one would notice my eyes. Then during my doctors check, Dr. Nakayama asked me to remove my shades. When he saw the swelling in my eyes, he looked very concerned and he asked me how I felt.

I tried to sound as convincing as possible as I answered, "I'm fine. I feel great!" Then when he shined a little flashlight in my eyes, it blinded me and I instinctively squinted and turned away from the light. He then asked with a concerned tone in his voice, "Are you sure you're okay?" I then smirked at him and said, "Of course! I'm ready to fight right now!" He then got up walked out of the room and apparently went to discuss my condition with the higher up Pride officials. My heart began to pound as I began to wonder if they would actually call my fight off. Then to my surprise, the doctor came back, stuck out his hand to me and said, "Good luck. Have a good fight." I was relieved and wanted to get out of the doctors room before they changed their mind so I put my shades back on and went straight back to my locker room.

While I was in the waiting area preparing to enter the ring, as my ring entrance song began, I felt really strange. Something was different inside of me. I don't know why but maybe it was because I knew it was my last fight. Tears kept filling my eyes and I tried my best to not to let them roll down my face. As I was walking through the crowd making my way to the ring, I could feel the energy in the crowd as if they also knew this was going to be my last fight. I got into the ring first then had to wait for Heath to enter. When we were both in the ring and the spotlights were turned on, I was completely blinded for a few seconds. I had to close my eyes and slowly begin to squint until my eyes adjusted so I could even open my eyes.

I knew Heath always starts off with a hard low kick so I decided to sit and wait for it to come and when it did, I planned to suck up his kick and step in with a huge right cross. The gong rang and as expected Heath came in with a big low kick. I timed it right and "Bang!" it connected. However I didn't step in enough so I hit the mark but it wasn't enough to hurt him. Then I felt like my fire had been lit and I couldn't wait so I continued with a big left hook and continued to charge Health. After missing a big wild roundhouse right, the straight left that followed hit its mark. Heath went down and I pounced on him.

Apparently, I didn't hurt him as much as I thought, because when I pounced on him he had more power and was more coherent than I expected. I thought he was really hurt so instead of taking his back and securing position, I stayed on the side of him and began raining down punches. To my surprise he was clear headed enough to grab one of my legs and had enough power to drive hard and put me on my back. Before I could adjust, he had my right arm in a deep key lock. What prevented him from breaking my arm completely or dislocating my shoulder was the fact that I had one of his legs wrapped up which prevented him from taking full side control. Without him taking full side control, it was very hard for him to get the leverage to break my arm. He then began to torque my arm so hard that my elbow began cracking. I heard a cracking sound so I knew I had to get out as soon as possible to prevent further damage. He had my right arm locked in tight so with my free left arm I began pounding the back of his head. He then torqued it again and there was more cracking.

Instead of continuing to torque my arm, he opted to look over to the referee and scream, "It's cracking! It's cracking!" The referee then looked at me and asked me if I wanted to give up so I shook my head to signify I was okay. Heath then turned to me and yelled, "Tap man! It's going to break!" To me, this was a sign of insecurity in Heath's mind. He was looking for a way out by trying to coax me to quit and the referee to stop the fight.

So I replied, "Go for it! If you can break it then go ahead and break it!" I then continued to pound the back of his head with my left hand wondering if and when my arm was actually going to break. I knew there was some damage already done to my arm because of all the cracking I heard but I wasn't about to tap just because I thought my arm was going to break. I wasn't about to give up on an assumption. Instead, I occupied my mind with waiting for an opening to slip my arm out while I pounded his head with my left hand.

Tapping out was never an option.

When you think about it, as I mentioned earlier, 99% of the fighters tap in anticipation of what they think will happen to them. The anticipation of passing out from a choke or a joint breaking from a joint lock, creates enough insecurity to help fear control fighters focus. Rarely do you see a fighter fighting until a limb breaks. Renzo is one of the few fighters that has done this and I really respect him for his heart and his samurai spirit.

I will never waste time or use any of my concentration on anticipating an outcome. I'll use all of my energy to get out by kicking, hitting, or stomping to distract my opponent or deter him from completing the damage that he is doing to me. I'm never going to try to anticipate an unpredictable fate, especially while my actions may change the momentum and the possible outcome. I'll do whatever I can to steer my fate into my favor, and if I'm unsuccessful, I will find out when I wake up from being choked unconscious or when one of my limbs snaps to a point where it is dangling and useless.

As I was hitting the back of Heath's head, I felt his grip loosen so I took the opportunity to slip my arm out and escape his ever so dangerous key lock. My arm felt a bit strange from the damage Heath did to my ligaments but it was still definitely functional.

We stood up again, and I immediately threw a 1-2 combination and we ended up in a clinch. Then, stupid me, tried the same ridiculous throw I tried on Mario Sperry. Again, with the exact same outcome, it failed and I ended up on my back giving Heath the top position. I put him in my guard and we then exchanged punches with neither of us doing much damage to each other. I got hasty and tried to force an arm bar and Heath was ready. He threw my legs to the side and secured side control. He threw a knee that missed, then another one that hit me square in the head. It was a solid knee but nothing compared to Igor's punches. The next two knees that he threw missed and to my surprise the referee stepped in and stopped the fight.

I was shocked. I wasn't hurt and the position Heath had me in wasn't a very dangerous position. I instantly held both hands up looked at the referee and said, "What? Why?" The referee then slapped my hand as if he resented my protest and I decided not to protest until I got to see a video to see how bad it really looked. I would look really stupid arguing a call when in everyone else's eyes the stoppage was justifiable. Sometimes what you feel and what it looks like to others are two totally different things. So I just accepted my defeat, congratulated Heath and then asked for the microphone. When I congratulated Heath, I remember him complimenting me on my Muay Thai and that made me happy.

Pride knew what I was about to do with the microphone so they tried not to pass it to me but I insisted. Finally, after I got the microphone, I said, "After I showed how durable I am in my fight with Igor, this fight shouldn't have been stopped so soon. However, it was my fault for letting myself get in that position. I am fine."

I then went to the center of the ring, took a deep breath, and got ready to drop a big bomb on everyone in the arena. I didn't tell anyone of my plans, I just kept everything to myself. I then took another deep breath, closed my eyes for a few seconds, and said, "Today was... Enson Inoue's... Yamatodamashii's... last fight!"

First, the arena fell dead silent. Everyone was shocked. Then slowly there was a lot of mumbling, followed by a lot of people screaming their protest and some even shedding tears. As I walked out of the arena, I made sure I held my head up high and raised my arms up in the air to signify that my spirit is still alive and in my heart I never lost a single fight.

I heard screams like, "No Enson!", "You can't retire!", "We need you to fight!" As I walked out of the arena ,for possibly my last time, I wasn't sad but instead, I was more relieved because all I was doing was closing one chapter in my life and looking forward to opening a new one.

Chapter 43

EGAN VS. GUY – PRIDE PLAYS GAMES WITH ME.

In the very next event, Pride 13, my brother Egan was offered a fight with Guy Mezger. Guy was more my rival than Egan's because when I got pulled out of UFC 13 by the doctor, I was supposed to fight Guy next. However, I had just announced my retirement in Pride 12 and Guy was matched up with my brother.

They had a good fight, with Guy getting the upper hand in the standing and eventually knocking Egan out. I ran into the ring to check on Egan and as I passed Guy he whispered to me, "Remember, this isn't personal." I was confused. It was a clean fair fight where Guy was the better man so why would it be personal?

So after briefly checking Egan, I walked up to Guy, shook his hand and asked him, "What isn't personal?"

He then said, "You don't know? I have to call you out, and I mean in a bad way. So just remember, it isn't personal."

Still holding his hand I couldn't believe what I was hearing. So I asked Guy, "You're going to call me out? I'm retired!"

He then replied, "I know. I don't want to. But I have to."

I was blown away. I was thinking…if he didn't want to then why is he going to do it? I could feel my blood beginning to boil so I clenched Guy's hand hard and began to corner him into the corner. I then told him, "If you don't want to do it, then don't fucken do it!"

He then replied, "I have to Enson, it's in my contract." That backed me off a bit, for now I knew it really wasn't personal, it was a ploy from Pride to pull me back into the ring. Now it became personal with Pride! Guy then grabbed the mic and said, "I had a great fight with Egan but the one that I think I really should fight is his brother, Enson."

I was furious… not at Guy, but at Pride for playing games. Pride was known to play games and bully some of the fighters, but they never tried anything like this with me. I thought the fear mixed with respect that they had for me prevented this sort of thing but now that was in the past.

I grabbed the mic and responded, "I'm retired and I will not come out of retirement for a stupid challenge like that. This is fucked up." Then I spiked the mic on the ground and left the ring. Walking back to the locker rooms all I could think about was finding out who put Guy up to this and why he did it.

The minute I got back to the locker room I was surprised to see Guy walk in. He came straight to my locker room to explain his side. He explained to me that his contract stated that if he beat Egan then he was supposed to call me out. They also told him that I was in on it so it would be okay to do it in a bad way. I explained to him that I knew nothing about it and I appreciate him coming out honestly with everything. I appreciated Guy being up front with me and I respected him for coming to talk to me face to face. Guy is a class act and I now not only respected him as a fighter but as a person, too.

After Guy left the room, I turned to one of the part time workers and demanded that he brought to me the president, Mr. Morishita or the vice president, Mr. Sakikabara. He was terrified and ran out of the room. Five minutes passed and a different part time worker came. I was so angry that it didn't matter that this poor guy had nothing to do with this. I walked up to him and said, "Get me the president NOW or I'm going to do to you what I plan to do to him!" Then I kicked him in the ass as he began to leave.

Another 10 minutes passed before another different part time worker came in... and this time it was a girl. Damn, that was my weakness. I have a hard time raising my voice to girls so I bit my tongue and waited. Five minutes passed and although I knew they were busy because there were still fights going on, I told myself that if another five minutes passes and no one showed up, then I was going to walk to ring side and drag the president to the locker room.

Just then in comes a higher up Pride official. It wasn't the president or the vice president. It was Mr. Kawasaki, the matchmaker. He walked up to me and asked me what was wrong and I instantly grabbed him, threw him to the ground, and mounted him. I clutched his throat, raised my other fist and gave him one chance.

"What the fuck is going on?! Who authorized this?" I screamed. I saw terror in his eyes like he was looking at death straight in the face. "I don't know! I had nothing to do with it! Please don't hurt me," he pleaded.

My grip tightened around his throat and I felt I was losing control. I felt like I was in my own bubble where just me and Mr. Kawasaki with nothing else around us. I'm not sure what I would have done next but when I heard a stern familiar voice say, "No Enson... Stop it! Let him go." Egan's voice popped the bubble and brought me back to reality.

It wasn't his fault. I needed to talk to higher ups, I thought. So I released Mr. Kawasaki's throat and picked him up off the ground. I looked into his eyes and sternly said, "Get Morishita or Sakakibara now." He told me he understood and briskly walked out of the locker room. I was flustered thinking about what I had just done but I knew that to get prompt answers from Pride, this was how I had to do it.

Then to my surprise, in walks Mr. Sakakibara. He calmly walked into the room straight up to me and began saying, "Enson please. It was someone in the office. We'll find out who it is." I didn't know what to believe so I asked him for a deadline on when he would produce me the name. He told me he would find out the following week and I let him know that if he didn't call me I would hold him personally responsible. He agreed and I let him leave.

Four days later I got a call from Mr. Sakakibara and he asked me if we could meet at the hotel restaurant. I agreed and we met. Before we sat down he started off by bowing his head really low and apologizing for what happened. He then sat down and said, "Please forgive us. We don't know who did it in the office but I'll take responsibility." How can they not know? I explained to Mr. Sakakibara that every time I fight I am prepared to die in the ring and I cannot die in a ring that I don't trust. I don't even want to associate with people that play games like that. He could see in my eyes and tone that I was dead serious as I glared intensely at him. I could see insecurity beginning to brew in him and I felt I was looking directly into his soul.

He then slowly reached down and reached into his briefcase and handed me a fat envelope. He bowed his head as his arm was extended out to me holding out the envelope. I knew it was cash and I wasn't sure how much it was but it looked over $5,000. I reached out, accepted the envelope and without opening it slipped it into my pocket. He seemed relieved that I accepted it and then again said, "I'm really sorry. Please forgive us."

I then explained that playing games like that will dissolve the trust I have in them and this should never happen again. He agreed, we shook hands and I left the meeting $10,000 richer.

Chapter 44
MARRIAGE – THE NEXT CHAPTER

The new door opening in my life was marriage. When I met Miyu I already had a steady girlfriend, Takako that I'd been dating for the past four years. I was young and weak to temptation and never turned down the chance to play and be sexually intimate. Then one night I was hitting the clubs with my sponsors and we were partying in a VIP room in a club in Shibuya, Tokyo. We were checking out all the hot chicks in the club when my sponsor pointed out a famous wrestler girl, Seiko Yamamoto, whom I'd seen on television many times, outside the VIP room sitting on the stairs with a friend.

I told John, one of my students from Guam, to go outside and bring them both into the VIP room to party with us. Seiko was very cute and athletic - just my type. So when John brought Seiko and her friend Yumiko in the VIP room to sit by us, I ordered them drinks and we began to introduce ourselves. Just as we were finishing introducing ourselves we heard glass breaking and beer bottles were flying all over. A big Yakuza fight broke out and we were in the middle of it all. So instead of hanging around, we grabbed Seiko and Yumiko and quickly left the club. Seiko then mentioned that she wanted to meet my dog Shooto Kun, so we took them to my car where Shooto Kun was waiting. Shooto melted their hearts and while we all played with him we exchanged phone numbers.

As the months went by Seiko and I became very good friends, going to dinner and occasionally she would come to my Omiya Gym to train. Then one day, she was going to meet me at my gym to hang out, but she called me, informing me that she had to cancel because her older sister Miyu had had a big fight with her husband. Miyu was an emotional wreck so she didn't want to leave her alone.

I suggested that she bring Miyu with her, so all three of us could hang out. She liked the idea so the both of them headed down to my Omiya Gym. When they got there we all went to dinner, and Miyu confided in me, about her problem with her husband. We talked a lot and she calmed down, so after we finished eating they both decided to head home to Yokohama since it was so far away.

I still felt that Miyu was a bit unstable, so I told Seiko to give her my phone number and to tell Miyu that she could call me anytime if she ever wanted to talk.

I went back to my apartment, did all my usual stuff, and then, just as I was about to go to bed, Miyu called. She was hysterical and crying, telling me that this time it didn't look like her husband would forgive her and that it looked like it might be the end of their marriage. She seemed like she was out of control, so I asked her if she wanted me to come over, and she said that she would really like that.

Although Yokohama was about a 90-minute car drive from Omiya, Miyu seemed to really need someone, so I jumped in my car and headed to Yokohama. When I got there, because she was still officially married, instead of picking her up at her father's house we decided to meet at a gas station. We met, drove to a nearby park, and I listened to her problem until she calmed down. I felt a connection to Miyu and the feeling was mutual. However, there was a small problem. What about the friendship with Seiko? I felt caught in a storm, a big storm that I had no clue how to get out of with everything intact. The next week I got a call from Seiko. She told me that she had heard what had happened between Miyu and I, and that Miyu really liked me. She also said that she hoped this wouldn't affect our friendship and wished the best for the both of us. So Miyu and I began dating – despite the fact that she was still married – and kept it very discreet and undercover. She was going through the divorce, but just the fact that it wasn't finalized yet, made me feel like we were walking on broken glass.

With the mixture of my fame and Miyu's fame and the circumstances we were dating under, it was a very difficult thing to do (to date her). We would go to events and make sure there was always someone with us; we would purposefully not sit together and stagger seats so the press wouldn't have the opportunity to start rumors. However, at one Rings event, Miyu and I went with Seiko and John Calvo. We naturally just took our seats and it so happened Miyu and I were sitting next to each other. Then a reporter that covers a lot of wrestling – Mr. Higuchi – who was an acquaintance of Miyu, approached us and informed me that there was a reporter trying to start something up in the press room by suggesting they get pictures of us sitting together for the weekly gossip magazines. This was something I took very seriously, so I left my seat and walked Mr. Higuchi to the back. I asked him to take me to the press room and show me who the reporter was. He refused. I asked him again in a more aggressive way, letting him know that if he didn't show me who this reporter was there would be problems between him and I.

He went on to explain to me that there is a "Writers Code" that you don't reveal discussions that are being made in the press room between reporters. I felt that was very hypocritical, given what he'd just told us so I insisted that he continue what he just started by directing me to that certain reporter. He again refused, and this time I could see by his demeanor that he wasn't going to tell me.so I took it a step further and grabbed him by the back of his shirt. I called John Calvo to come with me, and dragged him downstairs to the toilet. When we got into the toilet, it wasn't empty. One guy was washing his hands while a couple others were at the urinal. I was angry and just blurted out for everyone to get out now!!! Within a few seconds the toilet was empty. It was just me, John Calvo and Mr Higuchi. I instructed John to watch the door so no one could get in and I proceeded to drag Mr. Higuchi to a toilet stall. I roughed him up a bit and left him in the stall flustered and terrified that more was to come.

I was then no longer in the mood to watch any more fights so we all jumped into my car and went home.

215

Chapter 45

Paparazzi – Feeling Of Being Stalked

A couple of weeks later, a good friend in the media informed me that the media caught wind of our relationship so we must be very careful of the paparazzi. If we were caught by the paparazzi, and our affair was made public, Miyu would have a big black mark against her for her divorce hearings. A big black mark would affect her chances in her divorce case and possibly cause her to lose custody of her son.

To be safe, we decided to stop seeing each other for a whole month, only meeting up at events and with other people around us. When things subsided we slowly began seeing each other very discreetly until Miyu's divorce was finalized.

We planned a big wedding ceremony in Hawaii where hundreds of friends and family gathered. I flew her whole family over and through a good friend, James Tanaka, I rented out the fabulous Paul Mitchell Estate for an affordable price. It was a fabulous mansion that was on a 1.3 acre private lot with 7 bedrooms, 9+ baths, saltwater pool with waterfall, tropical saltwater jacuzzi, a grotto, pool house, pool bar with big screen TV, gym, office, furo, water features, ponds, and a private beachfront. It was a vacation paradise and the day before my marriage, instead of having a bachelor party, Rei (Miyu's son) and I just went back to the mansion and hung out together until we both fell asleep at the poolside.

The wedding went really well and it was a very beautiful and memorable wedding. However, the next morning after wedding party we threw at the mansion, we met with a problem. The boyfriend of Miyu's friend who was invited to the wedding was acting out of line. At the wedding and at the after party, although he had his girlfriend with him, he was hitting on Seiko, Miyu's sister. He gave her his phone number and even told her they should get together when they get back to Japan. But, what upset me the most was the night of the after party he even found his way to Seiko's room to check her out.

Miyu begged me to let it slide for she didn't want me to create a commotion after such a good wedding. Although I really didn't like this guy and I was dying to confront this idiot, I sucked it up and agreed. Then one of Miyu's friends, Naoko blurted out, "Yeah and I couldn't believe he tried to make Rei drink beer 3 times."

I couldn't believe my ears!

I was fuming! I turned to Naoko and Miyu and said, "This idiot tried to make 4 year old Rei drink?! Fuck. I can't overlook that!!!"

I stormed out to the beachfront lawn where he was sun tanning with one of my sponsors. I walked straight up to him and palmed him in the face and he went tumbling on the lawn. I beat him severely and through all the commotion the doorbell rang and we noticed that the police was at the front gate.

We let them in and greeted them at the door and they told us that they got a call from someone saying there was a big fight going on here. My friend's boyfriend was bleeding and half unconscious in the backyard and when they asked me what the commotion was about I told them the truth. I said, "This fucker tried to make my 4 year old son drink beer! Wouldn't that piss you off?" Then to my surprise, just as I thought they were going to ask to see the guy I beat, one of my good friends, Sogo stepped up and said, "I'm sorry. I was being stupid. I'm lucky Enson controlled himself and didn't lay a hand on me. I was caught off guard but caught on to what Sogo was doing and played along.

"Yes, I stayed in control but I'm sorry for making such a big commotion." They believed us and apologized for bothering us and promptly left. I got lucky… if they had just stepped into the backyard they would have seen the idiot all bloody laying in the yard with a swollen face and a fractured cheekbone. If they found him I probably would have been arrested and been booked for assault. I was still upset so I called them a taxi and sent them back to their hotel.

We had a very good marriage for three years, training together and traveling all over the globe. The love her son Rei and I shared was better than any father/son relationship I had ever seen. We even decided to change his name to a name similar to mine. We considered names as Exson, Ebson, and Edson until we finally decided on, Erson. Miyu and I had a nice relationship because we understood the sacrifices of training hard and were able to help each other from training all the way to dieting.

Chapter 46
Deceit – Relinquishing The Shooto Belt

I won the Shooto belt in 1997 and we ran in to a small problem. In the Shooto rules, there is a clause that a champion needs to make a mandatory title defense within two years or he will be stripped of the belt. I was ready to fight but the Shooto association wasn't able to afford a quality fighter qualified to be an opponent for a title match.

About a week after the Rings event, I got a call from Shooto telling me that Mr. Higuchi called them informing them of the incident in the bathroom and that he wanted to press charges. The guys that contacted me from Shooto were Wakabayashi the Amateur Shooto director, Ogata the head referee, and Suzuki another referee.

This would be very bad if charges were pressed. I was the Shooto Champion so I represented the association. Shooto told me that Mr Higuchi wanted them to do something to reprimand me, so Shooto suggested that I relinquish my belt from my side showing remorse. They told me that that would look good in the Japanese eyes and would actually look good for me. I believed them and waited for them to set a date for me to make the announcement.

At the time, although I was the current Shooto Heavyweight World Champion, I was also fighting very successfully in Pride. I voiced my concern of the situation to Mr. Sakakibara, the Vice President of Pride and he told me not to worry and that everything would be taken care of. I was relieved and informed Shooto that everything was going to be taken care of by Pride. They seemed relieved and I believed all would be taken care of.

Then a day later I got a call from Mr. Noguchi, a Yakuza working with Pride and he told me that they contacted Mr. Higuchi and it's all over. I was elated and called Shooto to tell them the good news only to be told by them that Mr. Higuchi had called them saying he still wants something done to reprimand me. I was confused. Mr. Noguchi told me everything was settled, but Shooto was telling me it was not over yet.

I decided to take the initiative to speak to Mr. Higuchi myself in person. I found out that Mr. Higuchi was going to be at a wrestling event so I went down there to find him. I got to the arena and he wasn't hard to find. I walked straight up to Mr. Higuchi and told him I wanted to talk to him. He looked scared so I assured him nothing was going to happen and we went out back to talk.

I started out by apologizing for what I did to him and then continued by asking him if he was contacted by Mr. Noguchi. He said he was contacted and thanked me for the apology. I was a little skeptical so I told him, "Shooto is telling me that you still want me to be reprimanded in some way, is this true?" He looked surprised as he said, "You and Pride apologized so as far as I'm concerned, it's all over."

I was a bit disturbed that Shooto was telling me something totally different but I was grateful to Mr. Higuchi and thanked him again. I then called Shooto and told them that I just talked to Mr. Higuchi and he said all was forgiven. They seemed pleased and finally I thought it was all over. However, again I got a call from Shooto saying that now, Mr. Higuchi's company, The Naigai Times newspaper wanted something done.

This was now going back and forth, so I decided to have the two sides meet. I set up an appointment with Mr. Higuchi's boss, picked up Suzuki, a Shooto representative and drove to The Naigai Times head office. In the meeting Mr. Higuchi's boss told me that Mr. Higuchi said everything was over so he feels the same way. Suzuki was still uneasy about it but he nodded in agreement. He really had no choice because the plaintiffs themselves were saying right in front of him that all was good.

Now, I began to feel like Shooto was playing games with me. I hated being played and I was determined to get to the bottom of it. Shooto kept making false claims so I knew once and for all, I had to get all the players in one room so no one could bullshit anymore.

Shooto had scheduled a press conference to announce my relinquishing of the belt before a fight. Because I was determined to get all this bullshit straightened out before I actually relinquished my belt, I set up a meeting at 12 noon before the press conference with all the Shooto guys, Wakabayashi, Suzuki, and Ogawa at a hotel. I called Mr. Noguchi, the Pride Yakuza, and told him to meet me at 12:30pm at a restaurant near the hotel I was meeting the Shooto guys at. Then I called Mr. Higuchi and asked him also to come to the restaurant at 12:30pm too. Everything was set and ready to go. I was going to get all three parties in the same room and they had no clue that this meeting was going to happen.

The day of the meeting arrived and I drove over to the hotel to meet the Shooto guys. They greeted me and asked me why I called the meeting. Without saying a word, I stood up and said, "Let's go." They were lost but had no choice and followed me to the restaurant. As we walked in the restaurant the Shooto guys saw Mr. Noguchi and Mr. Higuchi and they were surprised. I then directed everyone out of the restaurant and into the area where the press conference was going to take place. There was still an hour, enough time to find out the truth.

I started by asking Mr. Noguchi, "You told me you talked to Mr. Higuchi and everything was settled. Is this true?" Mr. Noguchi nodded in confirmation so I turned to Mr. Higuchi and asked, "So it is true? Everything was settled?" Mr. Higuchi then said, "Yes. I spoke to Mr. Noguchi over the phone and I told him everything was forgiven."

223

I turned to all the Shooto guys who all looked like they had seen a ghost. I felt betrayed and the press conference was about to happen so we had to sort things out fast.

I sat down and told Mr. Wakabayashi from Shooto that I no longer needed to relinquish my belt. This problem got solved before it made it to the press. They agreed but then Wakabayashi said, "We need to ask you for your help. The mandatory two year title defense is coming up and we can't get you an opponent and we are going to be in a hard situation. The two year deadline is coming up and in the rules we must take your belt away, but we can't because it was actually our fault that you couldn't make that defense." He went on and asked me, "So we would like to ask you a favor...can you still relinquish your belt because it would still make you look honorable and it would help us avoid this difficult situation."

I really didn't want to relinquish my belt but I really wanted to help Shooto out of this predicament. It also didn't seem like Shooto was going to be able to get me a title defense for awhile and I was having great success in Pride, so I figured why not.

The press conference started and I sat there with my belt ready to face the press. When my turn came I told the press that to show remorse for my behavior with Mr. Higuchi, I will punish myself and relinquish my belt. I then excused myself, got up, and left the room. It was done. I was no longer the Shooto Champion, but for a good reason.

Then to my surprise in the newspapers the next day it stated that Shooto said some disrespectful things about me, was giving me a suspension from fighting in the Shooto ring, and they were suspending my promoter's license. I couldn't believe my eyes. I quickly got on the phone, called the Shooto association, letting them know that I was going to put my fists through their faces one by one. Ogata never answered and Wakabayashi and Suzuki pointed the finger at Ogata. It seemed that Ogata was the one making the calls and it was also he who spoke to the press. He avoided talking to me and I really wanted to hurt him bad, but instead I vowed to make sure he never ever refereed in the Shooto ring ever again…and he never did.

This however wasn't over for me. Although Ogata was to blame and he was punished for it, I know the rest of the Shooto commission members had a part in it. That's what destroyed my faith in Shooto and I knew it would never be the same again. Until this day, no one, not a single fan knew all the details of why I relinquished my Heavyweight Shooto belt. Since then, Shooto has shown remorse by giving me the Shooto World Championship belt for me to keep and even presented me with a Shooto World Championship ring. However, the betrayal I felt in this incident still feels heavy in my heart so I'm still careful and keeping my guard up.

Chapter 47

BOUGHT MY HOUSE – THE HOUSE THAT FIGHTING BUILT

As soon as Miyu and I got married, I began looking for a house to buy. I was no longer going to be single and because Miyu had Erson from her previous marriage I was immediately stepping into a "family" setting. Living in an apartment as a single man or even as a young couple was okay with me but I didn't want to be a family living out of a small apartment so I went shopping for a house.

I looked at many houses until I found one I really liked. It had a big yard, and unlike all the typical Japanese houses, it had a high ceiling. There were 4 bedrooms, a big indoor greenhouse, and a huge living room. I could imagine having BBQ's in the yard and Shooto having lots of space to run on the 5000 square feet property.

The other big reason why I decided on this house was because the previous owner had a debt that he had to pay off so he was desperate to sell this house ASAP. This made the negotiation of the price a lot easier and the sale was made. I was excited because I was so proud that this beautiful house was bought through all my hard work and sweat in the MMA ring. I loved to tell people whenever they came to visit, "This is the house that MMA built!"

Chapter 48

NORIFUMI YAMAMOTO – THE BIRTH OF "KID"

While I was dating Miyu I met her younger brother Nori. He was an exceptional athlete but always in trouble. He was one of the top wrestlers in Japan with hopes of participating in the Olympic games someday. He was a great kid, and always left in the shadows, while his two famous sisters shared the spotlight.

At times it got so bad that some people didn't even know Miyu and Seiko had a brother. He wasn't a World Champion like his two sisters, but yet he was a very good wrestler. He was mischievous and always getting in bad situations. He was attending a big wrestling college named Yamanashi, a college far away from home where he had to live in a dormitory.

One day when Miyu and I were attending a wrestling event, Miyu got a call from Nori with some troubling news. Nori was in trouble! Miyu began to speak louder and by the look on her face I could tell there was a problem. She got off the phone, came directly to me, and told me that Nori needed help. I could tell it wasn't an ordinary problem and when I asked her, she told me that Nori had gotten himself in trouble with the Yakuza.

In order to help him I needed more information so I called him to get more details. He told me that he was scared and in a restaurant, hiding from the Yakuza members. He said that last week he was in town with his friends playing with an air gun. He unknowingly shot someone in the face, unaware that he was a Yakuza. They took the license plate number of his car and found his apartment.

In the morning they appeared at his third story apartment looking for retaliation. Afraid, Nori jumped from the balcony of his apartment and fled. They chased him to where he currently hid so I advised him to stay in public until they left. He did but it still wasn't over. They showed up to his school and the school had no choice but to release Nori.

The school didn't want the Yakuza problem to become public so they released him, pretending that the reason they released him was because he broke the rule of driving a car off campus during school hours. Nori's father was also a teacher at another big university and if the story went public, it could jeopardize his job too. The Japan Wrestling Association also heard of the incident and put Nori on probation for a whole year. This probation meant he was not allowed to enter any wrestling tournaments for a year.

Chapter 49

KID'S(NORI'S) NEW LOVE – MMA

A year was a long time for Nori to stay inactive so I had an idea. I suggested to Nori that he train MMA while he was on probation to stay in shape and because MMA incorporated a lot of wrestling, his movement wouldn't be rusty when he returned to wrestling. He liked the idea and the very next day he joined me at my gym, Purebred Omiya. He trained hard and I was surprised at how well he did on his first day. His natural athletic ability combined with his wrestling skill allowed him to hang tough with some of the seasoned fighters, even getting the better of them at times.

I was impressed but was also aware that this was still just a temporary thing. The training was going well and I could tell that Nori was really beginning to have a passion for MMA. Then one night at dinner when we were casually talking about training, out of the blue, Nori tells me that he wants to become a professional fighter. It caught me off guard. I loved the passion but I was afraid that he wasn't that serious. Training for fun and training to become a professional fighter are two different things. I decided to cut through the bullshit and get to the point, so the next day in training I made him put on the MMA gloves. I told him that he was going to do three hard MMA rounds with me and I planned to make him feel true MMA. He was game, and I was curious to see how it would go. Would he break and rethink his desire to become a MMA fighter like so many dreamers that stepped into my gym before or would he be able to tough it out?

We went hard and I gave him controlled ferocity and pounded him for three rounds. By the last round, his face was bloody and swollen but the game in him was alive and well.

I was impressed and after he expressed the same desire to become a professional MMA fighter I decided to change the tone of his training and work with him full time. He joined me in my training for two years and his level improved by leaps and bounds. He travelled with me to Thailand, Guam, Hawaii, Watanabe Gym, everywhere. Within a year he had improved so much that I felt he was ready for his first test, the All Japan Amateur Shooto Tournament.

It was an amateur Shooto tournament where all the best aspiring Shooto practitioners gathered to try to earn a ticket into the profes-sional Shooto ring. He won without much of a problem so I decided to take it a step further. I put him into his first professional fight, and decided to do it in Guam where the level wasn't too high. The fight would be kept undercover unless we wanted it to be known. He fought well, beating his opponent in all aspects of the fight, and finishing him off with a rear naked choke. However, he lost control. Although his opponent was tapping for mercy Nori held on to the choke refusing to release it even when the referee tried to pry the choke loose. The foul was so flagrant that, although he clearly won the fight, they decided to disqualify him and reward the victory to his opponent. He was also banned from fighting in Guam from the Guam commission for a year and I decided to keep this fight quiet for now. This was Nori's first professional MMA fight and his first official loss on his professional record. However, because we kept this quiet, until this day, this fight is not on his official fight record.

Although Nori showed promise to be a great MMA fighter, when his one year probation period was finally up, his father demanded that he drop fighting and return to wrestling full time to prepare for the Olympics to be held two years later. I discussed this with Nori and he expressed to me that his love was now fighting and he didn't want to stop. I supported his decision and to our disappointment when he told his father, his father was upset. He demanded that Nori quit fighting immediately and to return to wrestling again.

Nori defied his father, which made his father call me, hoping that I would make Nori stop training, but instead I told his father that I would support whatever Nori wants to do. This infuriated Mr. Yamamoto to the point that he disowned Nori and cut all support for him. This was unfair so I decided to take responsibility and took care of Nori. Food, bills, rent, and I even let him use one of my cars. Although Nori's father refused to support Nori unless he went back to wrestling, I was behind him to support him in whatever he decided.

Nori and I were getting close. He was like my little brother and we did a lot together. Then one day we had a crazy encounter with the Yakuza. It was the year 2000 and we had just finished our day of training. Nori and my best friend from Hawaii, Darren Suzuki, decided to go out on the town to check out a drinking place where young hostess girls served you. My sponsors and promoters have taken me to these drinking places for entertainment but I rarely ever go on my own. If you're not careful, when the bill comes you could be out $2,000 to $3,000 easy.

That night we decided to venture out on our own and headed to Omiya Station in Saitama where a lot of drinking places were clustered. We went to a place called Modern Times, which was in front of Omiya Station. We entered the bar, sat down, and enjoyed conversing with the girls. Nori got a few phone numbers while I drank my diet Coke, and Darren just sat back and enjoyed his first day in Japan. Darren had just come from Hawaii to visit me and was planning to hang out with me for about a week.

It was our first night out and everything was going great. After our hour was up instead of extending another hour we decided to move on and check out a different bar. As we exited the bar, we were flocked by guys trying to lure us into their bar next. We took our time feeling each guy out to see which bar would be the best to go to next. As I was talking to one of the guys, I suddenly heard a Japanese guy speaking in a loud voice, cussing and slurring in Yakuza language. When I glanced over to see what was going on, to my surprise this angry Japanese guy was directing his insults to Nori. Holy Shit!!! What's going on?

I could see that this guy wasn't just an ordinary angry civilian. His demeanor and aggressive behavior went beyond an ordinary angry person. This bar was located right in the heart of the nightlife and all his aggression and screaming attracted a crowd that was curious about what the commotion was about. Then in the midst of all his screaming, in front of the people gathered, as if he loved being in the spotlight, what he did next just confirmed my hunches. He ripped open his shirt to display his body full of underworld tattoos screaming "Hora" Which means, "Look" in Japanese. Then as he raised his hand to show us that he was missing his pinky finger he said, "This is what you're fucking with!"

In Japan, when an underworld guy fucks up bad, instead of just a verbal, "I'm sorry", which may not show enough sincerity, some like to give one joint of the pinky finger to show remorse. They feel that anyone can blurt words out of their mouth so a verbal apology is not a good gauge to determine if the apology is made from the heart. However, if you cut off your finger and present it to the person you are apologizing to, that shows that you really meant it from your heart that you regretted your mistake. Giving up part of your pinky is a big sacrifice let alone having to cut it off yourself. So now I knew two things... one he was a Yakuza and two he fucked up bad in the past.

Then Nori turned around, looked at me and asked, "Can I fuck him up?" I could imagine that if Nori fucked up this guy bad, we would have to deal with the repercussions. Now because this Yakuza clearly informed us about his status in the underworld, there was something good and something bad that came into play. The good is, now whatever he does would reflect on his family. If he fucked up with this problem, because he acknowledged his status, both he and the family will take full responsibility to fix things.

The bad thing was that if I beat him up now it would also be taken as a direct insult to the family. I told Nori "No" then asked him what happened.

Nori told me that as he was standing on the edge of the road, and although there was more than enough room to pass, this Yakuza's side mirror bumped Nori in the ass. The Yakuza told Nori to get the fuck out of the way and instead of shutting up, Nori replied, "What!?" The Yakuza are accustomed to getting their way and are rarely spoken back to.

This guy was on his claimed turf and he had to save face. I was aware that this guy was a Yakuza and had to keep his "tough guy" reputation so by all means I wanted to avoid trouble with him so I stepped in, told Nori to step aside and I promptly apologized. Then as if he drew power from my submissiveness he screamed at me, "Who the fuck are you?" I then said, "My name is Enson Inoue, we don't want any problems so how about we just forget what has happened and go our separate ways. Then, as if he didn't hear me he screamed, "Get the fuck out of the way!" He was now getting unreasonable because I was standing on the side of his car so if he got into his car he could drive off without any obstruction from me. He then screamed again, "Get the fuck out of my way!"

At this point I was really getting frustrated. I was being nice and respecting that he was an underworld figure but this guy was stepping over the line and being an absolute dick. I took a deep breath and repeated a bit more sternly, "We really don't want any problems, so get in your car and drive off." He then yelled again, "Get out of the way!!!" Now it was obvious to me that this guy wasn't interested in resolving this confrontation but instead, was throwing a power trip on me in his turf with everybody watching. Like a neon light in my head, like a big lit up billboard you see in Las Vegas "What a dick!" took over my thoughts and eventually my emotions. I was still holding back my frustration, controlling my intonation and trying to stay as polite as possible, but I was through with being nice. So in a harsh tone I replied, "It seems that you want a problem with us...if so, why don't you push me or physically touch me, then you'll have a problem."

He looked at me, took a deep breath, and then said, "Okay, now you pissed me off!!! I'm going to run you over and kill you!!!" He then proceeded to instruct all the cars that accumulated while this altercation was going on, to back up.

As I watched him getting all the cars to back up I thought, is this guy for real??? Was he really going to run me over? I had a hard time comprehending that over a bump of his mirror, he was willing to take a life. Something told me this guy was not thinking straight and this may be a bit dangerous, but something else didn't allow me to believe that he would actually do it. Just in case, I gave my wallet and cell phone to Darren, told him to get on the sidewalk because this nut said he was going run me over. I then turned to where he was coming from to see what he was actually going to do. As I was waiting to see what he was going to do I had decided that if this idiot tries to really hurt me, then I would have a solid reason to fuck him up."

It took about five minutes for him to finally get all the cars to move then he backed his car up about 20 meters and revved his engine like a race-car driver. He grabbed a secure hold of his steering wheel, took a deep breath, and floored the gas pedal. The back wheel spun, burning out, not moving forward for a couple of seconds before his car rocketed out speeding towards the first one in line, Nori. Nori stepped to the left just as he swerved to hit him and avoided being hit head on, but not enough. Nori was side swiped and knocked down, but fortunately, lucky enough to avoid any major injuries.

Then next in line was Darren. In his wildest dreams, he didn't expect that someone could be so crazy, so he felt safe on the sidewalk and had his guard down. By the time he realized that he was in danger from seeing Nori get hit it was too late. The car had already climbed the sidewalk and was headed directly towards him.

With no time to jump out of the way, BOOM, Darren was down, on the pavement along with all the contents that was in my wallet scattered out around him. Then it was my turn. Although it must have been just a few split seconds for the car to get from hitting Darren to where I was, it seemed like forever. I got myself ready...for what, I wasn't sure. I'd never been banged by a car before... but here goes!!! Then his car came within six feet of where I was standing and that's when I finally realized,

"Shit...I'm really going to get hit!" So without a split second of hesitation, I instinctively jumped.

I landed on the hood, rolled over the windshield, half way across the roof, and then back to the pavement on the side of the car. As I rolled off the roof down the side of the car, I was lucky to land on my feet. As I landed I realized that I was inches away from being crushed in between the Yakuza guys' car and a parked car. God must have been watching over me because I narrowly got by. Like Jackie Chan, I didn't get sand-wiched between the two cars and landed on my feet. I knew I just got banged but as I landed on my feet, the first thought in my mind was to grab that the Yakuza and give him a beating.

I began chasing the car, drooling at the thought of catching up with the car and pulling him out. This incident happened in a crowded area of town and he was speeding through people weaving and swerving almost like he was playing a video game. He was going too fast and began pull-ing away from me so I then began trying to take down his license plate number. As I was remembering his number, there was a bang and from the side of his car tumbled an elderly man.

Without stopping he continued on until he drove out of sight. Realizing that he got away for now, I then ran back to check Nori and Darren only to find out that Nori was up and chasing the car alongside me while Darren on the other hand wasn't so lucky. When I got back to where Darren was, he was still down on the ground while some of the workers around him were helping gather up all the money and papers that got scattered when he got banged. I noticed he couldn't get up and both his knees were red and beginning to swell up. Then as I was checking Darren, I noticed the elderly man that got hit too, staggering down the street bleeding from the head. I ran up to him asked him if he was alright and asked him for his name. He refused to tell me saying he was fine and didn't want any trouble.

I was speechless. Just because this lunatic that banged us was a Yakuza, the elderly man wanted to drop everything. In disbelief, I contested, "We can all pursue him together. Yakuza or no Yakuza, let's get him."

The elderly guy just shook his head and repeated, "Boku wa kankei nai. Sumimasen." Which meant, "I want nothing to do with this, I'm sorry." Amazing how the Japanese people will totally disregard anything that was done to them, willing to forget, if it involved a Yakuza.

This reputation and aura of fear is what gives the Yakuza power in Japan.. If Mr. A owes money to Mr. B, and is late on payments and/or he refuses to pay, all Mr. A needs to do is hire a Yakuza to collect for him. Of course, the percentage for a Yakuza is 50% but sometimes, half is better than nothing. Now the money Mr. A took years trying to collect to no avail, a Yakuza could collect in a day or two depending on the amount. All they do is visit the person who owes money, show them a business card with the mark of the family and give them a deadline. You'd be surprised at how easy problems are solved when a Yakuza gets brought into the picture.

So, I let the elderly man go on his way and proceeded to gather my things and get Darren home where we could start icing his knee. After we dropped Darren off at home, Nori and I proceeded to the Omiya Police Station to file a report. When we got to Omiya police station we were greeted but not attended to. I was wondering if the lack of importance they showed was due to the fact that I was foreign because attempted murder is a serious offense.

Then when we were finally helped we were sat down in a room where we began telling our story of the incident. When we were finished telling the entire story we were then led to another room where a different detective came in with a piece of paper and asked us to start from the beginning, to tell our story again but this time he was going to file the report. We had just spent about two hours explaining the story and now, we were being asked to repeat ourselves and tell it all over again. That's Bullshit!!! I glanced at the clock and it was already 3 a.m. and something told me we were wasting our time. So I told the detective to forget it and that I'll take care of the problem myself because they are good for nothing. Remember... we weren't here to talk about a parking ticket... a Yakuza guy just tried to run us over with his car. We were almost killed.

Our lives were just threatened, which is not an everyday thing. In fact, most people don't have something like this happen to them in a lifetime. These police acted like they didn't care so I said fuck it, I'd rather do this myself...and that's what I decided I was going to do and walked out of the police station.

When Nori and I got back home, Darren was laying down with bags of ice on his knees. His knees were stiffening up and he was in pain. What if Darren was killed? What if we were all killed? Those thoughts raced through my mind as I picked up the phone and called my boys to gather up more boys.

I wanted to find out who this Yakuza was, find him, and then face off with him face to face. Not behind a steering wheel, nothing between us just him and I, man to man. We all gathered in the same area that we were banged the night before and to my surprise, we were a strong 40 plus guys. I gathered everyone together, told them that we were looking for a Yakuza that works in the area, described him, then everyone scattered. The incident was so big that by now everyone in the area knew about it and was gossiping about it behind closed doors.

However, when we moved from shop to shop asking who that Yakuza was... no one would talk. They were not talking in fear of retaliation from the Yakuzas and this frustrated me to a point where I lost control. When I asked the manager of the game center that was located right across where the incident happened his response triggered me off. Although I remember seeing him standing right there as it was all going on, I calmly asked him if he was aware of the incident that happened yesterday and he replied, "No." When I heard him say no, my heart churned and the blood rushed towards my head. I reached out grabbed him by the neck and pulled him close to me so I didn't need to raise my voice.

Although I was furious inside I calmly but sternly said, "You fear the Yakuza? You don't fear me? I can get pretty scary too you know." He started quivering and shaking but still refused to talk. I then threw him into his shops neon sign and then palmed the arm wrestling machine right beside me. To my surprise my hand went right through it. As I pulled my hand out I noticed a gash on the palm of my hand where blood started gushing out. I didn't care. I was pissed that nobody was talking. We were then almost out of options when I remembered a Mahjong Parlor down the street that all the Yakuzas hang out at and gamble. Normally I wouldn't even consider going there but I was pissed and out of control.

I walked towards the Mahjong parlor and was about to enter when four older Yakuza men came walking out. As they stepped out onto the road in front of the parlor, they noticed me walking towards them, my hand dripping blood, and if looks could kill, they would all be dead. They were confused but seemed a bit curious about what was going on. Then without a greeting I addressed the senior looking Yakuza assuming he was the one with the most power. "You're Yakuza, huh. Yesterday a Yakuza tried to kill me. You guys want to kill me? Come and get me, I'm right here."

They all stepped back, looked at me like I was crazy, which I may have been at the moment, and replied, "What are you talking about?" Before I could answer a little guy I didn't notice earlier, stepped out in front of everyone and said, "Enson.... what's wrong?" I then realized it was the Number 2 Yakuza in the second largest family in Japan, the Sumiyoshi Gumi. This Yakuza, Mr. Nakajima, was the Yakuza behind the Shooto Association. (Yes, you read correct. He is the unseen back of Shooto even though they claim to be Yakuza free.) A familiar face, I regarded as a friend, was able to calm me enough to stop me from going crazy. We exchanged numbers and he agreed to find out for me who it was and help me clear it up.

I must have waited about two weeks without a call so I decided to call from my side even though the agreement was that he was going to call me. When I called him, he said that he needed more time and that he'd call me as soon as he found the guy. In the meantime one of my boys got all the inside scoop. He managed to get his name, hometown, territory, and most importantly, his family and his rank. His name was Mr. Hishino from Iijima Gumi, a family within Mr. Nakajima's Family.

It was ridiculous that Mr. Nakajima couldn't find someone in his own group? Unlikely...very unlikely. So I called Mr. Nakajima and informed him about something he probably already knew, the Yakuza guy's name and affiliation.

As I expected, he pretended like he didn't know and said he would call me back when he found this guy. I didn't expect a call but about three days later he called. He informed me that he got ahold of Hoshino and asked me what I wanted to do. This question caught me off guard so I said, "I would like you to bring Mr. Hoshino to my gym, close the door, and give me five minutes to do whatever I want." There was a long pause and then he asked, "What are you going to do?" I chuckled, and then answered, "What am I going to do? I'm going to fuck him up!" I then continued, "Not Enson vs. Sumiyoshi Gumi, not Enson vs. Yakuza, just two men with a problem hashing it out. I want no retaliation or hard feelings toward me. Put the Yakuza title aside just for five minutes." Mr. Nakajima quickly snapped, "Muri." Muri in Japanese means impossible.

Then I thought, why the hell did they ask me what I want to do if they aren't going to do it? So I said, "Okay, how about you make him work for me for a month?" Mr. Nakajima asked me what kind of work he would do, and I replied, "He will be my sparring partner." Again, he blurted out the word "Muri." It was obvious to me that this phone conversation wasn't going anywhere so I suggested they come in to my Omiya gym to talk in person. I could feel a sense of hesitation in his voice as he agreed. We were set to meet on Thursday of the following week at 6 p.m. at my Omiya Gym.

Thursday finally arrived and I decided to go in early to get some training in before the meeting. I arrived at 4 p.m., got a good 90 minutes of training, took a shower, then began waiting for Mr. Nakajima to arrive. Time was ticking and I was getting impatient. 5:50 p.m.... 6 p.m.... 6:10 p.m.... 6:30 p.m.... 7 p.m. What the fuck???? Is he just late? If so why didn't he call? Is he going to come? As I was about to call him my phone rang. My ringtone was the song from Godfather which was set to go off whenever I get a call from an underworld figure so I knew it was Mr. Nakajima calling. I answered and before I could say anything he babbled, "I'm running late and it would be rude to you to make you wait so let's meet next week." I bit my tongue, agreed to change the meeting to next Thursday, and then hung up the phone, disgusted with his lack of integrity.

Yakuza usually base their beliefs on integrity and honor but obviously this piece of shit was on a different channel. What's this shit about being rude to me so let's change the date? Wouldn't that be my decision to make? What a loser. I was beginning to lose my patience, not because it was taking forever to begin to get this settled, but because of the lack of respect he showed me. Not calling me to set the appointment and then calling me one hour after the set time to change the appointment was totally disrespectful. Now I did realize he was the #2 Yakuza for the second largest group and I was just an up and coming fighter with no Yakuza rank, but I didn't see it that way. I was a man just like him who wanted to be respected and not taken for granted. I value my Pride and Honor so much that I am willing to die to keep them and Mr. Nakajima was pushing the wrong buttons.

Against the fire in my heart, I decided not to make an issue of it, to avoid any unneeded problems, especially from a Yakuza group. However, what happened the following Thursday was the last straw. Again, I waited at the gym at the scheduled time except this time he was a no show and did not even bothering to call. Okay... I understand his Yakuza group could smash me in a day but that wasn't a reason to let him treat me like a dog.

I was in a big dilemma on what to do because, in the underworld scene in Japan, if I disrespected a person without knowing anything about his underworld affiliation, then there was a problem between just the two of us. But, on the other hand, if I knew he was affiliated to a big underworld organization and I disrespected him, there would be a problem between me, him and his family. The last thing I wanted was a problem with the Sumiyoshi Gumi, but the lack of respect Mr. Nakajima showed me had to stop.

Weeks passed by with no contact from him and I was wondering what was going on. I wondered if he was hoping it would just fade away or he was planning to take care of it at a later date. I didn't want to jump the gun, so I decided to wait and see what his next move would be. Weeks passed and I was getting a bit impatient when amazingly our paths crossed.

It was a sunny afternoon in Japan and there was a big Yakuza gathering for the death anniversary of a high ranked Yakuza and the place they were gathering was next to my Omiya gym. The place was a health center called Yunosato and just standing in the parking lot of my gym gave us a good view of all the Yakuza coming and going. When I got to the gym, the president of Yunosato, Mr. Ikeda, greeted me and stood by me as we watched the cars driving up to the parking lot with Yakuza from all over the country coming. Bentleys, Benzes, Rolls Royces and other high-class cars were driving up which made it look as if we were watching a movie. It was an incredible sight and I was in awe.

Then suddenly, I heard someone call my name, "Enson!". When I turned to see who it was... low and behold... it was Mr. Nakajima. As he approached me he was followed by five of his lower boy or as we say in Japanese, his *kohai*. He then said to me, "Hey Enson! How are you?" This took me by surprise. I really did plan to bite my lip again and suck it up, but when I saw this piece of shit coming towards me with his hand out, like we were on good terms, my emotions got the best of me. "What do you care? You ignored an appointment without having the courtesy to even call and now you stick your hand out in friendship like nothing's wrong?!?!!"

My intonation and choice of words indicated that I was upset and was totally disregarding his status in front of his *kohais*. Mr. Ikeda could sense the tension in the air and began to sweat anticipating an ugly confrontation. He then started subtly hitting my hip with his hand while uttering the words "Onegai! Onegai!" which means, "Please! Please!" He was begging me not to have a confrontation, hoping I would just shut up and suck up my pride again. Although I did plan to, I couldn't find the strength to bite my lip. "Obviously you're not my friend and you're not interested in making peace. You make an appointment and with no call you didn't show up. That's not something friends do to each other. So put your hand back in your pocket because I'm not shaking your hand."

Mr. Ikeda cringed expecting the worst when, to our surprise, Mr. Nakajima didn't get upset. Usually someone of his status isn't spoken to like that, especially in front of his *kohai* where he had to maintain his reputation. He just replied with a small forced chuckle, "What makes you say that? I'm going to take care of the problem. I'll call you tomorrow," Of course I didn't believe him so I replied, "Okay, if you call, we can talk, but until then I don't consider you a friend." Then we parted ways, giving a small nod to each other acknowledging we understood each other.

The next day came and to my surprise he called. He said he wanted to come by tomorrow to settle the whole incident. I agreed, we set a time, and as I hung up I wondered if, this time, he would keep the appointment. The next day I got to the gym early again to workout and Mr. Nakajima came right on time. He was accompanied by two other guys who apparently were supposed to be witnesses to our transaction. I showed them to the back room of the gym and we all sat down. Before anything was said, Mr. Nakajima pulled out an envelope and put it on the table in front of us. He then took out a piece of paper and set it besides the envelope. In the envelope there was $3,000 cash and the piece of paper was an agreement of closure he wanted me to sign.

I first picked up the envelope, flipped through the cash, and then handed it back to Mr. Nakajima. I let Mr. Nakajima know that $3,000 was like an insult. Mr. Hoshino tried to kill me and all he brought was $3,000. Was he saying that my life is worth only $3,000? No amount of money would have been acceptable to me in place of my life and I didn't want to take money from him. If I took money, then it would make us even, but I wanted them to feel like they owed me or for them to feel grateful to me because I did them a favor.

They were also the Yakuza that ran the area where my Omiya gym was located so being on their good side was a good thing. I decided that instead of receiving a monetary apology and making them think that we'd broke even, I chose to forgive them and have them feel like they owed me one, which was much more beneficial. So as I handed the envelope back to Mr. Nakajima, I said, "This is not about money; it's about integrity and honor. If you can have Mr. Hoshino come in to my gym and apologize from his heart, I will forgive him. If he doesn't apologize from his heart, then we still have a problem. And my judgment will be final." I figured Nori and I lived in Japan, so settling it this way was to our best interest.

However, Darren didn't live here, he had to get surgery on both knees, so his negotiation was a bit different. I told Mr. Nakajima that the day Darren arrived in Japan is the day he got banged. He was bed ridden for the entire trip and needed surgery on both knees. I asked Mr. Nakajima to pay for the total cost of Darren's surgery and when he heals, give him a full expense paid trip, first class, back to Japan. He seemed a bit reluctant to agree but finally did and we shook hands on it. He then told me that he would bring Mr. Hoshino in to apologize within a week so he'd get in touch with me again soon.

The next week, as promised, Mr. Hoshino and Mr. Nakajima came in to my Omiya gym. When Mr. Hoshino walked in he had two big bags of offerings to me. In Japan, when you visit someone of importance, you usually don't go empty handed. Gifts to bring are usually food like rice cracker or manju and drinks like beer or Sake. Mr. Hoshino brought boxes of different types of manju and rice crackers.

To my surprise, he was just a normal guy., not spastic or irrational, but instead a very calm, soft spoken guy. He kneeled down in front of me then began bowing down deep and low until his head touched the ground. When his forehead touched the ground he kept it there and said in a stern voice, "Moshiwake gozaimasen!" which is the way to apologize to people of higher status or when you are showing deep remorse.

After his verbal apology, he kept his forehead on the ground for a few more seconds before slowly raising his head. I looked him in the eye, asked him to get up, then extended my hand in friendship. He grasped my hand firmly with both hands, we looked into each other's eyes, gave a slight nod of acknowledgment with our heads, and as our hands parted we both understood that this problem was now in the past and in the past it must stay. Then Mr. Nakajima told Mr. Hoshino, "You remember this. You owe Enson. If Enson has any problems, you must fix it up for him." Wow, I realized that this Yakuza was now in debt to me and in the long run that would be much more worth it than a measly $3,000.

He apologized from his heart, so I forgave him unconditionally. Who knows, maybe someday Mr. Hoshino will come in handy when I get in a sticky situation. If not, better yet, because that means I'm not encountering any big problems. All in all, it's nice to know you have that kind of back up when you need it.

Chapter 50

NORI'S JAPAN DEBUT –
BEGINNING OF A SUPERSTAR

After the Guam fight, Nori began training intensely in anticipation of his professional MMA debut in Japan. We got an offer from one of the biggest associations, K-1, which was great, but it wasn't MMA rules. It was K-1 kickboxing rules. Nori was getting much better in his kickboxing techniques but nowhere near the level of the opponents he would have to face in the K-1 ring. His opponent was to be Murahama, a world class shoot boxer.

Since Murahama was a class above Nori in fame and kickboxing level we figured he had nothing to lose. The game plan was to give all he had and if he ever felt like he was in deep trouble due to stamina or technique, he was going to lift Murahama up and dump him out of the ring. To our surprise, Nori manhandled Murahama and landed big punches, stopping Murahama in the second round via KO. This was a great feat but, because this was a tournament, it meant that Nori would have to make preparations for another fight. We really didn't expect to get by the first fight so we were caught off guard. I talked it over with Nori and didn't want to continue because he was tired so I pulled him out claiming injury.

Although he wasn't injured, I felt that a victory over Murahama was huge and could be tainted if he had a bad showing in the second round in which he wasn't up to fighting. The next day, the press went wild. A new star was born.

Chapter 51

Nori failed the dope test – Marijuana

Only a week had passed and the victory celebration was disrupted by a call from K-1. Nori had failed the drug test and tested positive for marijuana, an illegal substance. This was bad. The victory could be overruled and become a loss. He could face criminal charges, be temporarily banned from fighting and he would lose all his sponsors as well as many fans. I immediately called the head of K-1, Mr. Tanigawa, and set up a private meeting. During the meeting I convinced him that it would be in our best interest to keep this undercover, not only to avoid major problems for Nori, but to save their new star and a possible big money maker for K-1. Tanigawa agreed and it was kept a secret, until now.

Nori winning and moving to superstar status was of mutual interest to myself and to K-1, so I negotiated a two year fight contract for Nori requiring him to fight four fights a year, making $50,000 per fight. That was a $400,000 two-year contract, unheard of for a lightweight fighter and a huge pay raise from his Shooto fight money of $2,000 a fight. When I broke the news to Nori, he was in disbelief and just elated to be able to fight in the K-1 ring again! After the negotiation for Nori's salary, I opened the next stage of discussion, what I would get out of it. I explained to K-1 that he was one of my instructors at my Purebred Gym and his fight training would take him away from his work. K-1 agreed to pay me $10,000 every time Nori fought for them. I liked the deal and the contract was signed.

NO, I FAILED THE DOPE TEST — MARIJUANA

Chapter 52

PUREBRED TOKYO, KILLER BEE –
YAKUZA RUN

While I was training Nori, there was a group of Yakuza guys who needed a place to train. In Japan, the majority of the gyms, fitness centers, and
spas do not allow gang members or Yakuza in the gym. Some go as far
as to deny entry to anyone that has a visible tattoo on their body. They do
that because many Japanese people do not want to associate with Yakuza
in fear of the possibility of dealing with a problem and having to deal
with the consequences. For example, if you accidentally hurt someone in
training, ordinarily, there isn't a problem, but if it is a Yakuza figure they
may use the fear people have of the Yakuza as leverage to demand ridiculous amounts of compensation. However, everyone at my gym knows the
respect and influence I have in the underworld so from this respect, there
would never be a problem like that.

The head guy of this Yakuza group, Eiji Aikawa, was a very nice man,
well-mannered and polite. The name of his group was called Kyokutou,
Aikawa Gumi. It was a smaller Yakuza group where he led his own family. They came to train about three times a week and I put Nori in charge
of them. They would get private instruction from Nori, who would make
about $150 a class. I set that up so Nori made the money because he
needed the cash since his father disowned him for refusing to go back to
wrestling.

As time passed I got close to Eiji and one day he had an interesting proposal to me. He wanted to run a fighting gym and be affiliated with me.

He wanted to do it in Tokyo and wanted to name it Purebred Tokyo. I liked the idea of expanding the Purebred family so I agreed on one condition: He had to hire two of my students so they could train and fight for a living. He agreed and I appointed Nori and Ryan Bow to this gym.

There was a big grand opening ceremony and the media and many famous people in Japan attended. Nori wanted to name the gym "Killer Bee" and I obliged. Purebred Tokyo: Killer Bee was born.

For Nori's next three fights, Japan's Yasuhiro, USA's Tony Valente, and Mongolia's Naranton Narantungalag and I arranged something that has never been done in the K-1 ring. I got K-1 to have the matches be mixed rules, where the first, third, and fifth rounds were to be fought under K-1 rules while the second and fourth rounds would be MMA rules. K-1 agreed and Nori scored impressive wins over big names and he shot to superstar status.

Chapter 53

2001 PUREBRED KYOTO
NICEST MMA GYM IN JAPAN

In my career I have met many people and one was Mr. Nakano, who lived down south in Japan's beautiful Kyoto Prefecture. A fellow fighter, Kanehara, introduced us, and our relationship grew to a point that Mr. Nakano asked me if I wanted to run a gym in a building he just bought. I liked Mr. Nakano but was always wary on how he would try to impress people and was rarely being himself. It was against how I carried myself but I understood that that was his way. He told me that he wanted no rent money and all he asked was that when his son grew up I would train him to be a fighter. I told him that as a friend I would train his son for free no matter what and a gym sounded very exciting. When the talks of making a gym got serious I decided to finally go down to Kyoto and take a look at this building he bought. I was amazed.

The building I imagined was a small two story concrete building but what Mr. Nakano bought was beyond my imagination. It was an 8 story beautifully tiled building in the heart of Kyoto. He took me up to the 6th floor and said that I could use this whole floor for a gym. I couldn't imagine what it would look like because I wasn't expecting the space to be so big. We soon began planning on what we needed to do with the floor and what we needed to purchase in order to have a full scale MMA gym. Mr. Nakano was the type of guy that was really concerned at how people perceived him so he always got the best in whatever he was buying. Even the cars he owned looked like they were from an exotic car dealership.

We finally decided what we needed to do and the cost of the renovation of the 6th floor and the purchase of the ring, mats, weights, and everything else that was necessary for a MMA gym would cost close to a quarter million dollars. We agreed to pay $125,000 each and the gym was on its way. When the gym was finally done, it was fabulous. By far it was the biggest and nicest MMA gym Japan had to offer. We had a big grand opening and Purebred Kyoto was born.

Chapter 54

2002 FEBRUARY COMEBACK FIGHT – NOGUEIRA RICHARD LEE RIP

I was retired, content, and happily raising the greatest boy in the world. Even though he wasn't my blood he was a part of my heart and I saw him as my own. Then something happened that disrupted everything. I remembered on this particular day, September 11th, I was training at Gold's Gym in Saitama. As I walked past the treadmills, where they have a bunch of televisions mounted on the wall, it seemed as though four out of the six televisions were playing the same channel, or so I believed. It was a program of a building on fire and I thought it was one of the "Die Hard" series. I noticed that although the four televisions were showing the same scene, they all had different angles. They were actually all on different channels, just showing the same thing. Then I felt a knot in my chest when I noticed the word "live" in the top corner of the screens. One of the buildings on the screen was on fire with thick black smoke gushing out of the building.

As I was trying to figure out what was going on, my heart dropped when I saw a plane fly straight into the other building. There was a big explosion and just then the words "World Trade Center, New York" flashed out on the screen and I got chills down my spine realizing that I wasn't watching a movie, I was watching live news! I couldn't believe it. The televisions at the gym had no volume so I left the gym and jumped in my car, rushing to get home to watch the news to see what in God's name was going on!

I got a call from Miyu and she was hysterical. She screamed, "The building is gone!!! It's gone!!!"I couldn't believe my ears!!! What did she mean, one of the buildings was gone? How could a building disappear? When I finally got home I couldn't believe what I was seeing. It was like David Copperfield did some amazing magic illusion making one of the towers of the World Trade Center disappear. As my eyes were glued to the television I couldn't believe what was being said. Two planes had crashed into the World Trade Center and one of the buildings had collapsed! Just then, the other building began to crumble.... it went down and wasn't there anymore. The World Trade Center was GONE!!! I had a strange feeling run through my whole body. What the fuck is going on!!! It was on CNN so this was no bullshit; I couldn't believe what I was watching. I felt like I was dreaming, like everything around me was surreal. I've been to the top of the World Trade Center twice, and to me, one of the things New York was known for was the World Trade Center.

I picked up the phone and called my mother and she was freaking out too. My mother then told me that one of her best friends, Susan, had a son, Rich, who worked in one of the towers. Susan would always visit my mother so Egan and I met Rich numerous times. She said that Rich worked in the second tower and there's a great possibility that he made it out. New York City was like a war zone, it was mayhem so there was no way to find out whether Rich made it out alive or not. As Susan and I were exchanging emails I began to feel her pain and my heart was pulled into the drama. I began to feel for Susan and was scared about what had happened to Rich as I began to dread her next email.

The emails I got were like a roller coaster ride of emotion and it was very hard to bear. At first Rich never came home so they began calling and searching all the hospitals in the New York and Canada area. Nothing for a few days until one day there was a bit of hope. They found one of Rich's co-workers who was with Rich when the first plane flew into the first tower. He said he was with Rich when the plane hit and everyone went into a semi-panic. They were contemplating what to do when an announcement came out on the intercom telling them that the building that they were in was safe so everyone should return to work. They both returned to work for a moment, while the majority of the people were evacuating, until they both had second thoughts and decided to evacuate too. They both ran towards the staircase and because of the chaos in the staircase, they lost track of each other. He made it out but Rich was still nowhere to be found. I felt that if he made it out, then there was a good chance that Rich made it out too so my hopes went up!

Then a week later, the dreaded email came. They found Rich's body, he didn't make it. He was one of the many that jumped from the building. My heart hurt. I sat at my computer in disbelief. Did he suffer a lot from smoke inhalation before he jumped? Did he pass out before making impact? All kinds of questions were scrambled in my head. Because I was getting frequent updates from Rich's mother, I was deeply emotionally attached to hoping Rich made it out. For weeks after, I was an emotional mess. One minute I was enjoying myself at a game center, then the next, I was overwhelmed with what just happened in New York and felt a sense of helplessness.

Then I began to feel guilty that I could sincerely hurt in my heart one minute then laugh and have fun the next. Sometimes before lunch I would see some coverage on 9-11 on the news and my heart would drop, then after lunch I would go to a game center with my friend and be able to laugh and have fun as if nothing happened. How could my emotions be so erratic? Then I wondered if I was truly a man of honor. Would a man of true honor have so much guilt and not do anything about it?

Then in the newspaper it said that over 30,000 Americans had enlisted to help fight the war against terror. That's when it hit me. 30,000 people have enlisted and here I was doing shit about it. Feeling bad when I see it on the news then going out and having fun... I felt like a loser! Out of all the people that enlisted, because I've been training 80% of my life, I'm sure I was more physically fit than 60% of them, and for me not to offer my services was hard for me to deal with any longer. I felt like my pride and honor was slipping out of my hands. To cry and hurt in my heart for Rich and the poor souls that perished on 9-11 and not do shit about it was killing my spirit. So in my heart I decided that I had to enlist and go to war!

When I mentioned it to my wife Miyu, she hit the roof. Her words pierced my heart, "What about Erson and I? Are you just going to leave us alone?" I didn't know what to say. I could see her point and it was obvious that she couldn't see mine. Was it because she didn't fully understand the Yamatodamashii way of thinking? Was I being stupid? I explained to her that I know that my duty as a husband is to take care of my wife and child but over all that, it is my duty to myself to take care of my pride and honor as a man.

So in other words, if I didn't constantly build and keep my pride and honor as a man, then I wouldn't be able to properly take care of my family as a husband and father. I felt that if I didn't do everything I could to assist with the war on terror, I would be killing my honor which would result in me not being able to walk the walk of a real man, therefore making me incapable of properly taking care of my family. Sort of like how can I keep my car clean when I don't have a car? I couldn't properly take care of anyone if I wasn't a man and to lose your honor is exactly the same as losing your manhood.

I explained it to her the best I could but I feel she didn't understand what I was trying to tell her. This broke my heart. Out of everyone around me, I had hoped that at least Miyu would understand. All she was concerned about was how she and Erson would survive. She didn't work and was living off what I brought home so if something happened to me, paying the bills was her big concern. I secretly cried myself to sleep many a night, never revealing my real pain to my wife, in fear that she would get angry at me for being torn between what to do. In her mind there was no question. I was to stay home and watch over the family.

My heart was torn, like something was ripping my chest apart piece by piece. It was already hard enough to fight this battle inside of myself because I didn't want to go to war! I really didn't want to die yet. If I had a choice I would choose to not go but I didn't have a choice. Honing, strengthening, and saving my honor was, without a doubt in my mind, the right thing to do. To keep my honor and spirit intact and at peace I had to go. Sitting here not even trying to do a thing is something I couldn't live with. For a moment I did think that maybe I was being a little bit selfish; but I thought, how can thinking about Rich and all the other people who died and suffered at 9-11 and wanting to do something in memory of them be selfish?

This was the beginning of when I began to see deeper into Miyu and how she thinks. She was basically so concerned with her feelings that many times she would disregard that I had feelings too. Without trying to understand my deep feelings she would be convinced that her feelings were the most important. There was never any way to negotiate this.

As difficult as my decision was, I had decided to enlist. The pain of living everyday knowing I didn't do all I could to help was killing my soul. Now that I had decided to enlist, I also decided to do a final fight. I didn't know in what kind of condition I would come back in physically and mentally or if I would even come back at all so in order to show my gratitude to all my fans for all their support, I decided to fight one last time for my fans.

Instead of contacting Pride directly I had a great plan. I had my manager at the time contact Pride and, without my knowledge, he secretly told Pride that I was planning to enlist in the military. He told them that before I enlist, I probably would be interested in fighting one more time. Pride didn't know that I personally wanted to fight one more time before I went and that I'm the one who told him to call. Now my manager at the time, Shoichi Sakai, was frequently doing credit card scams and evaded taxes for years so he was a pro when it came to deceiving people. Needless to say he had Pride fooled. I also told Sakai to tell them that if they offered me Wanderlei Silva the chances for them to get me to fight would be greater.

Then I got the call. Pride asked me if I was interested in fighting Wanderlei Silva for $100,000. I actually would have fought Wanderlei for free but I played the game and acted just semi-interested. When I didn't give them an answer for about three days, I got another call and instantaneously the fight money went up to $150,000. I wanted to jump through the phone, shake the Pride official's hand, and sign the contract right there but I played it cool and told them I'll have to think about it and I'd call them back. A week passed and just when I was about to wonder if that was their maximum offer I got another call. Now the offer was $200,000. I wanted to scream "yes!" but again I sucked it up and asked them for more time to think it over. Then when two weeks passed without a call I was afraid that I might lose this fight so I picked up the phone and made the call.

A dream come true!!! I would be able to fight a fighter I'd been dreaming of going up against for a long time and get paid close to a quarter of a million dollars doing so. I was stoked and immediately began training hard. Wow, I was actually going to fight Wanderlei Silva! One of the few fighters that I really admired and the image of throwing down toe to toe with him gave me chills up my spine! Every time I saw Wanderlei fight he was like a beast from the press conference to the stare down to the last punch.

This is what MMA should be like all the time. Every punch was thrown with bad intentions and the electricity that could be felt in his ferocity was unexplainable. I felt like this was the perfect fight to end my career. Like the finale of a fireworks show where the end is continuous flashes of light and ceaseless repetitious pops and explosions, followed by silence with the smoke settling with either Wanderlei or myself left standing.

The intensity I got in training was considerably greater than any fight I ever trained for. This fight was contracted at 205 pounds so I had to drop 7 kilograms, which wasn't going to be a problem at all. Enson vs. Wanderlei seemed too good to be true, and, unfortunately, it was.

Two months before the fight, I got a call from Pride and they informed me that the fight with Wanderlei fell through so they instead wanted me to fight Minotauro Nogueira, the older and bigger of the Nogueira brothers. I couldn't believe my ears!!! No Wanderlei??? I expressed my displeasure in the change and told them I was set on fighting Wanderlei and Wanderlei was the only fighter I was interested in fighting. So I straight up told them that if it's not Wanderlei then I'm not interested in fighting at all! Then they told me something I still can't believe today, they told me that Wanderlei didn't want to fight me. That he declined the fight. This was a lie and I knew it! Wanderlei was a warrior and by no means would he ever decline a fight.

Then a few days later my hunches were confirmed. Pride had a press conference where they announced Kiyoshi Tamura vs. Wanderlei Silva! "Those mothefuckers!" I thought. Fuck their games, I was fed up, tired of it. I was not fighting. Then a week later I got another call from Pride and they were literally begging me to take the fight with Nogueira. I was pissed at all their bullshit so I told them that I did not want to fight a heavyweight and if I'm not going to fight Wanderlei, then I'm not fighting at all. Then Pride threw me a curve ball that I would have never guessed would be coming in my wildest dreams.

They said, "Okay, to show our apologies for not getting you Wanderlei, how about we double your fight money for you to fight Nogueira?" $400,000 to fight Nogueira??? With that kind of money I could put a down payment on a nice house here in Japan! Up until now my average fight money had been $80,000 and now they were offering me five times that??? I couldn't turn that down and in an instant Enson vs. Wanderlei turned into Enson vs. Nogueira.

I knew I needed to train hard so I called down some hard, heavy hitting heavyweights to train with. I called Wesley "Cabbage" Correria from Hawaii, "Big" John Calvo from Guam, my cousin Jared Fuchigami, and my brother Egan. Training was awesome and I had these guys beat up on me every day and even took a two-week trip to Thailand to train with Sangtiennoi! Almost every day in training I had to push myself to my limit and in the process strengthen my heart every second that passed that I didn't give in to the pain.

"Pain is weakness leaving the body"

I worked through every test that popped up in training and could almost feel my heart and spirit getting stronger by the day. Every day it was a chore getting up and the aches and pains felt like adversaries I needed to conquer.

Since this was going to be my final fight, I flew down my whole family to come and watch. My father had been to a number of my fights but my grandparents and my mother had never ever seen me fight live. When they saw the size of the arena filled with the 50,000 plus fans they were awestruck! I also invited Rich's mother to come and witness this fight ringside because after all I was dedicating this fight to Rich and all the victims of 9-11. I also got a nice picture of Rich printed up and hung it around my neck during my ring entrance.

For my ring entrance I asked Pride for a special favor. Because this was my last fight and I was planning on going off to war after it, I really didn't know how much longer I would be living. I wanted to show my gratitude to all the people that were close to my heart and had supported me throughout my career. I wanted them to be a part of this last fight. My ring entrance consisted of passing through two levels and on the second level I had some heads of other families, some Yakuza and some not, hold Yamatodamashii flags.

This was unheard of for heads of different families to stand on the same platform side by side holding the same flag in peace and harmony. But because this was a request from me and out of respect for me they stood as one family! On the last level, the last stretch to the ring, I had a whole bunch of my students from Guam, Saipan, Japan, and Hawaii line up the ramp holding the same flag, the Yamatodamashii flag. It was a long ring entrance and I made it a point to firmly shake hands with each and every one of my students.

Then because I always get too pumped up during my ring entrances I had Miyu pass me a Walkman so I could listen to Tenacious D's "I Wanna Fuck You". This song was so senseless it made me relax and not be too much in the kill or be killed mode. As I approached the ring, I noticed another one of my brothers, Chad Griffin, who was working security for Pride walk up to me and give me a hug as tears filled his eyes. I had all my Ichizoku with me and I was ready for war!

The fight started out with both of us just feeling out each other while keeping distance circling each other. Every time I faked a punch or a kick he was unwilling to engage and backed away quickly. Although Nogueira's kickboxing was a level better than mine, it was obvious that he didn't want to stand and trade blow for blow with me. He then ran in and attempted a sloppy tackle that I easily avoided which left him on the ground on his back with me standing over him.

I began kicking him on the ground catching him with two solid kicks before the referee stepped in and stood him up. Without trading any punches and kicks with me, he again ran in for a clinch. This time instead of backing away I threw a hard low kick that landed but wasn't enough to stop his forward momentum and he had me tight in a clinch up in a neutral corner.

We were exchanging punches to the head until his second attempt to take me down with a leg sweep was successful and we ended up on the ground. Instantaneously he sunk in a Kimura and began to crank it hard. I felt my elbow pop once as the referee ran in and asked me if I wanted to give up. I then made eye contact with the referee and yelled back at him, "No! I'm okay!" We rolled and exchanged the top positions and I caught him with four unanswered solid punches from his guard. I then got careless by throwing wild chops giving him the chance to sweep me and regain the top position. I then got on top again as he attempted to sink in a guillotine. I managed to slide my head out of the guillotine and regained the top position.

He then tried a tricky arm bar that I defended only to find myself in a deep Omoplata. As he had me locked in the Omoplata he put me in a foot lock that hurt a bit but nowhere near enough to make me contemplate giving up. I then unexpectedly caught him with a solid kick to his head that made him transition to his next hold that sealed my fate.

263

As I escaped the Omoplata, he put me in a deep tight triangle and in about 5 seconds rendered me unconscious for the first time ever. I tried to relax and breathe to keep the circulation of blood flowing to my brain when all of a sudden the next thing I remember is Egan standing over me asking me if I was okay and that's when I realized that I was choked unconscious. I gave my 100% and had nothing to be ashamed of.

I grabbed the mic and made eye contact with Rich's mother and relayed a message I had deep in my heart. I said, "I was a big underdog in this fight against Nogueira, like Rich was a big underdog to make it out of the tower to get home to you! But like me, he didn't make it. But I wanted you to understand that no matter how great the odds or how impossible the feat seems until he was stopped, he fought to the very bitter end. I hope you can remember it in your heart how much he wanted to get home and how hard he fought as you care for his wife and son he left behind. I'm so sorry I couldn't win this fight in honor of Rich, but like Rich I fought bravely with all my heart to the very end."

I fought hard and to the last second when I was choked unconscious by Nogueira's triangle choke never, not even for a split second, did I think of quitting or tapping out. Now that the fight was over I had a much more serious, delicate issue to deal with. I decided to still pursue the military to see what I could do to contribute to the cause.

I contacted the Zama base in Japan and was told that the cut off age for enlisting in the military was 34 and I was 36. Then, to make matters worse, they informed me that anyone that has tattoos that showed when you wore the uniform was out, and I had a tattoo on the palms of my hands and the back of my head that would show when I was in uniform. I was bummed and felt a bit hopeless but my honor was still intact because I did what I could to help.

Okay, maybe I couldn't enlist but I still wanted to contribute in any way I can so I made an offer that still stands today and will always stand for as long as I am capable. I made an offer to any military base in the world that I would give free seminars to any military personnel. All they would need to do is take care of my airfare and housing. I felt that if I can't personally go to help fight in the war, the least I could do was help and make a contribution to the ones that are going. So far I've done three seminars and am willing to do as many more as is desired.

Chapter 55

SEPARATED – THE END IS NEAR

My marriage with Miyu was normal. We had our occasional fights where we would lose our tempers, and besides those few fights nothing was out of the ordinary. A lot of times when we would fight, Miyu would drive home to her fathers. I played Mr. Mom, and Erson and I were together constantly during those times. I would get up, make his breakfast, send him off to school, pick him up from school, help him with his homework, make dinner, and put him to bed.

When Miyu made a comeback in wrestling I would practically take care of Erson every day, and I even took him to Thailand, Guam, and Hawaii with me when I had to make business trips there. Miyu was busy with her training so, even if it was very difficult at times, I did my best to take care of and raise Erson to the best of my abilities. It was very hard, and since I was also planning a comeback in MMA, Miyu and I talked it over and agreed that sending Erson to home-stay in Hawaii with my parents was a great idea. My parents were more than happy to care of Erson, and while he experienced living in Hawaii he would be able to learn the English language.

It would be so good for Erson's future and at the same time it would allow Miyu and I to properly train and prepare for our comebacks. This was financially difficult because covering Erson's cost of living in Hawaii was hard. My parents were kind enough to feed, house, and take care of all of Erson's daily necessities, while I sent them money for sports enrollment and uniform fees, school books and tuition, clothing, shoes, and all his airline tickets back and forth.

Whenever he flew to Hawaii, because Erson was only seven, he couldn't make the international flight by himself. It was either, ask the airlines for an escort to and from the plane, or I had to go with him. Ordering an escort would have been very convenient, but I didn't want to make Erson endure an eight-hour flight all alone. This was very costly and hard, but I loved Erson with all my heart and would do anything for him. I also called Erson every day, sometimes twice a day.

Chapter 56

Divorced at Narita Airport

The paperwork for a foreign child to home-stay in Hawaii was tedious, and I took care of everything except a document I asked Miyu to get for Erson to stay in Hawaii. This is what caused the final argument that led to us finally getting divorced.

It happened around one of the times I was about to take Erson back to Hawaii and we met at Narita Airport so she could pass Erson over to me. I asked her if she could help and get an immigration form from the American consulate in Japan, and she wasn't very happy that I was asking her to do this. Yes, in the beginning, I told her I would take care of everything, but the last two times I'd tried to get the form in Hawaii they didn't have any. Immigration in Hawaii advised me to get it from the American embassy in Japan so since Miyu was always in Japan I asked her to pick it up when she had time.

I couldn't believe it when she said, "I thought you said you were going to take care of everything." So I replied, "Yes I tried to, but they were out of the forms so can you get one for me from the American embassy sometime this week?" She then rolled her eyes and that's what pushed me over the edge. I lost it. "You can't do this one thing for your own son? What the fuck?!" She then replied with, "Okay! Forget it then!!! He's not going back to Hawaii then!"

After all the preparations and work we'd gone through the past six months, how could she so easily just say he won't go back? Erson's English was improving in leaps and bounds, and he was looking forward to getting

269

back to all his friends in Hawaii so I thought it was a good thing for him to return. We were at Narita Airport and Erson and I were about to enter the customs area when she grabbed his hand and began walking the other way towards the exit.

I couldn't believe what she was doing, so I screamed to her, "I can't believe you!" She then turned around walked over to me opened her bag up and pulled out a divorce form already signed with her name. I was blown away. First of all, I'm the one who asked for the separation. Second, she had the form ready to be signed. Third, we were at the airport. Last but not least... right in front of Erson???

I couldn't believe this was happening at the airport. I was wondering why it was happening now, here right in front of the Northwest Airlines counter. It was very unfortunate that it had to happen at the airport, in public, and in front of Erson. It was clear to me that she had made up her mind 100% that she wanted to get it done now for the divorce papers were already signed by her. It really caught me off guard because the last time I talked with her just two months ago, she was still asking to come back.

However, since that last call 2 months earlier, her calls did subside and this may be why. Since I was considering divorcing her when we separated close to a year ago, instead of fighting it, I decided to go along with it, but with her being so worked up, I didn't think it was a good idea to sign the other side of the divorce papers in her state of mind and in the heat of a fight. So I sat her down and talked with her for over an hour until she calmed down and until we were both in a levelheaded state of mind. Then finally after we both were calm and we both still agreed that a divorce was still what we ultimately wanted, I took the pen and signed the papers. We were now officially divorced after four years of marriage. Well actually three years together and one year separated.

Chapter 57

My Heart Broke –
I'm Sorry Erson

What broke my heart was that a second after I signed the papers, Erson, who had been tearfully watching all this happen, came running up to me and said, "Dad! Why did you sign the papers?" My heart dropped as I crouched down to Erson's eye level to see him eye-to-eye and said, "You don't want to see Mom and Dad fight all the time and begin to hate each other do you?" He shook his head. "Then this is the best thing." I continued, "Mom and I will still be friends and you will always be my boy."

Little did I know that Miyu and I were going to be hit hard by the tabloids about our divorce and she would blame it all on me, which caused tension in our relationship. It got hard for me to see Erson and I was devastated. When we got divorced, Miyu told me that because Erson didn't really remember his real Dad, I would always be Erson's father. Miyu told me that Erson's real father used to beat her, and Erson remembered him as Mom's friend that used to beat her up.

Although Erson wasn't my son by blood, he was my son in my heart, so I asked Miyu if she could keep Erson's name as Inoue for I loved him with all my heart and he'd already had his name changed four times. He was born as Rei Ikeda. When Miyu got her first divorce from Nobu Ikeda his name was then changed to Rei Yamamoto. Then when we were married it was again changed to Rei Inoue. She then wanted to change the name her first husband gave to him – "Rei" – to a name resembling mine, so again another name change to Erson Inoue.

However she wanted him to have her name so for the fifth time his name was changed - to Erson Yamamoto. I would secretly see Erson when he would visit some of the old friends he'd made when he lived with me, but the last time I saw him he was a bit different. He was shy and I could feel the distance that had grown between us during the time away. I was sad but had to go on.

I am currently 47 years old, single, and probably the only one in my high school graduating class that doesn't have a child of his own. This may be a surprise to some of you who saw the documentary "Rites of Passages," Erson was introduced in it. However, he is not my blood son. He was my son in my heart but not my biological son. Erson is Miyu's son from her previous marriage. I loved him like he was my own; I loved him with all my heart. For the five years that I took care of him he went with me everywhere. Training in Guam, Thailand, and Hawaii, to buy groceries, to watch fights, and even to some Yakuza gatherings. He was my life and I would have and still would do anything for him if he ever needed my help, even though I haven't seen him in eight years. Since I divorced Miyu about ten years ago, I've seen him secretly only about five times. However in the last eight years I haven't seen him once. I miss him so much and I can't count the nights I cried myself to sleep missing him.

Everyone says that when he grows up he will come to see me but he is already about 18 years old and hasn't visited yet. When I divorced Miyu never in my wildest thoughts did I think I would never see him again. We had a bond and a father/son relationship that was priceless. Whenever he did something bad, I was the one he was the most afraid to confront but when things were fine, I was the first one he'd come to kick and punch and make trouble to. We were like best friends.

Erson and I were like best friends.

I was so tempted to try and get custody but I knew it would be useless because I wasn't his real father and there would be only bickering and fighting. When we were married, whenever we fought the one who was suffering the most was Erson. Erson is a very softhearted boy who loves his Mother very much. I knew he needed his mother, so my last words to him were, "Don't worry, I will always be here for you. You must stay with Mom and take care of her." That was the hardest thing I had to do because in my heart I wanted him to stay with me. But I knew that a child at the precious age of 7 really needed his Mother's love.

There is nothing more important than the bond with his mother at that tender age. I decided to back off and remain quiet knowing that it was the best thing for Erson. Since the divorce, the few times I got to see him were just by chance. Every time I saw him I gave him my phone number but I never got a phone call from him. I figured that either Miyu found it and threw it away or he just misplaced it somewhere. I always hoped to run into him by chance because to see him just for a second would mean a million words.

The first time I saw him since the divorce was at a K-1 event. When I went to the back to wish Nori good luck before one of his fights, out of nowhere he came running, wrapped his arms around my waist, gave me a tight hug, and said, "I love you Dad!" Then as suddenly as he appeared he ran back where he came from. In a way, it seemed as though he didn't want to get caught hugging me. The next time I saw him was when the father of his friend called me and told me that he was spending the night. I dropped all that I was doing and drove down to see him. We hugged, told each other how much we missed and loved each other, talked for about 10 minutes and said our goodbyes.

The third time was when I had my 37th birthday party. My students surprised me and when he walked in, it brought tears to my eyes. I gave him a big hug, told him how much I loved him and missed him and to my surprise, he sang "Happy Birthday" to me, solo! It touched my heart and that memory will remain in my heart forever.

The fourth time was when he came by my Omiya gym to participate in the wrestling practice with the Purebred Omiya wrestling team. One of my students called me to inform me that Erson was at the gym so I waited until the practice was over and I met him in the parking lot across the street. When I came into his view he ran at me at full speed and gave me what we call a "jumping hug". It was where he would come sprinting at me and without slowing down he would jump into my arms straight into a hug! I got that meeting on video and it touched my heart!

The last and final time I ever saw Erson was when he was visiting a spa next to my gym and one of the workers called me to inform me of his presence. This meeting was a long eight months after the last meeting and for some reason things seemed to be a bit different. First of all there was no jumping hug and he seemed a bit shy. I could feel the distance between us that gave me mixed feelings.

I was really sad because I could feel the bond we once had dissolving but on the other hand I was a bit relieved to see that he was growing up and moving on. I then decided that I finally had to let go. Up until that final meeting I was always trying to meet up with him and desperately trying to keep in contact with him. It was a strange feeling because not only did he act different, but his hair was longer and he was about 5-6 inches taller. I couldn't believe that it was time to let go.

I can remember as clear as day when Miyu told me that I was the only one Erson knew as a father and I would always be his father. I was overjoyed and I asked her that since I will always be considered as his father, if it was possible if she could keep his last name as Inoue. To my surprise she declined. He wasn't my biological son but I did love him with all my heart. I believe to be his TRUE father, you don't need to be the one who conceives him but instead the one who cares for him, raises him, and loves him with all your heart... and that I did and still do until this day and until the day I die.

I decided that if I was going to let go I needed to let go 100%. I wanted to be a part of Erson's life so bad but didn't want to cause any stress and confusion in his life. I also knew that even if I did send him something from time to time the lack of integrity that Miyu's father had would be a problem. I remember when I was raising Erson and on one of his birthdays his biological father sent him a birthday present with a card. Miyu's father received it, opened it, threw away the card, rewrapped it then gave it to Erson saying it was from him. It was a present that was hard to find, so Miyu called her father and asked him how he'd managed to get a hold of it. He couldn't answer. He finally admitted what he did and got a long lecture from Miyu for it. I was angry and shocked and couldn't understand how someone could do something so cold.

God I miss him so much. So many years have passed but every time I see a picture of him or go somewhere we been together, I get a lump in my throat and sometimes even shed a tear. At this very moment I still have a picture of us displayed in my house. Everyone says that he will come to see me someday and I wonder if he really will. I guess that if it is what God's plan is, then he will. Whether he does or not, I just hope he knows how much I love him and miss him. I also hope he understands that if he ever needs me I'll always be there for him.

Even now, just writing about him makes me recall all the wonderful times I had with him. I now have tears in my eyes wondering why God made us go our separate ways. God especially knew the special love we shared and I know our separation was for a good reason. I also have faith that in time God will reveal the reason to me. I have to just have faith, be strong until that day and I'm sure I will understand then.

If I could speak to Erson just one more time, I would say:

> *"My dear son, in my heart you will always be my boy! I will never ever be able to express in words how much love I have in my heart for you and how much I've missed you throughout these years. I hear from many how well you are doing and, although it saddens me that I can't be a part of it, I am so very proud of you! If there is ever anything I can ever do for you please don't ever hesitate to ask. Take care of Mom and remember that there is not a single day in my life that passes by that I don't think of you. Be a good boy and remember I love you with all my heart!*
> *Love, Dad"*

In my marriage with Miyu I had a lot of trouble come about because of her father. He was a man who loved money and would do almost anything to obtain it. He came between Nori and I and even managed to create turmoil and drama between Miyu and I many times in our marriage. One morning we were awakened by Nori when he came over to my apartment with a sports paper in hand in shock that Miyu was covering the whole front page in color. The story was about Miyu making her debut in Pro Wrestling.

It was news to Miyu and I. Never had there been any offer, let alone any discussion, about anything of that sort. I contacted the newspaper and the pro wrestling association and asked them where they got their information. I was only told that they had a good source. I explained to them that their best source, Miyu, was here beside me and that she knew nothing about it, but they seemed to be confident that their source was reliable. Her father had told the Pro Wrestling Association that he could vouch for Miyu because she was his daughter and he can make her do whatever he wants. I met with all involved only to find out that the pro wrestling association was promised Miyu's participation for a $200,000 sponsorship by her father. Miyu refused to participate, so I finally met with the sponsors and declined their offer. His scene was ruined and I learned a good lesson on what this greedy man can do. When Miyu and I were finally divorced, besides the sadness of losing Erson, I felt like a big weight was lifted off my shoulders and felt free of stress.

I never felt any suffering while being married and really felt happy, but after I got the divorce I felt so free and like I had a new beginning. So in 2004 after four years of marriage I was single again and I came to the conclusion that God put me on this earth not to be married and have children but to stay single so I can run and take care of my Yamatodamashii Ichizoku with no interference. In order to lead and protect the Ichizoku properly, I believe that I never ever can be married again.

It's a bit sad, but it may be my calling. I feel the love between a man and a woman is great, but it is nothing compared to the love between the Ichizoku, and because I have the love from all my Ichizoku, I feel no need for the love of a woman. Some people will say that they feel sorry for me because I feel this way, and maybe they are correct, but for now this is how I feel. For the people who feel sorry for me because I don't have a lady that I feel I could be with to the death, that I would do anything for, or that I would die for, I have one question for them: If there were thirty bullets coming at you in slow motion and there was no avoiding it, can you name thirty names that would take a bullet for you? No? Well, I can, and still have a lot more left just in case there were a few more stray bullets coming. I can name thirty names within a minute. To me that is happiness, the love of the Ichizoku. The love of hundreds of guys ready to die for you at any time, and of course hundreds of guys I am willing to die for at any second. I feel the love for a woman is nice, but in a very different way. It's not as deep, and 99.9% of romances have an end. The love for the Ichizoku is forever and can never be broken, even in death. But who knows, life is an adventure and is always so unpredictable.

Chapter 58

2002 Purebred Osaka

Things were going well with Purebred Kyoto and I frequented the gym at least once a month. I was spending lot of time in Kyoto and met a man by the name of Mr. Nakabo. He was a big fight fan and his company, Wedding, was a big sponsor for Pride, K-1, and Masato, a famous K-1 fighter. He called me one day and told me a friend was opening a gym in Osaka and he was wondering if I would attend the ceremony. The guys who were opening the gym were two Yakuza brothers, the Ohta brothers. They were huge fans of mine and were excited that I was going to attend their gym opening.

I got there and it was a beautiful gym. Not a very good location in regards to access but very spacious. It was called Ohta Gym and it was merely a kickboxing gym. Although it was our first meeting the Ohta brothers asked me to be a part of the actual ceremony of pounding open a huge barrel of Japanese sake, just like the cutting of a ribbon.

The ceremony was nice and the Ohta brothers and I became friends. Then about a month after the opening, Tabo, the younger Ohta brother, called me and asked me what the chances are of his gym becoming a Purebred Gym. I liked Tabo and felt honored that he wanted to be a part of Purebred so I Okayed it. I put absolutely no money into this gym and I liked the idea that Purebred was expanding. We had another opening ceremony and Purebred Osaka was born.

Chapter 59
FALLING OUT WITH KID(NORI)

Everything was going well when the first sign of a red flag came. After Nori's victory over Mongolia's Narantungalag, Nori unexpectedly grabbed the mic and directly challenged Masato who was commentating ringside. I didn't know he was going to do that and I was just as shocked as Masato was. This was the first sign that the fame was getting to Nori.

I wanted Nori to train in Thailand for the Masato fight so I flew up with him, trained with him for a week then flew home ahead of him, leaving him there so he could get another two weeks of hard Muay Thai training. Not long after I got back I got a call from Nori telling me that one of his dad's friends, Kazama Ken, wanted to manage him in television jobs, commercials, etc. I was for it as long as they didn't interfere with his direct fight contract. I was a bit upset for the father's inconsistency in his association with Nori. He disowned Nori until he became a superstar then suddenly wants back in.

Fame and money were things Nori's dad loved and in my eyes that showed a lack of integrity and bad morals. Nori was in Thailand so the meeting was set up with just Kazama Ken and myself. We met at a restaurant and he pulled out a contract and asked me to sign it. Because it was written in Japanese I asked him what it said and he told me that it was about giving him rights to Nori's management.

As I questioned him on why we needed this contract he began contradicting himself to a point that I began to get very wary of his intentions. I could see his intentions were about making money off Nori and I was worried about him taking advantage of Nori. I also knew that Nori's father was behind this and that made me worry so much more for Nori's well-being.

I had experiences with Nori's father while I was married to Miyu that baffled me. This man would sacrifice anything, even his family, for money. One of the problems was with the Pro Wrestling incident and the other was an incident of him rewrapping Erson's gift from his biological father and giving it as his own present. These two incidents made it difficult for me to trust Nori's father.

So I refused to sign the contract that Kazama Ken provided and before we ended the meeting I snatched up the contract and took it with me. The moment I snatched it up Kazama Ken stood up and demanded that I return it. I refused, telling him I didn't trust him nor Nori's father and wanted to get one of my Japanese friends to read and translate to me exactly what it said. He resisted but there was no way I was returning the contract. I told him after I reviewed the contract I would get back to him.

Chapter 60

KAZAMA KEN – SCHEME REVEALED

I brought the contract to a friend, Kawana, who couldn't believe what he read. He explained to me the details of the contract and I was so glad I didn't sign it. The contract was an agreement that I was going to cut all ties with Nori and give all the rights to Kazama Ken and Nori's father.

To make it worse, because they were planning to breach the contract they actually had a clause that stated that any breach or violation that if Nori gets accused for up until this date, I would take full responsibility. It was literally a contract having me cut all ties with Nori and allowing Kazama Ken and Nori's father full rights to Nori's management, and stating that I will take full responsibility for any illegal actions Nori had committed. The bottom line was they saw dollar figures in Nori and wanted a part of the cash. I, on the other hand, never took any money from Nori and was just doing this all from my heart. My satisfaction wasn't financial; it was seeing Nori do well.

I explained to Nori what this contract actually said and he denied having any knowledge of the details. So I called a meeting between Nori, Nori's father, and Kazama Ken. I began to hash out the details and explain why I wasn't going to sign this contract. At the meeting I felt everything was going smoothly and that they understood that I was letting them do whatever they wanted with Nori's name outside of fighting for I had no experience in television, commercial advertisement, or sponsorship. However, as far as the fighting is concerned, they knew nothing about fighting so I wanted full control of all fighting issues. They agreed and I felt the meeting went well.

Another problem I had was an issue of integrity. They were planning to breach the current existing contract that was only on its eighth month of its two-year agreement. Nori seemed to forget the appreciation he had for K-1's decision to contract him as a K-1 fighter. He also failed to re-alize that K-1 and I changed the rules to accommodate his style so he could pull out wins to raise his stock because of the rule changes and the proper selection of his opponents.

Six months and four fights later he was a superstar. However instead of showing his gratitude he wanted, along with Kazama Ken and his father, to breach the two year agreement we had with K-1 and ask for more money to fight Masato. I was against this because one, I didn't think he was ready to fight Masato and two, the timing wasn't right. Along with me not signing the contract, I disallowed any thoughts of fighting Masato and asking for more money.

I wanted to stick to our agreement, fight the remaining 16 months on the contract, and then ask for more money when we renegotiated the new contract. As much as K-1 was making out on only paying Nori the initial fight money of $50,000 dollars we would have made out if Nori didn't do well. Even if Nori lost all his fights and wasn't a marketable fighter K-1 would have been obligated to honor the two year $400,000 contract. Unfortunately Nori's father and Kazama Ken had other plans.

Despite our agreement for them to stay out of all fight negotiations they decided to ignore what we decided and go down to the K-1 office and try to get $2,000,000 for Nori to fight Masato. I got a call from K-1 say-ing Kazama Ken and Nori's father were down at their office demanding $2,000,000 to fight Masato or he wasn't going to fight in K-1 again. They had this leverage because now that Nori was a superstar, K-1 needed him.

I was pissed and demanded that they leave the meeting immediately and then called Nori and had a serious talk with him. I told Nori that I couldn't work with his father and that if he can't tell his father to back off I was going to. To my disappointment, Nori couldn't tell his father so I backed off totally. I didn't corner him for his fight with Masato and I let his father handle all fight negotiation from there on. Nori breached his contract, threatening K-1 to never fight for them again if they didn't renegotiate a better contract for him. Although the initial two-year agreement wasn't even half way up, they did and paid double. 'A+' for Nori and his new team financially but a big fat 'F' for his honor and integrity. I decided that I needed to step back. I loved Nori as a brother but his integrity and values on loyalty were too different from mine. It was so hard to step away from someone I considered my brother and from a fighter I created throughout the years but I felt it was the right decision.

Chapter 61

Beating up a Yakuza – Aikawa Kumichou

As time passed, although I wasn't directly caring for Nori anymore I still was hoping he did well in his fights. I wouldn't miss a single fight silently rooting for him to win. Then something weird began to happen. The Yakuza, Eiji Aikawa, whom I started Purebred Tokyo with began avoiding my phone calls. For about a month I called his cell phone without an answer or call back and left numerous messages at the gym never to hear back from him. I was guessing he knew my disappointment in what happened between Nori and I so he decided to turn his back on me to be with Nori.

This was wrong for I had a relationship with him before Nori and I'm also the one who introduced him and Nori. Besides avoiding me, was now disrespecting me, which was the wrong thing to do. I was upset but knew that our paths would cross again someday and was in no rush to find him. Until…

When Nori was fighting in the final of an 8 man tournament against Uno Kaoru I was eager to see how he did so a couple of friends and I watched it on TV. We were planning to go out on the town after and meet some friends for drinks. I was relieved that Nori won but thought I was seeing things when I noticed Eiji in the ring on national TV hugging Nori, jumping for joy. Suddenly my head got really hot as I thought, how can this idiot who is trying to avoid me have the gall to go on national TV? My friends knew something was up when I called the friends we were supposed to meet and told them that we couldn't make it. I then called my boys Nachi and Ise and ordered them to find out where the celebration party was going to be so I can go get Eiji.

They made some calls, found out where they were going to be and I jumped in my car and sped down there. When I got there I planned to walk into the party, grab Eiji, and drag him outside for a beating. However, just as I was about to go in, Nachi and Ise suggested that I wait outside and they could go in and get him. I agreed and waited in a park next to where they were celebrating.

Three minutes later, I noticed Eiji walking into the park towards me. He had a beer in one hand and had no clue what was about to happen. He approached me and said, "Eh Enson! What's up?" I approached him and asked him, "You think you can run from me?" Then I gave him a swift low kick in his thigh. I then continued saying, "Maybe I should break your legs so you can no longer run from me anymore!" as I connected another low kick to his thigh that dropped him. He got back to his feet and I asked him, "Why didn't you return my calls?" as I backhanded him smack square in the face. He dropped to the ground so I grabbed him by the jacket and forced him to stand back up. Suddenly, another Yakuza by the name of Tanaka came running into the park begging me to stop. Tanaka used to be very close to Eiji until Eiji backstabbed Tanaka in his relation with Nori.

I couldn't believe what was happening. Tanaka had his head bowed down to my belly button getting between Eiji and I begging me to stop. Here is this guy who was trying to help a man that betrayed him. I just walked through Tanaka and went on beating Eiji. This went on for about 20 minutes as I lightly beat him not wanting to hurt him bad but just wanting to send him a message. His face began to swell up and his face was covered with blood when all of a sudden three guys came storming out from the bushes rolling their tongues angrily in typical Yakuza fashion. They were screaming, "How dare you beat up my little brother like this!!! You need to pay!!!" I noticed one guy was Hasegawa, the number two guy in a Yakuza group called Osekai. The cared and watched Eiji's back like an older brother. They were approaching me in a very aggressive manner so my boys got in-between them.

I knew this wasn't good for me and was anticipating this getting big really fast. I had no intentions of backing down for I believe I was wronged and I was justified to do what I was doing. As my boys were holding them back, they were trying to push their way through while screaming threats to me. I wasn't about to run or try to avoid this situation so I shouted out to my boys, "Let them through. I just have one thing to say so hear me out. If you still want to get me then we can get it on." They came through breathing and giving me a heavy stare. I wasn't afraid because I didn't do anything wrong. I was fair and if they were still going to stand by him I was ready for whatever they wanted to do.

I looked Hasegawa in the eye and asked him, "If I wanted to kill Eiji, how long do you think it would take?"

"About 5 minutes." he replied.

I then spoke, nodding my head, and said, "Yes, that's right. I've been beating him up for 20 minutes. If someone were to backstab you, wouldn't you want to punish him?"

He looked over at Eiji and I could see anger stir up inside of him as he angrily replied "Yeah, look at him! He's a bloody mess!"

Then I answered, "If you punish the guy you backstab, only 20% of what you really wanted to do, wouldn't you think that would be being a little too kind? Well, I only did 20% of what I really wanted to do. He's still alive, and he's still standing."

I could see the tightness in Hasegawa's face loosen up. His whole demeanor also changed as he reached his arm out, grabbed me on the shoulder, and directed me away from everyone to talk.

He said, "Okay, I understand what you're saying now. But you have to understand I can't have someone doing this to my little brother. I thank you for being lenient and I have a favor to ask – can you please back off for now and leave it up to me? I will make sure that he makes up to you what he has done, and if he doesn't I will kill him myself."

Hasegawa was known to be a man of his word. I could see the sincerity in his eyes and I knew it was time for me to step back. We shook hands and promised to put it behind us.

Chapter 62

HARD TIMES –
2003 SAKAI STEALS

The racquetball company I started in Japan was actually an offshoot of Egan's company, E-Force. I struggled to get this company on its feet, but with a lot of sacrifices and help from my brother Mashiko I got it done. I actually ran the Japan side of E-Force Japan and got Sakai to do it.

I felt the company had become very sturdy and I didn't need to be there anymore to run it. I wanted to go home to Hawaii but before I went home, I wanted to get in the ring at least once and if I was ever going to do it, Japan was where I could.

One thing led to another and fighting got big. I made Sakai president and made him take over the whole company. I put all the gyms under that company which meant my fight money, gym fees, and t-shirt sales all went through it. I trusted Sakai so I made him the president of E-Force Japan. I was the owner.

The thing is, he had all the stocks in the company but I was the owner and everybody knew that, but on paper, he was the owner. I made him the owner because in Japan there are fewer complications and fewer taxes if the owner of a business was a Japanese national. However, every big decision would have to go through me and nothing I disagreed with would go through.

After I retired, I looked into the business. I fought many big money fights and after every fight I put a big percentage back into the company. Yamatodamashii t-shirts also had a boom in sales averaging $2.5 million to $5 million in gross sales for five years. After my fight with Nogueira I was semi-retired, so I decided to be more hands-on with the company since I would have a lot of free time. I started looking into the books and I was surprised at what I found.

There was supposed to be a lot of money saved up in the company and when I checked the accounts I couldn't believe my eyes. There was only $30,000.00 cash and $200,000 in stock. I confronted Sakai and asked him where all the money went and all he could tell me was, "I'm sorry. Bad business. I don't know where the money went." For me that excuse wasn't good enough. If we were talking a couple thousand dollars I can understand, but we are talking about hundreds of thousands.

He continuously lied so I got sterner. I found cash in his home, $40,000 and ¥6,000,000 yen. I then confiscated the two cars he had. I also found he purchased a 3-bedroom apartment that he bought with a $250,000 cash down payment.

I took the apartment away too forcing him to move out and I moved in using it as a vacation home. However, the cash still didn't add up. So I then asked him to deplete all his accounts where he had an accumulation of another $200,000... but still, that wasn't enough. I began to question him again. Through all his repeated lies he cried and apologized repeatedly saying the same thing, "I'm sorry. Bad business. I don't know where the money went." I really wanted to beat the shit out of him but he wasn't a fighter and he was like a brother to me so I restrained myself. Then I had an idea. The next time we talked, every time he lied I would cut his hair. Like I expected he lied so I grabbed a handful of his hair and cut it off. He then lied again so I chopped off yet another handful of hair. By the third lie I was fed up so I just passed him the scissors and made him cut his own hair.

Chapter 63
CIVIL COURT CASE

By the end of the conversation Sakai had no hair and I was furious. He knew I was about to lose it so right after that meeting he skipped town. No one could find him or contact him for weeks. I was pissed. I left messages on his phone and called him a dozen times each day. What I wasn't prepared for was what he had planned.

As I was leaving all those threatening messages on his phone, he planned to sue me by filing a suit for extortion. He tried to file it as a criminal case but the police wouldn't allow it because of insufficient evidence so he filed a civil suit instead. The biggest thing in his favor was that on paper he was listed as the president of the company and I was listed as an employee. I trusted him so I didn't feel that I needed to cover my back for anything.

To make a long story short, he prepared well and he won the civil case. I couldn't believe it. I was instructed to return the apartment, the two cars, and all the cash I took from him. I didn't want to return a thing, because after all, these things were actually mine because he bought them with the money that he took from me. In fact, that was only a small portion of what he stole.

The apartment was hard to destroy so I had to return that. The two cars I destroyed and all the cash, I kept. The only problem with keeping the cash was that because it was a court order for me to return the cash, he could freeze any bank accounts I had and seize any valuable assets in my name. So I withdrew all the money in my accounts and took my name off any valuable assets.

When I didn't return the things I confiscated Sakai took it a step further. He filed a criminal case, which wasn't good for me. With the verdict of the civil case he had a good chance of winning the criminal case too. If I lost the case I could face up to 2-5 years in prison.

One of my brothers, Mr. Kaneda, a big pachinko parlor owner, was concerned and asked to see me. I met with him and was touched by what he wanted to talk about. He was worried about the criminal case Sakai was filing and wanted to help me pay the money back. It was close to a quarter of a million dollars and he was willing to make the full payment for me.

I appreciated his concern but I wasn't afraid of going to prison. Right is right and wrong is wrong and the bottom line is that this was actually all my money that Sakai stole from me. I was just taking my money back. So I explained to Mr. Kaneda that it's not prison I'm worried about, my main concern was not letting him get away with this scheme he conjured up. I explained to Mr. Kaneda that even if it were $1 dollar, I wouldn't pay it back. I was not wrong and the threat of a prison sentence wasn't going to scare me. His concern increased but he understood.

Sakai pursued the criminal case for seven years. However, his bullshit was slowly being revealed. The police started off thinking of me as the criminal and as the years passed the momentum shifted to the police trying to back me up. Because of all the inconsistencies in his story, after seven years, the police threw out the case and even tried to convince me to file a counter suit. I declined, for I really just wanted to move on and put this behind me. The thought of Sakai owning and getting income from the racquetball company I founded bothered me, but I knew I had to deal with it and tried my best not to think of it.

My basic theory is that I did no wrong in this. The money I took was rightfully my money. In fact, Sakai still owes me a lot of money. I wasn't really afraid of the outcome. I would try my best to win the case and if I lost and I had to go to jail then I believe it is destiny. I believe everything is destiny. I believe everything happens for a reason. If God wanted me to go to prison, then there is a reason why.

These are two scenarios that I can think God would be protecting me from by sending me to prison: 1) A car accident. Maybe I was supposed to die next year in a car accident but because I'm in jail, I cannot drive, I cannot get into the car accident – he might be saving my life. 2) Like I said, I'm surrounded by the underworld. I've got a lot of friends.

Maybe I was getting a little too deep within the Yakuza world. I do feel it sometimes. I feel like I'm part of the family, with all different families. Maybe if I went to prison for 1-3 years it would create the much-needed distance or possibly sever the ties. I believed that if I did lose a case when I'm in the right and I do go to jail, I'd go in there with a positive attitude thinking that there is a reason and in a way, I am being protected.

Chapter 64
PRO WRESTLING DEBUT –
NEW JAPAN PRO WRESTLING

I was semi-retired and teaching at my Purebred Gyms when a good friend/fellow MMA fighter got in touch with me. His name was Josh Barnett and he wanted to know if I was interested in participating in pro wrestling. I was really hesitant, knowing I was horrible at acting. I knew it would be hard for me to act angry when I really wasn't and it would be even harder to pretend to be in pain when I wasn't. I told Josh that I wasn't interested, but he was persistent.

He suggested that I first try cornering him in a match that he had coming up and get a better feel of what it is like. I really didn't want to, but I gave in to Josh's persistency. His match was against a famous pro wrestler named Yuji Nakata and it was held at the Tokyo Dome, which seats over 50,000 people. When we made the ring entrance it was similar to fighting so that wasn't a problem.

The problem was when I was in the corner for Josh's match I knew what was going to happen and I knew the outcome. I just couldn't act. Instead, I just sat quietly watching the match with absolutely no reaction. I was horrible and more than ever I knew I couldn't do pro wrestling. However, at the arena, I was approached by one of New Japan Pro Wrestling's head director, Mr. Uwai. He passed me his business card and said that he wanted to meet me for lunch and discuss me possibly doing some pro wrestling for them.

During my fighting career I have expressed my resentment for pro wrestling but it wasn't that I resented pro wrestling itself. I resented the fact that some so-called fighters like Takada were doing pro wrestling matches in the MMA ring. If he kept pro wrestling in the pro wrestling ring I would have nothing against that. But when you do pro wrestling in a ring where the other fighters are risking their lives, then that is being disrespectful to MMA and to all the fighters who were fighting REAL fights. New Japan Pro Wrestling used a pro wrestling ring so I was all good with that.

I met Mr. Uwai for lunch and the proposal he made was so tempting. It was a guarantee of $10,000 a month even though I wouldn't necessarily be having a fight every month. I was to appear at only the matches in big arenas or the ones that would be nationally televised.

So I was looking at 8-10 Pro Wrestling matches a year getting paid $120,000. Holy shit!!! How could I turn this down? I sucked at acting but maybe I could try. Who knows I might be good at it after all. I agreed and my first pro wrestling match was set.

As expected it was difficult. Between acting and remembering the skit, I was struggling. I also was not good at taking back drops, let alone doing it to others. In pro wrestling the way your opponent backdrops you is more important than you being good at taking a backdrop. The angle and the timing are all important. Even if you were really good at taking backdrops, if your opponent isn't good at doing them, then that is very dangerous.

So since I wasn't a seasoned pro wrestler, they kept my fight style as close to real fighting as possible. Therefore I didn't need to do or take many backdrops, didn't use the ring ropes, nor did I do or take the slaps on the chest. Another thing that was really different from MMA, was in MMA I try to avoid any type of interaction with my opponent before the fight. However, in pro wrestling, you have to meet up with your opponent before the match to script a skit for the match.

That was a weird thing, meeting your opponent before the match to decide what to do and who was going to win. Remembering the skit play-by-play from the opening gong to the finish was very difficult for me. There are many times I forgot what to do and had to go ad lib until I remembered or someone reminded me. It was difficult and I was just an average pro wrestler but I stuck it out for the whole year.

The funny thing is that I gained twice as much popularity with the fans doing just one year of pro wrestling, than my eight years of MMA. The reason was because the population of pro wrestling fans was three times that of MMA. Pro wrestling magazines came out twice a week instead of once a month like MMA magazines. Then there was TV. Pro wrestling was on public TV once a week while MMA never was on public TV.

Although pro wrestling was financially good to me, and I gained new experiences, made new friends, and gained more fans, I decided that one year was enough and closed up my pro wrestling career when my contract expired.

Chapter 65

FIGHT FOR MY SECOND HOME, GUAM

Although I was semi-retired from MMA and my career was coming to a close, I always felt I wanted to fight in the two places I called home. One was Hawaii and the other was Guam. One of my Guam brothers, Roman, was running a promotion called Fury in Guam and I was always there to give him advice and help in any way I could. For one certain event in particular, he was having a lot of trouble when the unimaginable happened. His main event fighter pulled out and signed with another production that could pay more money.

Roman was devastated. He didn't know what to do and was in a panic state but I had a plan. He would let his main eventer go and as a replacement, I suggested me fighting in the main event. Roman thought I was joking and when he realized that I was serious, the first words out of his mouth were, "But I can't afford you." I wasn't doing this for the money but to help a dear brother out of a dire situation. It would also be an opportunity to fulfill my desire to fight in my second home of Guam. The fight was on and it was blowing everyone on this little Micronesian island's minds away. However, there was one problem... my opponent. Roman couldn't afford a top name and we didn't know what to do.

Then we got word that Sochi Nishida, the 300-pound Karate guy I fought years back, wanted another shot! He was saying stuff like he wanted another chance to show me his Yamatodamashii and Roman contacted him and set up the fight. The media coverage was huge and I had an opponent. It wasn't a top notch opponent, but the objective was to help Roman and to fight on Guam and this was being fulfilled.

The fight went smoothly as I expected. After taking a few shots and getting put into a guillotine choke, Nishida tapped out and the fight was over. He was far from having the slightest bit of Yamatodamashii but the fight was a success and the two objectives were accomplished: Roman's event was a success and I fulfilled one of my dreams, to fight in my second home, Guam.

Chapter 66

2004 FIGHT IN HAWAII –
TOM SAUER

The second part of my dream was to fight in my hometown, Hawaii. I expressed my interest in fighting in Hawaii to the promoter of Super Brawls, T.J. Thompson so we touched bases to discuss my fight money. T.J. began asking me what kind of guarantee would I need and what percentage of ticket sales would I be happy with. My reply was "I'm going to trust you, so pay me what you think is fair. However, don't you ever try to fuck me... because if you ever fuck me, I promise...I will find you." He looked into my eyes and saw that I was dead serious and he agreed to put me on the next fight card. I really wanted to make a good showing for my family and hometown friends so I wanted to get into top shape. I called down a good friend, Phil Baroni from Las Vegas, to train with me along with one of my students, Riki Fukuda.

Because I was a ripe 37 years old, what I was most worried about was my conditioning and stamina. I also had a nagging knee injury that I was afraid to reinjure in sparring so I stuck to more weight training and running. I was training hard and Phil and Riki were great training partners so I got into top physical shape. My weight dropped fast and I knew I wasn't going to have a problem making the 93 kilogram weight limit. My fat percentage also dropped down so much that I actually could see my long lost six-pack.

I was concentrating on my conditioning so much, I didn't realize that my lack of sparring was going to be my biggest demon on fight night. When we got to Hawaii my best friend Darren made me vegetable soup and I was feeling great.

Me and my best friend Darren Suzuki.

I felt great and was ready to go. For this event a part of my agreement was that many of my Purebred fighters would also be put on the same card. Ryan Bow, Makoto Ishikawa, Norifumi Yamamoto, Joji Yamaguchi, Tetsuji Kato, Katsuhisa Nonaka, and Riki Fukuda all fought on one side and represented Purebred. The contracted weight was 93 kilos but I had such an easy time dropping weight that I came in at 91 kilos at weigh-ins.

On fight night all my Purebred fighters fought hard and, win or lose, they represented well. I was a little nervous as usual but knew I trained hard and was confident I'd do well. Phil was there to corner me and I got a good warm up in. For my ring entrance I chose the 9-11 remix of "I Believe" by the Blessed Union of Souls because I wanted to show the people that I haven't and we all shouldn't forget all the lives that were lost in New York.

Making my way to the ring felt different from all the other fights I had. This was the first time I was going to fight in front of my hometown, and as I made my way to the ring and I looked down at the people in the arena, I had this overwhelming feeling churning in my chest. I felt proud, and could literally feel the power and energy of support the Hawaii people had for me. I got to the ring, looked over at Tommy Sauer and was ready for war! I felt like I was in great shape and couldn't wait to get the fight started.

The bell rang and the fight was on! I planned to stand with Tommy so I moved in to range to begin striking. As soon as the distance was right I threw a straight right cross that missed and instead of following the game plan, I found myself clinching and pressing Tommy up against the ropes. I was confused. I planned to stay away and strike but here I was clinching which made it impossible to strike. Then I felt like Tommy's balance was off so I torqued my hips and tried to suplex him. It was rushed and not the right time and I ended up falling on my back with Tommy on top of me.

Instinctively I put Tommy in my guard and quickly locked on a triangle. Tommy then tried to turn out of the triangle but he was turning the wrong way, setting himself up for my patented arm bar. But to my surprise, instead of transiting smoothly into an arm bar, I tried to force the triangle and Tommy eventually slid his head out and he was suddenly in side control.

He then moved over for a North/South head and arm choke and put on the squeeze. I felt the pressure but didn't feel like I was in any danger of passing out so I threw knees from the bottom connecting with a few but nothing that hurt Tommy. Then Tommy caught me off guard and positioned for the mount and practically got it. He began raining down punches from the top position. I got hit with a few solid punches but felt I was okay when suddenly the referee jumped in and signaled that he was stopping the fight.

My first feeling was "Why?" but decided not to protest it because it may have looked worse than I thought. Shit, I was fine but the referee made his call and the fight was over. The referee's job is one of the hardest of the night so right or wrong, he made his call and Tommy was the victor. I fell off the game plan and it allowed Tommy to aggress me and control me enough for the referee to feel he had to stop it. Tommy was the better man that night and I wasn't about to cry over spilled milk. It was already bad enough that I finally got to perform for my hometown and I lose, so I wasn't about to make things worse by being a crybaby too. The fight was over, I was still alive and most of all I knew all things happen for a reason.

When I got back to the locker room I was honest with my feelings. I didn't feel like I moved the way I was capable of and honestly felt that maybe it was my time to retire. I never felt like this before and when Phil and I got back to the locker room I turned to him and said, "I think I'm done. I think this may be my last fight." I will never forget the look on Phil's face. His eyes filled up with tears, he gave me a big hug and said, "Don't you fuckin' say that! If you're done then so am I!" I felt his heart and it hit me as my eyes also filled up with tears and I began to cry too. I felt pain. Not pain from losing, but pain from letting down the people who care about me and pain of not knowing exactly how I felt and feeling lost.

Back at the hotel, the promoter, T.J., came to pay me. I didn't feel like I deserved the pay I was getting. So after T.J. left, I called each of my fighters one by one and gave them bonuses from my pocket for a job well done. I then got all my fighters together in my room, congratulated them on fighting their hearts out and for making me proud. I then honestly let them know that I wasn't sure exactly how I felt, but this could possibly be my last fight. We then turned on some Hawaiian music and let the party begin

Parting Words
DEATH

Many aspects of this book discuss my development as a man both physically and more importantly – spiritually. Fighting has taught me many lessons about life, about people and about the human spirit. These lessons, I believe, transcend this physical life and are intended to prepare me for the ultimate test, Death.

It is my wish for this to be read at my funeral:

> *To Live as a Man.*
> *To Die as a Man.*
> *To Become a Man.*

Death is one of the most dreaded words in the English dictionary. Everyone fears it, even the toughest and bravest men. It is the inevitable outcome for every living thing. No one knows when, where, and how but with each passing day it creeps closer and closer. To fear it or dread it is meaningless. Instead, you must learn to accept it unconditionally and be strong. I have... Everyone must accept that it is inevitable and unavoidable and must be prepared for when their time comes. Be prepared to face it like a man knowing in your heart that it can't be avoided and accept that it is one of the many things in life that cannot be changed.

> "God grant me...
> the courage to change the things that must be changed,
> the serenity to accept the things that can't be changed,
> and the wisdom to know the difference."

I've learned to accept that death will come to everyone, sooner to some and later for others. For me... I believe I'm in the sooner bracket, and I'm fine with it. If my time comes tomorrow, I'll be a bit bummed about all the things I still wanted to do, but instead of dwelling on that I will appreciate all the things I had the opportunity to do. I'm ready to go with my head up high facing this uncertain transition like a warrior with my 大和魂 flowing strong in my heart just like the tattoos that are permanently carved under my skin...etched in my soul.

Yes, I will be sad to temporarily say goodbye to my loved ones but I'm more curious to set foot in that wonderful place called Heaven.

Death is something that will come to us all no matter what we do. There is no way to avoid it, just ways to delay it. Whether it be a plane crash, a car accident, cancer, or just slowly dying from old age, death is inevitable. For me, rather than the fear of dying, my fear is the way I will die. Will I slowly wither at the hands of cancer? Will I die instantly in a car accident? It is unknown and besides the choice of suicide, there is almost no way you can have a say on the way you will go.

So for me, rather than my life being taken by some meaningless circumstance, if I had the chance to die for someone I loved, without a split second of hesitation I would jump at the chance. Even if it was tomorrow, if I could take a bullet in the heart for one of my Ichizoku, there would be absolutely no hesitation at what I would do. I would proudly stand tall, with pride in my heart, take the bullet in my heart and die with a smile on my face knowing that my life didn't end in a meaningless way. My life was sacrificed for a loved one whose life will go on because of my noble actions. Dying is much easier than watching a loved one go, and giving your life for an Ichizoku... to me, there is no better way to die.

No matter who dies, the orbit of the earth does not falter, everything continues and, as cold as it may seem, the fact is... Life goes on! After I pass, if some of the things that I did during my life on earth had a helpful impact on others' lives I will go in peace. For someone to face a tough obstacle in their life and think, "What would Enson do... "or to remember my fights or my words and be able to conquer an obstacle in their life, would make the time I had here on earth all worthwhile.

During my life here on earth I have helped some who contemplated suicide, helped people overcome the death of a loved one, helped people battle sicknesses, etc. And if even after I'm gone in flesh, if the memories I leave behind can continue to help people, words will not be able to express the joy and satisfaction I will have no matter where I am. Also, whether it be one year or ten years after my death, if people were to say, "Remember when Enson did this..." and smile or have a laugh remembering me, it would mean the world to me.

Do you believe in God? If so, then you believe in Heaven. What is Heaven? To me, it is the most wonderful place where everything is calm. No more worries. No more pain. Then why does everyone dread death? For we all must die to go to Heaven. If you live forever, you will never go to Heaven. Maybe it's because you'll miss the people you love... Yes, maybe, but in Heaven you will be reunited with the loved ones that moved on before you. In my lifetime I've seen so many people move on prematurely. Fellow fighters, students, relatives, pets, fans, and the most painful, people in my Ichizoku.

There were times that I sincerely, in my heart, wished God had taken me instead. Through the pain of watching the loved ones of the people who have passed struggle to move on, I've come to realize that dying isn't the hard part. Yes you may suffer before you die, but when you die you are at total peace. The real pain and suffering lies in the ones that are left behind. Yes I do still fear dying but what I fear a hundred times more is the loved ones I will have to leave behind. The insecurity of worrying if my Ichizoku will be okay will burn in my heart.

That's why before every single one of my fights, before I get into the ring, I write farewell letters to the ones I care about. Because if I were to suddenly die in the ring with no warning, I know that the words that I write will definitely make my passing much more bearable and their suffering will subside tremendously. To some I write things that are in my heart but never had the timing or chance to tell them these deep feelings. It is words that they have never heard from me before, but it is words that will definitely ease the pain of my passing. I hide the letters in a safe place that will definitely be found in the case of my death and it is addressed separately to each and every person in my heart.

If I make it out of the fight alive, the first thing I do when I get home is burn all the letters. These are words that will only be read when I am gone and before every fight I write a new letter putting the present feelings in my heart down on paper. While writing these farewell letters I sometimes have a smile on my face and at times a tear will run down my cheek. However, I am positive that these letters will ease the pain and suffering my Ichizoku will be facing with my passing. That is also why I have written this...

I believe there are two lives we live simultaneously, the physical life you live through your body and the spiritual one that you live in your soul. Compared to the spiritual life the physical life is short. 80-90 years is like a grain of sand on the beach compared to eternity. The way you die in the physical life will determine the glow of your aura your soul will shine with when it moves on to the spiritual life. The glow of the aura of your soul will determine what level you will start your spiritual life with and the status that you will have as you continue on your spiritual life.

If you die a coward then you will have no glow to your aura going into the spiritual life and will start on the bottom. If you die a regular death like a car wreck, cancer, or old age then the glow of your aura will be a normal glow and you will have a normal start. However, if you die as a samurai, for what's right, or for someone important to you; when you move on to the next world your aura of your spirit will glow and sparkle and you will begin at an elite level. To me the physical life is just a stepping-stone to the gates of the spiritual life! The spiritual life is forever and the most important. I would never sacrifice the glow of my aura just to extend my physical life. I will sacrifice my physical life without a moment's hesitation to die an honorable death and begin my journey in the spiritual life with a glow that can be seen for miles.

That is the reason why if someone from my Ichizoku has a big Yakuza problem or I needed to stand up for myself or for what's right, I would without a moment's hesitation, even if it meant death.

When someone dies, yes I agree that the tears will flow. But why? Tears aren't necessarily bad. For every tear that drops there is a deep feeling in your heart that causes it to flow from your eyes. Without the good times tears wouldn't flow. For every tear that flows, it represents a memory or a time of joy. If you have something good and it ends or is gone, there is sadness. If you have something you don't like or don't really care about, when it's gone not a single tear will drop.

If you want good times and unforgettable memories, you must accept that sadness is inevitable when it will come to an end. Like entering the ring, as well as the rush and happiness of victory comes the agony of defeat. To be able to experience the thrill of victory you must accept that there is a possibility that things might go bad and you may be overwhelmed with the agony of defeat. To get in the plane and fly home to beautiful Hawaii, I am aware that before I can absorb the beauty of the beaches, I might experience an untimely death if the plane were to crash. The majority of people, even with this horrible possibility of the plane crashing, will still without a moment's hesitation jump at the chance to get on a plane and vacation in Hawaii. It all boils down to what you focus on, the rewards to success or the penalties to failure... I chose to focus on the rewards.

When a loved one passes, the feeling of being sad because you won't be able to see that person for a long time and missing many things about them is fine. But the feeling of sympathy and pity for the one who has passed or the misunderstanding that death is the end of the road is not okay. Every tear that drops down the face of someone dear to me that I have left behind because of pity for me or for the misconception of death will pierce my heart like a knife cutting butter. So please don't waste your energy and time worrying whether or not I "didn't want to die". Of course no one wants to die. But, more importantly, before you mourn over my passing, the important question is whether or not, in my heart, I have accepted death or not. And because I have 100% in my body, heart and soul accepted death, instead of feeling sad, feel happy for my passing for it is merely just a transition to heaven and instead of goodbye, wish me "Itterashai" or "mata ne".... until we meet again!

Death is not scary...what is scary is
The Anticipation of Death.
From the moment you know
you are going to die
Until the moment you actually die,
that's the real terror.

The moment you die, you enter a world of
tranquility, serenity, and peace.
I will rest in Peace!